W9-AUB-049

# Holy Matrimony!

**BY THE SAME AUTHOR:**

*Celebrity Lies!*
*Celebrity Feuds!*
*Celluloid Gaze*
*The Lavender Screen*
*Hollywood & Whine*
*In or Out*
*Sing Out!*
*Hollywood Gays*
*Bette Davis Speaks*
*Hollywood Lesbians*
*Hollywood Babble On*
*Leading Ladies* (UK)
*Hispanic Hollywood*
*The Films of Jane Fonda*

# HOLY
# MATRIMONY!

Better Halves and Bitter Halves:
Actors, Athletes, Comedians,
Directors, Divas, Philosophers,
Poets, Politicians, and Other Celebs
Talk About Marriage

## BOZE HADLEIGH

**Andrews McMeel
Publishing**

Kansas City

# HOLY MATRIMONY!

Copyright © 2003 by Boze Hadleigh. All rights reserved. Printed in the United States of America. No part of this book may be used or reproduced in any manner whatsoever without written permission except in the case of reprints in the context of reviews. For information, write Andrews McMeel Publishing, an Andrews McMeel Universal company, 4520 Main Street, Kansas City, Missouri 64111.

03 04 05 06 07 RR2 10 9 8 7 6 5 4 3 2 1

Library of Congress Cataloging-in-Publication Data
Holy matrimony! : better halves and bitter halves ; actors, athletes, comedians, directors, divas, philosophers, poets, politicians, and other celebs talk about marriage / [compiled by] Boze Hadleigh.
    p.  cm.
  ISBN 0-7407-3325-7
    1. Marriage—Quotations, maxims, etc. I. Hadleigh, Boze.
PN6084.M3 H65 2003
306.81—dc21                      2002043161

## ATTENTION: SCHOOLS AND BUSINESSES

Andrews McMeel books are available at quantity discounts with bulk purchase for educational, business, or sales promotional use. For information, please write to: Special Sales Department, Andrews McMeel Publishing, 4520 Main Street, Kansas City, Missouri 64111.

**To Ronnie:
Twenty-seven years . . . every
day's a holiday!**

# CONTENTS

Introduction **ix**

Sex, and Before Marriage **1**

Women on Marriage **59**

Men on Marriage **107**

Broken Marriages **157**

Divorce **215**

Lasting Marriage **257**

# INTRODUCTION

*L*ove and marriage. If there's any topic that most anybody will gladly open up about, that's the one. Or ones. Everybody has a romantic history, a marital tale, or a theory. What makes a marriage last? Why don't most last as long, these days? Love and marriage, or love versus marriage? Does matrimony spell the end of romance? When is the honeymoon actually over? Marriage or honeymoon first? Is "sweetheart" really the past tense of "daddy"?

Love is the great common denominator. It's the one thing everybody shares in, regardless of outward differences and varying arrangements or duration. Of course the word has been so overexposed that the romantic souls who still write love letters may choose a more dramatic verb like "adore," to distinguish from usages like "I love cheesecake" or "We love our postman—he always rings twice."

The word "marriage" has also been modified. For instance, it's often used in regard to mergers, as in "a corporate marriage." *Webster's New World Dictionary* reminds us that marriage includes "any close union" and that to marry means "to enter into a close relationship." Marriage has expanded beyond a narrow legal term, for obviously two people can be a lifelong loving couple without having signed a contract.

The point is, although love is a universal language, in reality it's as varied as the individuals experiencing it. People routinely compare their own to others' relationships, measuring not just in years, but more important, in quality, compatibility, fidelity, affection, and so on. Connubial tips, clues, and news are a staple of daily conversation and weekly periodicals. If our neighbors' marriages appear too dull to comment on (perhaps because they're happily uneventful), we can always follow the real-life soap operas of celebrity marriages. We all have certain famous couples we root for, some we feel sure are doomed, and some we just don't believe (publicity-based celebrity mergers).

We root for romance, for lasting unions. We want love to conquer all. And when sometimes it doesn't, we like to know—even if we don't wish to seem like we want to know—what happened? And whose fault was it, really? (We often assume one partner is blame-free!) Our increasingly tabloidized era seems obsessed with love and marriage, love without marriage, marriages ending up without love, and so on.

The love affairs, marriages, and marital woes of celebrities—be they actors, politicians, or royalty—remind us that they're human too and reassure us that fame and fortune don't guarantee happy relationships. Reading about VIPs' domestic ups and downs brings them closer to us and can put our own less hectic, more stable unions into clearer, more appreciated perspective.

In many or most interviews with celebrities, the most interesting quote is one about love or marriage. The contents of this book were culled from hundreds of interviews and articles in magazines, newspapers, books, and on television. Hopefully these stellar nuggets will amuse, entertain, inform, surprise, evoke laughter, and possibly shock or amaze. They may also make you aware of how good you have it.

Whoso loves believes the impossible.

**—ELIZABETH BARRETT BROWNING**

When two are gathered together,
majorities shall not triumph.

**—E. M. FORSTER**

Marriage halves our griefs, doubles our joys,
and quadruples our expenses.

**—ENGLISH PROVERB**

# Sex, and Before Marriage

❦

A husband is what's left of a sweetheart after the nerve has been killed. **—LOU COSTELLO OF ABBOTT AND COSTELLO**

When two people are under the influence of the most violent, most insane, most delusive and most transient of passions, they are required to swear that they will remain in that excited, abnormal and exhausting condition continuously until death do them part.

**—GEORGE BERNARD SHAW**

If love is the answer, could you rephrase the question?

**—LILY TOMLIN**

One should always be in love. That is the reason one should never marry. **—OSCAR WILDE**

All marriages are happy. It's after the honeymoon, when you go home together, that the problems usually begin.

**—JULIA LOUIS-DREYFUS OF *SEINFELD***

The success of the marriage comes after the failure of the honeymoon.    **—ENGLISH WRITER G. K. CHESTERTON**

Isn't it a shame honeymoons don't last? Such a sweet, lovely time that is. Even if you aren't thinking all that logically. On my last honeymoon my husband Charles answered our hotel telephone and said, "Miss Channing's suite." And I said, "Now, Charles, don't flatter me, just find out who it is."    **—CAROL CHANNING ON HUSBAND-MANAGER CHARLES LOWE, OF WHOM SHE DECLARED DURING DIVORCE PROCEEDINGS THAT HE'D HAD SEX WITH HER NO MORE THAN TWICE IN FOUR DECADES**

Marriage is wild. I thought it was this perfect land of happiness and joy. Wrong! After you say you do, you don't for a long time.    **—JOHN LEGUIZAMO**

I lied on my honeymoon—said I was a virgin. In a situation like that, at least one person should know what they're doing.    **—WOODY ALLEN**

On my first honeymoon, everything was new to me. Even the sight of a naked man. In three words, it was appalling, hilarious, and terrifying.    **—COSMETICS TYCOON HELENA RUBINSTEIN**

It isn't known how sexually inclined [German writer] Goethe was toward his child-wife Christiane, but we do know that he wrote poems on her backside.    **—GOETHE EXPERT WILLI KORNGOLD**

Marriage is a book of which the first chapter is written in poetry and the remaining chapters in prose.    **—UK WRITER BEVERLEY NICHOLS**

Marriage. That's a meal where the appetizer's better than the dessert.                                        —DEAN MARTIN

The honeymoon is where "they loved happily ever after" . . . for a week or two. Then comes marriage. Realistically, shouldn't the honeymoon trip come after the first fifty weeks, as a reward, something to look forward to?                   —GILLIAN ANDERSON *(THE X-FILES)*

Getting pregnant on your honeymoon is like saving up for a big vacation, then being told you'll have to wait to take it until you're forty.                                        —PAMELA ANDERSON

I like men. I like 'em so much, I'd rather have the honeymoon than the marriage. . . . I'm single because I was born that way.
—MAE WEST, WHOSE HUSH-HUSH EARLY MARRIAGE WAS REVEALED
IN THE 1930S AT THE HEIGHT OF HER STARDOM

I like to wake up feeling a new man.      —'30S SEX SYMBOL JEAN HARLOW

Today, honeymoons are redundant. At best, an opportunity to travel. But the first time a couple has sex together? Puh-leeze. I wonder what a honeymoon must have felt like in the old days . . . the anticipation, the ecstasy of discovery, and the blessed end of frustration. It must have been glorious!                           —STEVE MARTIN

The first time my wife said she had a headache was on our honeymoon. Now, about a century later, I hear the experts are saying sex is a great cure for headaches. They say it releases chemicals inside you that make you happy and reduce the pain. I was born too soon!
—HENNY YOUNGMAN ("TAKE MY WIFE, PLEASE")

You can tell a man "I hate you," and you'll have the best sex of your life. But tell him "I love you," and you'll probably never see him again. —KIM CATTRALL *(SEX AND THE CITY)*

The thing that takes the least amount of time and causes the most amount of trouble is sex. —JOHN "THE GREAT PROFILE" BARRYMORE

Sex is emotion in motion! —MAE WEST

Sex between a man and a woman can be wonderful—provided you get between the right man and the right woman. —WOODY ALLEN

You know what the cynics say . . . in marriage, three's company and two is none. —SARAH JESSICA PARKER OF *SEX AND THE CITY*

In France there is a saying that the heaviest burden on earth is the body of a man one has ceased to love.
—CATHERINE DENEUVE, WHOSE TWO CHILDREN ARE BY MEN SHE DIDN'T WED AND WHO MARRIED A MAN WITH WHOM SHE HAD NO OFFSPRING

I fell in love with her smile. But I married the rest of her too. Drat.
—W. C. FIELDS ON HIS SOLE, UNHAPPY MARRIAGE

$\mathcal{I}$ dallied in the garden of love . . . and picked a lemon.

—DAVID LETTERMAN

$\mathcal{R}$unning after women never hurt anybody—it's catching 'em that does the damage.

—UK SCREENWRITER JACK DAVIES

$\mathcal{I}$ was [in Hollywood] with no money, and all these people saying they wanted to do this and that for me. People wanted to marry me. People wanted to put me in the movies. . . . I can honestly say, hand on heart, that I have dated nineteen guys in my life. And of those nineteen I have slept with fifteen.

—PAMELA ANDERSON LEE, AS SHE THEN WAS

$\mathcal{I}$ don't sleep with married men, but what I mean is that I don't sleep with happily married men.

—BRITT EKLAND

$\mathcal{Y}$ou mean apart from my own?

—ZSA ZSA GABOR, WHEN ASKED HOW MANY HUSBANDS SHE'S HAD

$\mathcal{A}$ girl can wait for the right man to come along, but in the meantime that still doesn't mean she can't have a wonderful time with all the wrong ones.

—CHER

$\mathcal{M}$ost of the girls out there are looking for Mr. Right, while most of the guys are looking for Miss Right Away.

—BEN AFFLECK

$\mathcal{M}$ost men have to marry to get regular sex, and most women have regular sex to get married.

—BRETT BUTLER

Women need a reason to have sex; men just need a place.

—BILLY CRYSTAL

Guys going out on a date wonder if they'll get lucky. But a woman already knows.

—WHITNEY HOUSTON

Men flatter themselves when they are a woman's first love. But women prefer to be a man's last love.

—SOPHIA LOREN

A jealous boyfriend can be rather exciting. A jealous husband would be excruciating.

—JULIA ROBERTS

A bad thing about jealousy is the element of pornography in it: the stimulation of visualizing one's darling in someone else's arms.

—COLETTE

Long engagements give people the opportunity of finding out each other's character before marriage, which is never advisable.

—OSCAR WILDE

My girlfriend says I should be sent out on lectures to teach men how to be. . . . He planned his proposal for about six months, to get it just right. Like writing a classic song.

—PAUL MCCARTNEY'S FIANCÉE HEATHER MILLS

Marriage is the last proposal a man is allowed to make, unchallenged.

—LARRY BLYDEN *(ON A CLEAR DAY YOU CAN SEE FOREVER)*

$\mathcal{B}$efore I married, I had affairs with older women. Girls my age were too demanding—always on the make, marriage-happy, manipulative, acquisitive . . . so dreamy-eyed to walk down the aisle and have babies. Older women just want to share a good time with you. And you learn so much from them.   **—PHIL HARTMAN**

"$\mathcal{H}$ome, Sweet Home" must surely have been written by a bachelor.
**—ENGLISH WRITER SAMUEL BUTLER**

$\mathcal{I}$t's good to enjoy yourself. If you don't want to do that, enjoy someone else. Which however sometimes entails having to marry them.   **—*POLITICALLY INCORRECT* HOST BILL MAHER**

$\mathcal{A}$ liberated woman is one who has sex before marriage and a job after.   **—GLORIA STEINEM**

$\mathcal{A}$ffairs and one-night stands are like dessert—eventually you want the more satisfying main course.   **—BRAD PITT**

$\mathcal{N}$o one has the right to deny us sex before marriage. Or the right to choose marriage. But I finally chose it because marriage includes one important thing that affairs lack: hope. . . .

**—KIM BASINGER**

$\mathcal{P}$eople tend to think of sexuality as the main ingredient young people have to offer. I beg to differ. I think older people exude bundles of sexuality. It's just that older men and women tend not to run around like cats and dogs in heat.   **—FIFTYSOMETHING JACQUELINE BISSET**

$\mathcal{I}$ used to believe marriage could cure my itch. Wrong. Then I thought middle age would diminish it. Wrong again. I think and assume that death must cure and diminish it.
>—CHOREOGRAPHER-DIRECTOR BOB FOSSE, WHO ADMITTED TO CHEATING
>ON ALL HIS THREE WIVES (AND SOMETIMES CHEATING ON HIS MISTRESSES)

$\mathcal{A}$ good lover isn't necessarily a good husband. It takes time to find out if a beau is marriage material. And by then, you're usually stuck.
>—FORMER COLUMBIA STUDIO CHIEF DAWN STEEL

$\mathcal{W}$e didn't marry, but it was wonderful. It's better to have loved a short man than never to have loved a tall.
>—STATUESQUE BLONDE SUSAN ANTON ON DIMINUTIVE ACTOR DUDLEY MOORE

$\mathcal{I}$ am always looking for meaningful one-night stands.
>—DUDLEY MOORE

$\mathcal{S}$ex without marriage being involved is like having a wonderful meal without later having to clear away the dishes and wash them up, stack them, and wonder if it's time to replace them and where are you going to get some that're reasonably priced and halfway attractive.
>—DIRECTOR RICHARD BROOKS *(IN COLD BLOOD, CAT ON A HOT TIN ROOF)*

$\mathcal{I}$t's so hard to know if the male of the species is excited about you or your body. Or both. Regardless, when you're young, it's terribly flattering. You don't see through it, see how mechanical and exploitive it is.
>—DEMI MOORE

Too many girls think that with their sex appeal they can handle most any man. Most of the time, they can't. The cards are stacked in men's favor, and the girls don't yet realize how replaceable they are to most men. **—ROBERT MITCHUM**

Look for romance, baby, not the glance. That glance is from glands, and is very random. **—AVA GARDNER**

I think unrequited love is a lost, special thing. Like in those tales of old, about love from afar . . . loving deeply but chastely. It's too bad. Because at least in unrequited love there's no disappointment.

**—SHARON STONE**

The reason a man or woman remembers that "lost love" is because it was lost, and never fulfilled; thus it always stays in that romantic, bittersweet stage of promise and mystery. **—LORETTA YOUNG**

I like being in a relationship. But it has to be just right. . . . I won't be in a relationship to be in a relationship.

**—FIFTYSOMETHING CHER**

If you wait for a knight in shining armor, you can wait your whole life long. Lower, I mean adjust, your standards, is my advice. Life isn't some perfect fairy tale.

**—DANA PLATO** *(DIFF'RENT STROKES)*, **WHO DIED FROM A DRUG OVERDOSE**

That nonsense about a girl expecting her Prince Charming to come along on his beautiful white horse? She'd be better off keeping the horse instead. **—JULIE NEWMAR**

$\mathcal{I}$ don't believe in missing the boat. I have friends of all sizes waiting at home for Prince Charming to ride up and find them. It's not gonna happen. You've got to go out and make your life happen. You've also got to notice the little guy who's holding Prince Charming's horse—he's probably s-o-o in love with you and he can't say a word about it. **—LARGE-SIZED SOAP STAR PATRIKA DARBO**

$\mathcal{W}$hen you're younger, you think one way must be right. But I don't feel that way anymore. . . . When I was with men, I didn't feel buffered from every storm because I was with them. You can't get that from somebody else. I did not buy the fantasy of Prince Charming and all that garbage. . . . Any kind of love is acceptable, and you don't have to do it in the usual way.

**—DIANE KEATON, NEVER CONTRACTUALLY WED**

$\mathcal{T}$oo often in our Western culture, especially with our daughters, the teaching is to look outside yourself for happiness, relief, and salvation. As a Buddhist, I believe in the advice: Be a lamp unto yourself. Ultimately it comes from within, if it's to last.

**—PETER FINCH, POSTHUMOUS OSCAR-WINNER FOR *NETWORK***

[$\mathcal{I}$t was] the end of my lifelong belief in the Prince Charming myth. And about time too. . . . I learned the hard way that just as I no longer have to save anyone, neither do I have to be saved.

**—LONI ANDERSON ON THE BREAKUP OF HER MARRIAGE TO THEN–BOX OFFICE KING BURT REYNOLDS**

$\mathcal{T}$he Prince was a prince but he proved not be Charming at all. [He had a] heavy iron door that held his secrets and hid all the shadowed bodies inside. The maiden, whom he called his only love, his Princess, glimpsed behind the door and saw too much. Then he brought all his power and darkness down upon her.

—FORMER ACTRESS AND DIRECTOR SONDRA LOCKE IN HER BOOK *THE GOOD, THE BAD AND THE VERY UGLY*, CHRONICLING HER RELATIONSHIP WITH CLINT EASTWOOD, WHICH ENDED IN MUTUAL LAWSUITS

$\mathcal{O}$lder men can make marvelous lovers or husbands, not to mention benefactors. But girls, if he's rich or powerful, and he turns on you, he can really turn on you. So a word to the wise and ambitious. . . .

—VIRGINIA GRAHAM

$\mathcal{O}$lder men are so grateful. Generous too, sometimes. But go elsewhere for marriage. Older guys want to be your lover and your dad. They use control and disapproval a lot, and their outlooks don't change much after their twenties. For a lasting, two-sided relationship, the boy should be within five years of you, either way.

—CYBILL SHEPHERD

$\mathcal{G}$irls usually think if a guy's fairly handsome, somewhat successful, and has the hots for them, they've got it made. But for how long? How many marriages will you settle for in one lifetime?

—ACTRESS LEE REMICK *(DAYS OF WINE AND ROSES)*

$\mathcal{I}$ wouldn't want to get married to someone who thinks settling down means settling.

—HALLE BERRY

*Y*our experience will be a lesson to all of us men to be careful not to marry ladies in very high positions.  **—DICTATOR IDI AMIN TO LORD SNOWDON ON THE END OF HIS MARRIAGE TO PRINCESS MARGARET (THERE ARE VIRTUALLY NO "LADIES IN VERY HIGH POSITIONS" IN UGANDA)**

*N*othing wrong with marrying a rich woman. Men are more secure these days. But find out if she's going to do the plastic surgery thing. You can start out with someone your own age, but . . . the surgery works better on women, and they don't get heavy around the middle if they're vain, so you could wind up married to someone that people will mistake for your daughter.  **—OLIVER REED *(GLADIATOR)***

*M*ichael Douglas and Catherine Zeta-Jones have been getting a bad rap that the wedding gifts they received are now being recycled. When *Usual Suspects* star Kevin Pollock celebrated his forty-fourth birthday, Michael sent him a bottle of Piper-Heidsieck champagne wrapped in a Jean-Paul Gaultier corset. Months later, Pollock discovered from a mutual friend that Douglas had been given a case of the bubbly as a wedding gift.

**—2002 ITEM IN ARLENE WALSH'S *BEVERLY HILLS (213)* COLUMN**

*W*hen Michael Douglas and Catherine Zeta-Jones recently visited the White House [in 2002] they had to undergo a security check first. Douglas found out that his wife is actually five years older than she'd told him. But this doesn't mean the honeymoon's over yet. Catherine is simply an old-fashioned Welsh lass who believes that a woman's age is her secret prerogative.

**—SYDNEY COLUMNIST PAMELA DUQUESNE**

When we married I said I was keeping my maiden name, and I am. But occasionally the Victorian spirit moves me. . . . I've ordered some engraved stationery that says Jennifer Pitt. It just feels good and looks good to me. So does my own name, of course.

—JENNIFER ANISTON, MARRIED TO MOVIE STAR BRAD PITT

You can keep the pretty party boys. They're just for show. I like a man who can make me laugh. Looks fade, but a sense of humor is for keeps. I'll take a Woody Allen over a Warren Beauty [sic] any day!

—BETTE MIDLER, LONG AND HAPPILY MARRIED TO A HOMELY, HUMOROUS MAN

People live longer now, they can afford to take more time choosing a mate. I also happen to think if you wait and take your time, it can last longer, hopefully for life.

—FORMER CLINTON AIDE GEORGE STEPHANOPOULOS, WHO DIDN'T WED UNTIL 2002

Every week I hear that Leonardo DiCaprio has proposed to super-model Giselle and every week I hear that she's accepted. I guess the real deal-breaker is scheduling the honeymoon for a time when Leo's best buddy, Tobey Maguire, is free!

—COLUMNIST CATHY GRIFFIN IN *BEVERLY HILLS (213)* ON MARCH 28, 2001

Brazilian model Giselle Bundchen wised up and got rid of *Titanic* star Leonardo DiCaprio. Giselle arranged a modeling assignment in Los Angeles so she could hang out with Leo in his home. But Leo found it more interesting to run off to Las Vegas with his pals. By the time Leo returned, she'd packed her bags and left him a note telling him it was over.   —COLUMNIST ARLENE WALSH ON DECEMBER 12, 2001

Liza [Minnelli] and I had a very gay wedding . . . our best man was Paul Jasmine, an artist who did the voice of Mother in *Psycho* and was Tony Perkins's closest pal. . . . Van Johnson was one of the guests. . . . Oh, yeah, the honeymoon was also rather gay!

—SINGER-SONGWRITER PETER ALLEN, WHO REPORTEDLY
SPENT THE WEDDING NIGHT WITH HIS BOYFRIEND INSTEAD

I'm very deeply romantic, also very private, so I think it's going to take me a very long time to find the right person.

—SINGER RICKY MARTIN

I don't have any plans on getting married again, and I never thought I would have children. But now that I'm not married, I'm thinking about it.

—SINGER JANET JACKSON (ONCE ANNULLED, ONCE DIVORCED)

Will I have to be married to have kids? Maybe I won't be—just to piss off [then-vice president] Dan Quayle.

—GEENA DAVIS *(THELMA AND LOUISE)*

The word "honeymoon" is the opposite of "parenthood." Don't confuse them.

—RICHARD BURTON

Having children is like having a bowling alley installed in your head.

—MARTIN MULL

I used to take my kids everywhere. But they always found their way back home.

—PHYLLIS DILLER

These days, why marry unless you're going to have children?
—WINONA RYDER

These days, only closeted gay actors get married. Everyone else in Hollywood just lives together.  —OPENLY GAY ACTOR CRAIG CHESTER

Liza Minnelli's close pals may be skeptical about her running into marriage with her forty-two-year-old, never-married producer fiancé David Gest. The longtime bachelor is proving he's got Liza's best interests at heart . . . he had her staff throw away all the no-no's that were in her house. Now Liza's getting back the glamour she was once famous for and David may end up a hero.
—ARLENE WALSH'S JANUARY 30, 2002 COLUMN

It takes guts to call it off. You don't want to lose a man you've really felt something for. But if the future isn't going to be what you hoped for . . . it does take guts.  —ACTRESS MINNIE DRIVER, WHO BROKE WITH FIANCÉ JOSH BROLIN (JAMES'S SON), THEN HAD A BRIEF RELATIONSHIP WITH HARRISON FORD

Sometimes a little selfishness, healthy or not, seems to get in the way. . . . Women ask for a lot. Maybe they have a right to.
—RUSSELL *GLADIATOR* CROWE, WHOSE RELATIONSHIP WITH MEG RYAN BEGAN WHILE THEY WERE FILMING THE EVENTUAL FLOP *PROOF OF LIFE* (THE AFFAIR EVENTUALLY ENDED HER MARRIAGE TO ACTOR DENNIS QUAID) AND ENDED WHEN CROWE CHOSE TO SPEND CHRISTMAS AT HOME IN AUSTRALIA WITH PALS RATHER THAN WITH RYAN

Can you imagine a world without men? No crime and lots of happy fat women.  —ATTORNEY MARION SMITH [1884–1947]

It's one thing to tolerate a boring marriage; a boring affair does not make sense. **—WRITER JANE WAGNER**

Married or unmarried, men have sex on the brain. Also on their palms, their soles, and all points in between.
**—KYLIE MINOGUE, AUSTRALIAN SINGER-ACTOR**

Do you know that 15 percent of American women send themselves cards or flowers on Valentine's Day? Isn't that sad, or pathetic?
**—RICKI LAKE**

It's too bad you can't marry yourself. There'd be no divorce. And less pressure from relatives to find the right person who's going to disappoint you anyway. **—ROSEANNE**

To love oneself is the beginning of a lifelong romance.
**—OSCAR WILDE**

The problem with loving someone so much is that pets don't live long enough and most spouses last too long. If your husband's a dud but you're old-fashioned and antidivorce, then it's interminable. And if your husband's a gem and your one and only, then widowhood is long and miserable. **—VIRGINIA GRAHAM**

The easiest kind of relationship for me is with 10,000 people. The hardest is with one. **—SINGER JOAN BAEZ**

*I*'ll tell you why intimacy is so difficult. Even more so for men. Because it means dropping some of the facade . . . it means getting vulnerable.

—HUMPHREY BOGART

*Y*ou give a woman an inch, she'll criticize you for not giving her seven.

—OLIVER REED

*N*ow all the gals are saying they like men more sensitive. Sure, when they're in a good mood. But later, they'll stick you where they know you're most vulnerable.

—EDDIE MURPHY

*T*he men I knew [intimately], most of them became anything but friends. . . . As Diane de Poitiers said, to have a good enemy, choose a man you have loved—he knows where to strike.

—BRIGITTE BARDOT

*S*cratch a lover, and find a foe.

—DOROTHY PARKER

*W*ith women, I've got a long bamboo pole with a leather loop on the end of it. I slip the loop around their necks so they can't get away or come too close. Like catching snakes.

—MARLON BRANDO

*A*n anthropologist once asked a Hopi why so many of his people's songs were about rain. The Hopi replied, "It is because water is so scarce. Is that why so many of your songs are about love?"

—WRITER GREGORY MCNAMEE

*I* want everybody to be thinking I'm having the time of my life, but I'm single and miserable. I'm experiencing the best things in my life and have no one to share them. I'm a hopeless romantic.

**—FRED DURST OF LIMP BIZKIT**

*I*'m just looking for a guy who has his own car—and doesn't live in it.    **—GAY COMEDIAN JASON STUART**

*Y*ou marry a man, you marry a house. It's unavoidable, unless he's homeless. . . . Housework is a concomitant of marriage. . . . The Rose Bowl is the only one I've ever seen that I didn't have to clean.

**—HOUSEWIFE HUMORIST ERMA BOMBECK**

*B*ack when women didn't have outside jobs, I can understand why they did the housework. But can someone rationally explain to me why, when both mates have full-time careers, it's still the wife who gets stuck with the housework? I really think men should see shrinks about why they find housework so demeaning, and why if it's so demeaning they dump it onto their beloved wives.

**—MELANIE CHISHOLM, A.K.A. "SPORTY" SPICE OF THE SPICE GIRLS**

*B*eing in therapy is great. I spend an hour just talking about myself. It's kind of like being the guy on a date.    **—COMEDIAN CAROLINE RHEA**

*W*omen speak because they wish to speak, whereas a man speaks only when driven to speech by something outside himself, like for instance he can't find any clean socks.    **—PLAYWRIGHT JEAN KERR**

Men are always asking what women want. That's because most of them don't listen. And you know what? The sincerest form of flattery is not imitation, and it's not compliments. It's listening.

—OPRAH WINFREY

Women want men, careers, money, children, friends, luxury, comfort, independence, freedom, respect, love, and a three-dollar pantyhose that won't run.   —PHYLLIS DILLER

Most husbands want good sex, good food, a halfway decent place to live in when they're there, and sooner or later a girlfriend.

—COMEDIAN SAM KINISON

Two is company, three is fifty bucks.   —JOAN RIVERS

We gotta talk. My wife loves Brad [Pitt], so tell him to call.
—AEROSMITH'S STEVEN TYLER, AFTER JENNIFER ANISTON'S CONFESSION
THAT THE ONE MAN BRAD SAYS SHE COULD "HAVE" IF THE OPPORTUNITY
PRESENTED ITSELF IS TYLER

Yes, I have fantasized about having sex with Tom Cruise and his [then-]wife Nicole Kidman.   —TORI SPELLING

Like everyone else, I want to sleep with Leonardo DiCaprio. But I guess I'd want to marry Tom Cruise because he's much more reliable.
—*DAILY SHOW* HOST JON STEWART, BEFORE CRUISE'S SECOND DIVORCE

When you date a guy, it can be fun. Parties can be fun. Going to dinner together. There's a limit, and after you marry, if he's still acting and partying the same way he used to, the marriage is probably doomed. **—DREW BARRYMORE, REFERRING TO COMEDIAN TOM GREEN, HER EX**

You have such a good time together when you're courting, that in time you're not so happy separately with the life you had. It can get to the point, if you're lucky, that you just can't live without each other . . . finally you have to live together, so you won't be unhappy.
**—SARAH MICHELLE GELLAR ON HER ESCALATING RELATIONSHIP WITH FREDDIE PRINZE JR. (THEY'VE SINCE WED)**

Young couples say they have sex first to find out if they're compatible. Or is it an excuse to indulge in nonpersonality—in sex and bodies, you know, sensation and fun? These are admittedly pleasant diversions, but they can be had with most any other good-looking human being, in distinction to the one unique person you intend or hope to spend your life with. **—WALTER MATTHAU**

I used to believe there was one special someone in the world meant just for me. And that I was meant just for him. If that's so, I guess we forgot to synchronize and meet during the same century. My knight in shining armor probably really was a knight in shining armor.
**—COMIC ACTRESS KATHLEEN FREEMAN (BROADWAY'S *THE BIG MONTY*)**

I was young, romantic, rather lonely, ambitious. I asked my agent for advice. How do I become a successful writer? He said, "Marry money." **—JOHN OSBORNE, FIVE-TIME HUSBAND**

𝒮trange word . . . and it starts out like "monotony." Ends up the same way too. . . . I was on an English "chat show." The host asked my opinion of monogamy. "Oh, I've only heard good things about it. I've heard it makes the best coffee tables."

—LEE VAN CLEEF *(THE GOOD, THE BAD AND THE UGLY)*

𝒲omen have no shame. . . . You really wouldn't believe what I have to put up with. Women come right up to [Brad Pitt] and press their bodies against him from behind. And I'm right there!

—PITT'S LONGTIME GIRLFRIEND GWYNETH PALTROW

𝒟on't marry on an empty stomach or a starved libido.

—JOHN TRAVOLTA

𝒲hat I learned . . . is don't marry everyone you fall in love with.

—STOCKHARD CHANNING *(GREASE, THE WEST WING)*

𝒥 dated for pretty, but I married the woman I thought would be the best mother to our sons. Turned out she's pretty anyway, and turned out we have all daughters.

—STAR EDDIE CANTOR, WHO FOUNDED THE MARCH OF DIMES

𝒢ood-looking people turn me off. Myself included.   —PATRICK SWAYZE

𝒥 kept dating this man because he thought I was so attractive. He gave me confidence in myself. Then he met my friend Ana, a waitress. Face like a lemon. He thought she was attractive too. What do men know anyway?

—STAND-UP COMIC TOTIE FIELDS

𝒟ahling, any husband of yours is a husband of mine.
—TALLULAH BANKHEAD, ON MEETING GINGER ROGERS'S HUSBAND
(ROGERS WAS NOT AMUSED)

𝒞onrad [revealed] that for the first year of his marriage he had slept with his bride in their double bed in total innocence. Only when they consulted a doctor about their childlessness were they enlightened on how to get the stork to visit them. Until that doctor's visit, neither the minister's son nor his wife had the slightest clue.
—JOAN FONTAINE IN HER MEMOIRS, ABOUT HER FIRST LOVER, ACTOR CONRAD NAGEL

𝒥 never touched my first wife at all. We got married in New York in 1920, on a Saturday morning. She made me marry her. She loved me so much that she just swept me off my feet. We would ride across town and she would stick her head out the window and yell, "I love Rudy Vallee!" We went together for a week and then got married, and on our wedding night I said, "Leona, I just can't go through with it."
—SINGER-ACTOR RUDY VALLEE

𝒫oor Kiefer [Sutherland] and what he had to go through [after Julia Roberts canceled their wedding]. I worked with him on *Article 99,* and I think that's why I've stayed away from going out with actresses.
—RAY LIOTTA

𝒲hile he was still dating actress Eva Duarte, Juan Peron found out the extent of her jealousy and star complex. Evita got her hands on every photo and memento of Peron's first wife and destroyed them all.
—HISTORIAN MARTIN GREIF

*I* married one of the few actresses with a great head on a great body. I hate to say it, but most actresses—and the same goes for a lot of actors—are mentally deprived.

—JACK LEMMON, HUSBAND OF FELICIA FARR

*My* advice to most actors on the upswing would be to date a model, a starlet, an actress. So what if she thinks a thesaurus is an extinct reptile? After the guy achieves stardom, he can date or marry a college professor, anyone he wants. Well, almost. . . .

—THEN-CLOSETED HOLLYWOOD SUPERAGENT STAN KAMEN

*I* remember way back when, Jerry Lee Lewis the singer married his little cousin. She was thirteen. Big backlash. Later on, Don Johnson, the *Miami Vice* guy, he was dating Melanie Griffith when she was fourteen, I think. . . . Now it's Jerry Seinfeld and his teenage fiancée. The young guys now, they can get away with anything. Unless the girl's a guy!     —MOREY AMSTERDAM *(THE DICK VAN DYKE SHOW)*

*I* wouldn't even mention it if Mrs. Reagan and her husband weren't setting themselves up as such arbiters of public morality. But the record shows that when Nancy and Ron got married, she was already pregnant with their [daughter]. And at that time, that was a very serious thing. About which people were ready to be extremely judgmental—as the Reagans themselves now are.

—SCREEN STAR MYRNA LOY

*I* was engaged when we were shooting *U-Turn,* and one day Sean Penn said, "If I weren't married and you weren't engaged, would this have been a very different movie?" and I go, "Yeah! Very different."

—JENNIFER LOPEZ

$\mathcal{A}$ctually, before we were dating, my wife Phoebe [Cates] said she saw me in *Sophie's Choice* and assumed I was gay. I said, "Hmm, really? Why is that?" She said, "Well, because you moved your hands so much in that movie. And you seem so, uh, clean."

—KEVIN KLINE *(IN AND OUT)*

$\mathcal{D}$ahling, you're divine. I've had an affair with your husband. You'll be next.

—TALLULAH BANKHEAD TO JOAN CRAWFORD, THEN MARRIED
TO DOUGLAS FAIRBANKS JR.

$\mathcal{T}$he best way to attract a man immediately is to have a magnificent bosom and a half-size brain and let both of them show.

—ZSA ZSA GABOR

$\mathcal{N}$othing risqué, nothing gained!    —PERPETUAL STARLET JAYNE MANSFIELD

$\mathcal{P}$ornography tells lies about women but unfortunately tells the truth about a lot of men. Find out if your Romeo is heavily into porno. A little of that goes a long way. Especially in marriage.

—DR. RUTH WESTHEIMER

$\mathcal{I}$ don't know what percentage of men it is that's apt to cheat. But there's a smaller though sizable percentage of husbands who, even with a wife handy, excuse my drift, are do-it-yourselfers. Which is fine and dandy for a bachelor, or once in a blue moon, married. But is this fair to needy wives? Even if it is the best birth control method.    —TV JOURNALIST RUTH BATCHELOR *(A.M. AMERICA)*

The drawback with video is it makes porn available to anyone, anywhere, all the time. It's a lifestyle for some men! I dated one very successful, charming businessman until he confessed that he was a porn addict and couldn't give up his X-rated tapes.

—**LEADING ARTISTS AGENT ANN DOLLARD**

First off, I have dated black men. But a woman with power is a problem for any man but particularly for a black man because it's hard for them to get power. I understand that, but I have to have a life and that means dating the men who want to date me.

—**WHOOPI GOLDBERG**

I've never had sex with a woman, but I've been on dates with a woman.   —**SHARON STONE**

There hasn't been a studio head I've worked for who hasn't come out and asked me if I'm a lesbian. I say, "Normally this would be none of your business. However, I will answer you. . . . It's possible. I'm not practicing at the moment, but I will not say it will never happen or hasn't happened in my past."

—**WHOOPI GOLDBERG IN THE EARLY '90S**

The homophobes raise the old stereotype of gay promiscuity. Yet they're the same people opposing gay marriage and relationships.

—*POLITICALLY INCORRECT* **HOST BILL MAHER**

There are no Ten Commandments when it comes to love. There is only one: unconditional love.   —**MARLENE DIETRICH**

Marriage is a friendship recognized by the police.
—BRITISH AUTHOR AND WIT QUENTIN CRISP

I said I refuse to do a scene with a naked woman, I don't care who she is. —STAUNCHLY CATHOLIC ACTOR JIM CAVIEZEL DURING FILMING OF *ANGEL EYES* WITH JENNIFER LOPEZ

Jim took me aside and said, "You know I'm married and very faithful." And I said, "Jim, it's a Disney movie."
—ACTRESS DAGMARA DOMINCZYK TO JIM CAVIEZEL DURING A LOVE SCENE FOR *THE COUNT OF MONTE CRISTO*

Not if it delays the ceremony. —ROBIN WILLIAMS IN THE 1970S, ASKED IF HE BELIEVED IN SEX BEFORE THE WEDDING

A woman for duty, a youth for pleasure, a goat for ecstasy.
—NINETEENTH-CENTURY WRITER-EXPLORER SIR RICHARD BURTON ON PURPORTED SEXUAL TASTES OF NORTH AFRICAN MEN (ANOTHER VARIATION WAS: "PROSTITUTES FOR PLEASURE, CONCUBINES FOR SERVICE, WIVES FOR BREEDING, A MELON FOR ECSTASY")

I'll come and make love to you at five o'clock. If I'm late, start without me. —BISEXUAL ACTRESS TALLULAH BANKHEAD TO A MALE ADMIRER

There are many things better than sex, but there's nothing quite like it.
—W. C. FIELDS

Henry's idea of sex is to slow down to thirty miles an hour when he drops you off at the door. **—JOURNALIST BARBARA HOWAR, FORMER COMPANION OF HENRY KISSINGER**

My father told me, "Anything worth having is worth waiting for." I waited until I was fifteen. **—ZSA ZSA GABOR**

The last time I was inside a woman was when I visited the Statue of Liberty. **—WOODY ALLEN**

At certain times I like sex—like after a cigarette. **—COMEDIAN RODNEY DANGERFIELD**

I used to think "promiscuity" meant when you said "I promise" a lot. **—STAND-UP COMIC FRANK MAYA**

I learned several tricks of the trade from my wife, Uta Hagen, one of the greatest acting teachers. But I never learned how to sing from Rosemary Clooney—we made children, not music, together. **—OSCAR-WINNING ACTOR JOSÉ FERRER**

I had this girlfriend . . . I would cringe because she wanted to sing to me just because I'm a professional singer. It's like in most musicals—if something's too stupid to say, they sing it. **—KURT COBAIN**

Singing the praises of marriage, period, is like praising eating, without regard to what's being consumed. The difference is, eating is essential to life; marriage is not. **—LEONARD BERNSTEIN**

woman has got to love a bad man once or twice in her life, to be thankful for a good one.

—WRITER MARJORIE KINNAN RAWLINGS *(THE YEARLING)*

Till it has loved, no man or woman can become itself.

—NINETEENTH-CENTURY POET EMILY DICKINSON

Most people, certainly most women, love because we feel the need so to do. Not because we've found someone deserving of all our love.

—EMMA THOMPSON

My boyfriend and I broke up. He wanted to get married, and I didn't want him to.

—RITA RUDNER

A wedding invitation is beautiful and formal notification of the desire to share a solemn and joyous occasion, sent by people who have been saying, "Do we have to ask them?" to people whose first response is, "How much do you think we have to spend on them?"

—JUDITH MARTIN, A.K.A. MISS MANNERS

It is a truth universally acknowledged that a single man in possession of a good fortune must be in want of a wife. —JANE AUSTEN IN 1813

Wife and servant are the same, / But only differ in the name.

—POET LADY MARY CHUDLEIGH IN 1703

If the right man does not come along, there are many fates far worse. One is to have the wrong man come along.
> —LETITIA BALDRIDGE, PUBLICIST AND WHITE HOUSE SOCIAL SECRETARY

An athlete can make for a good boyfriend. A rich man can make for a good husband, anyway a good provider. . . . When I met him, I couldn't believe my luck.
> —NICOLE BROWN SIMPSON IN 1988 ON O. J. SIMPSON

Why do they call them boyfriends when they're almost never your friend?
> —SINGER SHERYL CROW

To a man, marriage means giving up four out of five of the chiffonier drawers; to a woman, giving up four out of five of her opinions.
> —WRITER HELEN ROWLAND IN *REFLECTIONS OF A BACHELOR GIRL* (1909)

As so often happens in marriage, roles that had begun almost playfully, to give line and shape to our lives, have hardened like suits of armor and taken us prisoner.
> —FILM CRITIC MOLLY HASKELL

In courtship as in marriage, a woman should say no a lot. If you switch to yes, fine. But if you begin with yes, then you can't suddenly switch to no.
> —BIANCA JAGGER (FORMER WIFE OF MICK)

Ah, the relationships we get into just to get out of the ones we are not brave enough to say are over.
> —FILM PRODUCER JULIA PHILLIPS *(THE STING)*

$\mathcal{A}$ good premarital test, one that'll prove much better over the long run than sex, is this: Can he just sit with you for fifteen minutes and hold hands? Even thirty minutes—without petting? Just affection. Because sex will always fade, but affection should remain—and grow.

Conversely, after you've been married—a long time—can you have just sex for thirty minutes? Not fifteen, but thirty. . . .

—**BRITISH ACTRESS RACHEL KEMPSON, WIDOW OF MICHAEL REDGRAVE**

$\mathcal{P}$eople in show business are notoriously bad judges of potential mates. . . . In Hollywood, you send out for happiness—and sometimes for love.                                                    —**HUGH GRANT**

$\mathcal{A}$ bride is a person with lots of happiness behind her.

—**HELEN MIRREN** *(GOSFORD PARK)*

$\mathcal{A}$ man is known by the woman he keeps.

—**JULIA PHILLIPS, AUTHOR OF** *YOU'LL NEVER EAT LUNCH IN THIS TOWN AGAIN*

$\mathcal{F}$ernando Lamas said to me, "I really would like to marry you, but could you stop being Esther Williams?" I said, "That's a really interesting question. I've been Esther Williams since I was twelve, when I started competitive swimming. . . . Could you stop fooling around?" He said, "I don't know."     —**ESTHER WILLIAMS, WHO DID WED THE LATIN LOVER**

$\mathcal{N}$o partner in a love relationship—whether homo- or heterosexual—should feel that he has to give up an essential part of himself to make it viable.

—**AUTHOR MAY SARTON IN** *JOURNAL OF A SOLITUDE* (1973)

You need someone to love you while you're looking for someone to love. **—PLAYWRIGHT SHELAGH DELANEY**

When a woman says "love," she usually means that. When a man says "love," well, save yourself some possible grief and ask if he means love or sex? **—CAMERON DIAZ** *(CHARLIE'S ANGELS)*

The media has gotten out of hand. You can't go to lunch with a member of the opposite sex without it getting reported and enlarged. Suddenly, supposedly, you're "in love" with this person. **—MEG RYAN**

I got filmed going out of a restaurant by *Hard Copy.* They said, "Here Antonio is, getting into this car with his new girlfriend." It was my sister! I went out with my sister to dinner. **—ANTONIO SABATO JR.**

. . . "the opposite sex"—though why "opposite" I do not know. What is the neighboring sex? **—MYSTERY AUTHOR DOROTHY L. SAYERS**

There is more difference within the sexes than between them. **—BRITISH AUTHOR IVY COMPTON-BURNETT**

In today's press, they still protect you. You go out to a restaurant with your boyfriend, his sister comes along, they take a photograph and say you're out with your new girlfriend! It's the business of show, pretending every celebrity is straight. They still prefer to hide anyone gay. Even if you don't want to be "protected." **—OPENLY GAY ACTOR DAN BUTLER** *(FRASIER)*

All the women in America are hating me! Matthew [McConaughey] and I are not dating, we're not married. I'm not with Matthew. He's a single man. **—SANDRA BULLOCK**

Call me naive, innocent, whatever. But I did hang out with [madam to the stars] Heidi Fleiss three times before I caught on what her profession was. It's not like she handed out business cards or anything. **—SINGER DAVID LEE ROTH**

Misha [Mikhail Baryshnikov, the ballet dancer] was more like a friend, and there was a lot of distance. Monogamy wasn't in his book—he had a long-term girlfriend who, unbeknownst to me, got pregnant while we were going out. But I was in love with him. **—JANINE TURNER**

Warren's conquests of women are not totally unsuccessful. His percentage is about 50-50. **—*SHAMPOO* COSTAR LEE GRANT ON WARREN BEATTY**

Frankly, who in Hollywood hasn't made love with him? Not having sex with Warren Beatty is like going to Rome and not seeing the pope. **—BRAZILIAN ACTRESS SONIA BRAGA**

Brad [Pitt] is a good friend of ours, but he did not donate the sperm for our baby. **—MELISSA ETHERIDGE, ON HER AND JULIE CYPHER'S CHILD**

I think Brad [Pitt]'s a good friend and he's awfully cute, but I think he's afraid of commitment. **—FORMER GIRLFRIEND JULIETTE LEWIS, AFTER PITT AND GWYNETH PALTROW SPLIT UP**

Some men are either so fond of sexual conquest and/or so afraid of committing to one female that they avoid marriage as long as they can. For a lifetime, or until their looks are gone and they have to start paying for sex. That's when such men turn to matrimony—as a last resort, and a cheaper alternative.

—ELIZABETH MONTGOMERY *(BEWITCHED)*

If girlfriends and mothers didn't push like they do, I wonder just how many men would ever marry?   —DEBORAH HARRY OF BLONDIE

Sure, I'm for gay marriage. But not for me. I'm just commitment-phobic, I guess.

—NATHAN LANE *(THE BIRDCAGE* AND BROADWAY'S *THE PRODUCERS)*

Love means never having to say you're single.

—ACTOR RUPERT EVERETT *(MY BEST FRIEND'S WEDDING)*

I experimented with girls, but it wasn't just that I preferred my own kind. The real proof of your sexual orientation isn't who you have sex with, but who you fall in love with.

—SIR NIGEL HAWTHORNE *(THE MADNESS OF KING GEORGE)*

All of my sexual experiences when I was young were with girls. I mean, we didn't have those sleepover parties for nothing.   —MADONNA

Particularly for a young woman in a world of AIDS, I've said [lesbian sex] seems to be a safer way to explore your sexuality, rather than screwing around with a lot of boys.   —SUPERMODEL CINDY CRAWFORD

Fooling around today with a whole bunch of guys, seems to me you could get something terminal—like a kid.

**—COMEDIAN HENRIETTE MANTEL (*THE BRADY BUNCH MOVIE*)**

With children no longer the universally accepted reason for marriage, marriages are going to have to exist on their own merits.

**—ATTORNEY ELEANOR HOLMES NORTON IN 1970**

If marriage is supposed to be for procreation, then millions of heterosexual marriages without children—like that of Bob and Elizabeth Dole—would have to be legally dissolved.

**—GAY ACTOR AND PLAYWRIGHT HARVEY FIERSTEIN (*MRS. DOUBTFIRE*)**

Biological possibility and desire are not the same as biological need. Women have child-bearing equipment. For them to choose not to use the equipment is no more blocking what is instinctive than it is for a man who, muscles or no, chooses not to be a weightlifter.

**—TV JOURNALIST AND AUTHOR BETTY ROLLIN (*FIRST, YOU CRY*)**

If you never want to see a man again, say, "I love you. I want to marry you. I want to have children"—they leave skid marks.

**—RITA RUDNER**

Being a housewife and a mother is the biggest job in the world, but if it doesn't interest you, don't do it. It didn't interest me, so I didn't do it. Anyway, I would have made a terrible parent. The first time my child didn't do what I wanted, I'd kill him.   **—KATHARINE HEPBURN**

$\mathcal{H}$aving a child is a big, messy, great human process. I feel like I either will or I won't in my lifetime. I don't feel this "I am nothing unless I have children," like women do perhaps at a certain age. I don't think I'm nothing if I don't have kids.  —JODIE FOSTER, WHO LATER
HAD TWO CHILDREN VIA ARTIFICIAL INSEMINATION

$\mathcal{P}$arenthood: That state of being better chaperoned than you were before marriage.  —WRITER MARCELENE COX

$\mathcal{W}$hen you are a new mother and you are breast-feeding, there is nothing about it that is sexy. You can't just say [to your husband], "Okay, I am yours tonight. Let's get down and have a good time." You have to talk a lot with your partner.  —CÉLINE DION, WHO BECAME
A MOTHER AT LAST IN 2001 VIA IN VITRO FERTILIZATION, AFTER "SIX YEARS OF TRYING"
WITH HER TWENTY-SIX-YEARS-OLDER HUSBAND-MANAGER

$\mathcal{L}$ong ago, someone said that the first half of our lives is messed up by our parents, and the second half by our children. If you have children, be sure you want them. Don't do it because it's done. Do it, like marriage, for love. In big matters, love is the best reason for doing anything.  —DIRECTOR ROBERT ALTMAN *(NASHVILLE, GOSFORD PARK)*

$\mathcal{W}$e were bought and used, and when our usefulness was over, we were dismissed. I was sent to boarding school at ten and never lived at home again. I never had a family, nothing that could remotely be called normal.  —CHRISTINA CRAWFORD, ADOPTED CHILD (ONE OF FOUR) OF
IMAGE-CONSCIOUS JOAN CRAWFORD

Guys, watch out—ever since the sexual revolution, there's less space than ever between flirtation and fatherhood.
—JAMES KOMACK, PRODUCER *(WELCOME BACK, KOTTER)*

Flirtation is merely an expression of considered desire coupled with an admission of its impracticability.    —WRITER MARYA MANNES

I can always be distracted by love, but eventually I get horny for my creativity.    —GILDA RADNER IN *IT'S ALWAYS SOMETHING* (1989)

The best index to a person's character is a) how he treats people who can't do him any good, and b) how he treats people who can't fight back.    —COLUMNIST ABIGAIL "DEAR ABBY" VAN BUREN

I'm looking for a partner, a soul mate. Not a boss. An adult woman doesn't need a third parent.    —BRITNEY SPEARS

Anyone who marries for a reason other than love is all but guaranteed to wind up having an affair.
—FORMER CANADIAN PRIME MINISTER PIERRE TRUDEAU

Where there's Marriage without Love, there will be Love without Marriage.    —BENJAMIN FRANKLIN IN 1734 (FOR THE SECOND LOVE, READ SEX)

During courtship, he must respect your boundaries. It's during this time that he learns whether you stand by your principles. For, once married, his respect is voluntary and your boundaries virtually nonexistent.    —HOLLYWOOD GOLDEN-ERA COLUMNIST LOUELLA PARSONS

Boyfriends are sort of like little kids toward their girlfriends: it's only by going too far that they discover how far they can go.

—BEN AFFLECK

When women go wrong, men go right after them.    —MAE WEST

The average man is more interested in a woman who is interested in him than he is in a woman—any woman—with beautiful legs.

—MARLENE DIETRICH, RENOWNED FOR HER LEGS

Cleopatra was no beauty. But she charmed powerful men, and apparently did so by making them believe they were each wonderful and unique. Of course it didn't hurt that she also had a kingdom to offer.

—SCREENWRITER HELEN DEUTSCH (KING SOLOMON'S MINES)

Sex can intimidate a man at times, particularly if the woman is very beautiful or exceptional. More than a few men prefer a sex partner with flaws. It makes him feel more at home.

—BENNY ANDERSSON OF ABBA

We were sitting around for days, sort of naked between takes, and Nicole and I would look at each other and say the most godawful stupid things like, "Can you believe this weather?" or "Do you think they'll have the good fish for lunch?" It's almost like being in a doctor's office. You can't wait until it's over, even if it's Nicole Kidman across the bed from you.

—BEN CHAPLIN ON HIS LOVE SCENES IN BIRTHDAY GIRL

I loved the way Nicole looked. If I saw her on that sidewalk right now, I'd pull over and hit on her.   **—PRESUMABLY NOT LITERALLY; O. J. SIMPSON SPEAKING OF HIS MURDERED EX-WIFE, IN 2001**

So long as women are slaves, men will be knaves.   **—AMERICAN SUFFRAGIST ELIZABETH CADY STANTON (1815–1902)**

Women have served all these centuries as looking-glasses . . . reflecting the figure of man at twice its natural size.   **—VIRGINIA WOOLF**

. . . and by the way, in the new Code of Laws . . . I desire you would Remember the Ladies, and be more generous and favorable to them than your ancestors. Do not put such unlimited power into the hands of the Husbands. Remember, all Men would be tyrants if they could. . . . Such of you as wish to be happy, willingly give up the harsh title of Master for the more tender and endearing one of Friend.   **—ABIGAIL ADAMS, WIFE OF JOHN ADAMS, IN A LETTER TO HER HUSBAND IN 1776**

I had this one boyfriend, it was getting serious, except whenever we'd argue, his way of trying to win was to say that I took everything personally. How *else* can you take anything?   **—JULIE WALTERS *(EDUCATING RITA)***

I'd never say who, but I broke off with one guy who, every time before we had sex, . . . liquor. If he needs that as a stimulant so early on in the relationship, well, you can imagine. Sex should be in and of itself stimulating enough, don't you think?   **—CYBILL SHEPHERD**

Creative men, men in the arts, do tend to be more in touch with their feelings. Therefore more aware of yours. . . . Notice that when women get together, they usually talk about people. By contrast, most men will avoid people and relationships for talk about sports . . . and sports are okay, if it's not obsessive. But they can be a shield against reality, feelings, and self-knowledge.   **—SUSAN SARANDON**

Friend of mine was going steady with this girl who was driving him nuts. Nothing could be simple, everything a ceremony, some little ritual . . . a toast before every glass of wine, a prayer for this, a saying for that, weird and repetitive preparations for sex. After he dumped her, he said, "Don't get involved with someone who's obsessive-repulsive."   **—JACK KLUGMAN** *(THE ODD COUPLE)*

Ritual is the act of sanctifying action—even ordinary actions—so that it has meaning: I can light a candle because I need the light or because the candle represents the light I need.

**—WRITER-EDUCATOR CHRISTINA BALDWIN**

Women have sent me everything, from pictures of themselves nude to their actual underwear—used. What really impressed me, got to me, was when a woman sent me flowers.

**—CROONER ENGELBERT HUMPERDINCK**

He never sent me flowers. But he had a steady job and he didn't drink. . . . I don't know: Do we settle for too little?

**—PRODUCER JULIA PHILLIPS, ON A FORMER BEAU**

A fox is a wolf who sends flowers.   **—ACTRESS RUTH WESTON**

*I* like dates. Love going on dates. But I'd have to know a man awfully well before ever making that huge matrimonial commitment.

—YASMINE BLEETH *(BAYWATCH)*

*I*'ve never been an anonymous-sex kind of person. I need to know who he is, where he comes from, and how many brothers and sisters he has. —MULTI-GOLD-MEDAL-WINNING OLYMPIC DIVER GREG LOUGANIS

*H*ey, if he's breathing, I don't turn him down. Not enough men are that interested. Most want sex, not a nest.

—ROSE MARIE *(THE DICK VAN DYKE SHOW)*

*T*here are far too many men in politics and not enough elsewhere.

—HERMIONE GINGOLD *(THE MUSIC MAN)*

*A* man in the house is worth two in the street. —MAE WEST

*L*oneliness is the poverty of self; solitude is the richness of self.

—WRITER MAY SARTON

*O*nce you have lived with another it is a great torture to have to live alone. —WRITER CARSON MCCULLERS *(THE HEART IS A LONELY HUNTER)*

*N*o matter how lonely you get or how many birth announcements you receive, the trick is not to get frightened. There's nothing wrong with being alone. —PLAYWRIGHT WENDY WASSERSTEIN

$\mathcal{B}$eing alone and liking it is, for a woman, an act of treachery, an infidelity far more threatening than adultery.

—FILM CRITIC MOLLY HASKELL

$\mathcal{W}$hen you live alone, you can be sure that the person who squeezed the toothpaste tube in the middle wasn't committing a hostile act.

—COLUMNIST ELLEN GOODMAN

$\mathcal{P}$sychiatrist was dating this girl. Says to her, "You're crazy." She says, "Oh, yeah? I want a second opinion." He says, "Okay. You're ugly too."

—HENNY YOUNGMAN

$\mathcal{I}$'m whatcha call hyperheterosexual. I like all kinds of women. Even the ugly ones. I've known some in my time, some of 'em kinda nice. Love means never having to say you're ugly.     —REDD FOXX

$\mathcal{A}$ female lover would have to look exactly like me to really turn me on!     —ROSEANNE (WHO HAS A GAY BROTHER AND A LESBIAN SISTER)

$\mathcal{M}$e with a guy? Never happen! . . . Well, maybe Brad Pitt.

—RODNEY DANGERFIELD

$\mathcal{I}$ was far too polite to ask.     —GAY AUTHOR GORE VIDAL, ON BEING ASKED
WHETHER THE FIRST PERSON HE HAD SEX WITH WAS MALE OR FEMALE

As I grow older and older
And totter towards the tomb,
I find that I care less and less
Who goes to bed with whom. —ENGLISH NOVELIST DOROTHY L. SAYERS

As to marriage, I think the intercourse of heart and mind may be
fully enjoyed without entering into this partnership of daily life.
—U.S. WRITER, EDITOR, AND CRITIC MARGARET FULLER IN AN
1848 LETTER TO HER SISTER

All my relatives want me to marry. They say it's a great life. But
what about the *days* . . . ? —JERRY SEINFELD, PREMARRIAGE

Strange to say what delight we married people have to see these
poor fools decoyed into our condition. —SAMUEL PEPYS IN 1665

I've come to the conclusion it's not for everyone. I'm sorry, but I
would tell my son, "Son, marriage is like boarding school. After
you've been through it, you can appreciate, deeply, the rest of your
life." It would be up to him if he wanted to gamble on that
experience. —DUDLEY MOORE

I advised my daughter, "Treat your husband like a permanent
roommate and guest. Be on your best behavior, but let him find his
way gradual-like. Marriage isn't a natural state for a man." I also told
her if he cheats on you, throw the bum out. When you have daughters, it makes you a bit of a feminist. —ACTOR RORY CALHOUN

An undutiful Daughter will prove an unmanageable Wife.
**—BENJAMIN FRANKLIN IN 1752**

I pity the man who ends up marrying my daughter.
**—ALEX TREBEK ON THE SET OF JEOPARDY! ON JANUARY 7, 1998**
**(THIS AUTHOR WON THAT DAY)**

If a woman came into my life who was absolutely stunning and sat-isfied me emotionally, intellectually, and sexually, I'm not going to draw the line and say, "I can't because you're a woman." I find it hard enough to find someone to be with, why narrow the field?
**—AMANDA DONOHOE *(L.A. LAW)***

Do I like women? I like women. Do I like them sexually? Yeah, I do. Totally. . . . It's weird. Women are so much more selective with women than they are with men.   **—DREW BARRYMORE**

In suburbia they thump you for anything. . . . People still think het-eros make love and gays have sex. I want to tell them that's wrong.
**—BOY GEORGE**

A slip of the tongue is often meaningful. They don't call it a Freudian slap—I mean slip—for nothing. Like my ex-boyfriend . . . we were talking about adolescence, and he said, "You mean that time between puberty and adultery?"   **—NICOLE KIDMAN, PRE-TOM CRUISE**

$\mathcal{I}$f a woman loves you, I don't think it's ever too soon to ask her a favor. You got your mum and you got the current love of your life. In fact, when I met my first wife she was already engaged and I tried to get her to sell her ring, I was that hard up. . . . I married her anyway. She was a model, you understand?    —OLIVER REED *(WOMEN IN LOVE)*

$\mathcal{T}$his one guy I dated once. Once. He thought a Caucasian was a gay Chinese or something.    —TÉA LEONI

$\mathcal{T}$his girl I was going with, she didn't know from sex. I suggested foreplay for Saturday night; I went over to her place, she'd invited two other people.    —JERRY SEINFELD

$\mathcal{Y}$ou like sports? I like sports. Why can't girls like sports? One girl I broke up with, she hated sports. Thought a quarterback was a refund.    —BILL MURRAY

$\mathcal{I}$ kissed my first woman and smoked my first cigarette on the same day. I have never had time for tobacco since.    —ARTURO TOSCANINI

$\mathcal{I}$ wasn't kissing her, I was whispering in her mouth.    CHICO MARX, CAUGHT IN THE ACT

$\mathcal{B}$isexuality immediately doubles your chances for a date on Saturday night.    —WOODY ALLEN

$\mathcal{L}$ove is an obsessive delusion that is cured by marriage.    —DR. KARL BOWMAN (1888–1973)

$\mathscr{I}$t must be convenient, being a hermaphrodite. If you're heterosexual and horny, you just date yourself. —COMEDIAN SHIRLEY HEMPHILL

$\mathscr{M}$y God, when I discovered sex! The first time . . . the embarrassment, the shame, the disillusionment, the guilt and remorse. And this was just masturbation. —WOODY ALLEN

$\mathscr{W}$hat's better than roses on your piano? Tulips on your organ! —PIANIST-SHOWMAN LIBERACE

$\mathscr{E}$veryone thinks I hate penises. I don't! I have four of them at home. —LESBIAN COMEDIAN LEA DELARIA

$\mathscr{I}$ had this beau, let's call him a fiancé. The relationship was okay, but the sex was great. Then one day he said the most chilling thing: "I bet when you imagined eternity, you never thought it would be me. . . ." —FORMER PRODUCER JULIA PHILLIPS *(YOU'LL NEVER EAT LUNCH IN THIS TOWN AGAIN)*

$\mathscr{I}$t's not like I'll never be married. . . . I was with Elizabeth [Hurley] for fourteen years. I'm not exactly a classic lost cause. —UK ACTOR HUGH GRANT, TWO YEARS AFTER BREAKING UP

$\mathscr{W}$riting is like getting married. One should never commit oneself until one is amazed at one's luck. —IRIS MURDOCH

$\mathscr{I}$'m kind of afraid to marry an actress. They're so dumb and vain. I heard about one—her husband asked her to make up her mind, and she put lipstick on her head. —ACTOR STEPHEN BALDWIN

*I* feel sorry for people who worry about commitment or divorce instead of enjoying companionship today. —**DENZEL WASHINGTON**

*I* like to model and I love to party, but now I'm pregnant, so that's going to affect all that. —**KATE MOSS, TWENTY-SEVEN, PREGNANT BY COMPANION JEFFERSON HACK, AN EDITOR**

*It's* weird kissing somebody you don't want to kiss. Most girls would love to kiss Hayden. I just don't feel that way about him. —**NATALIE *(THE PHANTOM MENACE)* PORTMAN ON COSTAR HAYDEN CHRISTIANSON, ABOUT WHOM SHE WAS INITIALLY ENTHUSIASTIC**

*Seems* like there's always three stages on how you relate to someone new that you like. First, you have a crush, he's wonderful. Second, the faults come through, and you like him less and less. Third, you like him and see him as a human being. Same thing when I had crushes on teachers in school. —**CAMERON DIAZ**

*I* thought my steady was wonderful. And then he tried to explain that after we would marry, I wouldn't need a job. Oh, why? Because, he said, being his wife would take up all my time. So now my time would be his time. And my job wouldn't just be him, it would be his clothes, his food, his upkeep, his, his, . . . . I decided he was history. —**MADELINE KAHN *(PAPER MOON)***

*A* smart parent doesn't let his kids get a peek at the Christmas presents ahead of time. Or else the anticipation's gone, all that excitement. Likewise, a fiancée shouldn't let her guy get a sneak preview. He'll want to. He'll try to. But she shouldn't let him. —**ELVIS PRESLEY**

𝒜 couple is driving to Miami Beach in a brand-new car. As they're driving, he puts his hand on her knee. She says, "We're married now, you can go a little farther." So he went to Fort Lauderdale.

—**HENNY YOUNGMAN**

𝒪n my honeymoon, Fang told me to unbutton my pajamas, and I wasn't wearing any. —**PHYLLIS DILLER**

𝔐y parents want me to get married. They don't care who anymore, as long as he doesn't have a pierced ear, that's all they care about. I think men who have a pierced ear are better prepared for marriage. They've experienced pain and bought jewelry. —**RITA RUDNER**

𝔐y wife and I were happy for twenty years. Then we met.

—**RODNEY DANGERFIELD**

𝒥 asked my new bride to promise me, because I wanted so much to please her, to let me know—to be honest—when she had an orgasm. She was honest too; she said, "I will—if you're there."

—**GABE KAPLAN** *(WELCOME BACK, KOTTER)*

𝒯oo much of a good thing can be wonderful. —**MAE WEST**

𝒥n those days [the 1940s], young stars, male and female, were all virgins until married, and if divorced, they returned magically to that condition. —**SHELLEY WINTERS IN** *SHELLEY* **(1980)**

Women who miscalculate are called "mother."

—**ABIGAIL "DEAR ABBY" VAN BUREN**

A pretty girl should break her mirror young, while there's still time to save her character.

—**DAME JUDI DENCH**

There's a strain of young men who long for perpetual youth and idealize their boyhoods. Spare me! When you date them, you serve the sole purpose of an audience. Show me a man who waxes rhapsodic about his teenage years and I'll show you someone who has either no memory or no heart.

—**KAREN VALENTINE** *(ROOM 222)*

Whatever happened to wife-swapping? Talk about glamour and excitement. All that pre-AIDS stuff, the possibilities. Now it's just sexual nostalgia, the stuff envious dreams are made of.

—**DAVID SPADE** *(JUST SHOOT ME)*

Well, scientists now know [in 2000] that the AIDS virus originated in Africa and was transferred to humans from chimps. So much for these "God's punishment" people. Unless God was punishing chimps for being too smart for their kind or humans for living too near to chimps.

—**STEPHEN FRY, UK ACTOR-AUTHOR**

If we can take sex out of the realm of sin altogether and see it as something else to do with personal relationships and ethics, then we can finally get around to a phase . . . which deals with the question of sin as violence, sin as cruelty, sin as murder, war and starvation.

—**NOVELIST ANNE RICE**

Someone at a party one time mentioned wife-swapping, and I said that theoretically I wasn't totally opposed to husband-swapping, and the host stopped me and said, "That's shocking." He'd been carrying on about pro–wife-swapping! So I said, "What's the difference?" and he said, "Well, what you said, that's dirty . . . like a sin."
—JUDITH LIGHT *(WHO'S THE BOSS?)*

If a man, any man, in Hollywood offers to marry you, run, don't walk, for the nearest exit.   —UK ACTRESS STEPHANIE BEACHAM

Hollywood men are the most manipulative on earth.
—TERRI GARR *(TOOTSIE)*

The biggest impediment to real relationships with men is that they're, at heart, such sexual predators.   —TINA LOUISE *(GILLIGAN'S ISLAND)*

The thing you finally find out about women is how sexually manipulative they can't seem to help being.   —FRENCH ACTOR GÉRARD DEPARDIEU

Said a puzzled young bachelor named Claridge,
"Connubial life I disparage.
"Every time I get hot
"And poke some girl's spot,
"he thinks it an offer of marriage."                    —IRISH LIMERICK

You can discount all those romance rumors you've been hearing. There was nothing between us but air.   —UMA THURMAN ON
JOHN TRAVOLTA, HER *PULP FICTION* COSTAR

*I* told my intended I wanted a togetherness marriage. Not a social arrangement like my parents had. My mother once said of my father, "I see him so seldom, I feel like I took his name in vain."

—**BROOKE SHIELDS**

*B*eware anyone—your mother, wife, your fiancée—who solemnly informs you, "No one else will ever love you as much as I do." They're either trying to limit you or scare you.

—**JON LOVITZ**

*M*r. Mayer could not believe my cousin [Ramon Novarro] was homosexual. He did not really know what a homosexual was. He felt that if he forced Ramon to marry, he could convert him. Ramon refused, saying his private life was his own. You can imagine what happened to Ramon's standing at Metro [MGM] after that. . . .

—**DOLORES DEL RIO**

*R*elatives may or may not try and pressure you into marrying someone of the opposite sex, but corporations sometimes try to frighten you into it. You can compromise for your career, but how long do you have to compromise yourself, your love life, and the love of your life? —**ROSIE O'DONNELL IN 2002, AFTER COMING OUT FOLLOWING HER TENURE AS A PROFITABLE TV TALK SHOW HOST**

*I* fell in love with [costar] Cary Grant. . . . He did not reciprocate the emotion, and that disappointed me. . . . Cary and I became good friends. Not close friends, because he doesn't let you come too close. If we had gotten married, I doubt he would have let me get too close. . . . It is better to have a crush on Cary Grant than to have him for a husband. A crush allows you to keep your fantasies.

—INGRID BERGMAN

*I* married Vincent Price very late in both our lives. It was chiefly because . . . without a husband, even an actress doesn't get invited out much. In Hollywood, a woman without a [man] doesn't rate, socially. Here feminism is a foreign concept—something imported from New York or elsewhere.    —CORAL BROWNE

*M*en have an unusual talent for making a bore out of everything they touch.    —YOKO ONO

*T*he great thing about being thirty is that there are a great deal more available women. The young ones look younger and the old ones don't look nearly as old.    —GLENN FREY

*A*t least some of the men who write sex books admit that they really don't understand female sexuality. Freud was one. Masters is another—that was why he got Johnson.    —CRITIC ARLENE CROCE

*N*o sex is better than bad sex.    —WRITER GERMAINE GREER

*N*iagara Falls is only the second-biggest disappointment of the standard honeymoon.    —OSCAR WILDE

Men have always detested women's gossip because they suspect the truth: their measurements are being taken and compared.

—**WRITER ERICA JONG**

She: "You are the greatest lover I have ever known."
He: "Well, I practice a lot when I am alone." —**WOODY ALLEN**

Aren't women "prudes" if they don't and "prostitutes" if they do?

—**WRITER KATE MILLET**

Is it too much to ask that women be spared the daily struggle for superhuman beauty in order to offer it to the caresses of a sub-humanly ugly man? —**GERMAINE GREER IN *THE FEMALE EUNUCH***

Most plain girls are virtuous because of the scarcity of opportunity to be otherwise. —**WRITER MAYA ANGELOU**

Woman's virtue is man's greatest invention. —**CORNELIA OTIS SKINNER**

Abstainer: a weak person who yields to the temptation of denying himself a pleasure. —**AMBROSE BIERCE**

To my flaming youth let virtue be as wax. —**SHAKESPEARE IN *HAMLET***

Virtue is its own reward. —**JOHN DRYDEN**

Virtue is its own reward, damn it. —**BETTE MIDLER**

Virtue is its own revenge.

—E. Y. HARBURG, COCOMPOSER OF *THE WIZARD OF OZ*

If wives were good, God would have one.   —RUSSIAN PROVERB

A bachelor never quite gets over the idea that he is a thing of beauty and a boy forever.   —HUMORIST HELEN ROWLAND

Slightly icky and a little bit wet.

—THANDIE NEWTON ON KISSING *MISSION: IMPOSSIBLE 2* COSTAR TOM CRUISE

I'm so happy. It's so nice to go with a man whose clothes you can wear.   —BRITT EKLAND ON BEAU ROD STEWART, WHOM SHE UNSUCCESSFULLY SUED FOR $15 MILLION IN PALIMONY IN 1978

I didn't marry my high school sweetheart, Beavis, who had to repeat the twelfth grade twice. He was so unromantic, all the word "moon" meant to him was dropping his pants. He loved to moon people, and he had the hairiest rump you ever saw. I recently met up with him again, at a high school reunion, and his beautiful head of hair was mostly gone. But his personality hadn't changed. So I said, "Beavis, you should go for a hair transplant now, from your butt to your head."   —COMEDIAN JUDY TENUTA

The only two things that motivate me and that matter to me are revenge and guilt. These are the only emotions I know about. Love? I don't know what it means. It doesn't exist in my songs.

—ELVIS COSTELLO

*I* had a fiancé, he'd never say "I love you." He finally did say he thought the world of me. Of course, he was a misanthropic misogynist who didn't think much of the world. We did not marry.

—LEADING ARTISTS AGENT ANN DOLLARD

*It's* gotten so that if a man opens a door for a lady to go through first, he's the doorman.

—MAE WEST

*Like* Oprah Winfrey of Chicago, USA, I am black, female, and oversized. Unlike her, I got my man to marry me, and I let people read what they please.

—JAMAICAN CRITIC ROSE ACHEBE

*I'm* no virgin. I'm all for female sexuality and taking the sexual power away from the guys. They've had it for way too long. All this "Do not touch" nonsense is not me.

—CHRISTINA AGUILERA, DISTINGUISHING HERSELF FROM BRITNEY SPEARS

*A* Casanova is a man who never misses a chance to go on a date, shall we call it?—and never Mrs. a girlfriend.

—JACK BENNY

*My* ex-girlfriend was such a sex maniac, when she got the flu, the doctor came over, gave her a prescription, and said, "Don't worry, a few days on your feet and we'll soon have you back in bed."

—SAM KINISON

*The* more sex becomes a nonissue in people's lives, the happier they are.

—SHIRLEY MACLAINE

$\mathcal{I}$ think it's tiresome and ridiculous, the way they [the writers] make having a boyfriend the whole focus of Ally's life—getting a boyfriend, finding a new boyfriend . . . there's so much more she could do with her life. **—*ALLY MCBEAL* STAR CALISTA FLOCKHART IN 2002**

$\mathcal{F}$or married people, it's the only day of the year you can count on having sex. **—AISHA TYLER *(TALK SOUP)* ON VALENTINE'S DAY**

$\mathcal{T}$he average man starts considering getting a wife after he gets his first full-time job. That's because now he can afford her, and because after a long, hard day in an office or on an assembly line, a man needs a wife waiting for him at home to keep from going crazy—unless he's picked the wrong wife. **—DIRECTOR ROBERT ALTMAN**

$\mathcal{W}$e all marry strangers. All men are strangers to all women. **—MARY HEATON VORSE IN *McCALL'S* MAGAZINE IN 1920**

$\mathcal{A}$ woman who has known but one man is like a person who has heard only one composer. **—ISADORA DUNCAN IN HER MEMOIRS**

$\mathcal{M}$arriage is a great strain upon love. **—MYRTLE REED IN *MASTER OF THE VINEYARD* (1910)**

$\mathcal{L}$ord of yourself, uncumber'd with a wife. **—JOHN DRYDEN**

$\mathcal{I}$t's not that marriage itself is bad; it's the people we marry who give it a bad name. **—TERRY MCMILLAN *(WAITING TO EXHALE)***

You have to kiss an awful lot of frogs before you find a prince.

—GRAFFITO

Notoriously, women tolerate qualities in a lover—moodiness, self-ishness, unreliability, brutality—that they would never countenance in a husband, in return for excitement, an infusion of intense feeling.

—SUSAN SONTAG

Two fears alternate in marriage, the one of loneliness and the other of bondage. The dread of loneliness is greater than the fear of bondage, so we get married.

—CYRIL CONNOLLY

The truth is, when I think of my loneliest moments, there was usually somebody sitting there next to me.

—CALISTA FLOCKHART *(ALLY MCBEAL)*

A man is like a cat; chase him and he will run. . . . Sit still and ignore him and he'll come purring at your feet.

—HUMORIST HELEN ROWLAND

When I was terribly young I had an American friend. One day he asked me if I liked "tits." I said, "Well, they're rather small, but I suppose they're all right." The look on his face combined surprise, anxiety, and shocked interest. Tits, of course, are small birds. My friend then explained what he'd meant. He meant did I like "bristols"? I assured him I did like "birds," but the human kind, while he, being from the States, was very fond of "chicks."

—BRITISH ACTOR OLIVER REED *(GLADIATOR)*

*Y*ou marry a man who, to quite an extent, is drawn to your charms. Then, in marriage, you educate him about your personality and the importance of wife, family, and honoring an agreement. It's not easy, but few worthwhile things are.
                    —BEA BENADERET, MATRIARCH OF *PETTICOAT JUNCTION*

*G*irls sometimes ask me how to hook a man. I say, "Honey, it's simple: Turn him on, make him beg for more, and then don't give it to him." Which is also good practice for married life.    —ETHEL MERMAN

*F*rom a practical point of view, marriage has to be harder on the female partner. But psychologically, . . . I wonder.
                    —THEN-BACHELOR JERRY SEINFELD

*F*or as long as it's a man's world, average females will need that marriage contract. It's far from perfect, but until men move up the evolutionary scale or things progress to a more equitable level, sister, we need it!                    —RICKI LAKE

# Women on Marriage

❧

Marriage isn't a word, but a sentence.    —ANONYMOUS

Marriage is the biggest gamble going.
                    —DREW BARRYMORE, WHO'S HAD TWO BRIEF MARRIAGES SO FAR

Marriage is too emotional and thrilling to try just once.
                    —JENNIFER LOPEZ, DURING HER SECOND MARRIAGE

Why do such a lot of men think that settling down means giving up? Or giving in? I think most women view marriage as a beginning, whereas men tend to see it as an ending.    —SUSAN SARANDON

You know when people get married and they call it "settling down"? I'm an optimist. I think they should call it "settling up."
                    —PAMELA ANDERSON

Girls, hold out! Hold out for that wedding ring. Don't give in until then. After the soup course is over, who values the spoon?
                    —COSMETICS MAGNATE ELIZABETH ARDEN

*I* got married so many times because I was an old-fashioned romantic. —ELIZABETH TAYLOR

*S*oon after marriage, and even before motherhood, most females realize they are mothers at heart. Most husbands become fathers, but hardly any are fathers at heart. Alas, married or not, most men are bachelors at heart. —CARRIE FISHER *(STAR WARS)*

*B*efore you walk down the aisle, have a chat with his ex-girlfriend. Or better yet, his ex-wife. —AUDREY MEADOWS *(THE HONEYMOONERS)*

*E*at a meal with your intended. If he doesn't gross you out while eating, you just might be able to live with him. —ELIZABETH HURLEY, FORMER LONGTIME COMPANION OF HUGH GRANT

*M*y dream man, because I am a stickler for good grammar, is one who can put a sentence together. I don't like the "dees, does, and dems" guys. —MARIAH CAREY

*I*f there wasn't marriage, most men wouldn't feel any guilt at all about promiscuity or multiple partners. —MAUREEN O'SULLIVAN, TARZAN'S JANE AND MIA FARROW'S MOTHER

*E*verything about marriage used to be stacked against women. Now there's a little unfairness toward the men. Like the double standard where if a woman holds off from marrying, she's independent, but if a guy holds off, we say he has a fear of commitment. —KIM CATTRALL *(SEX AND THE CITY)*

$\mathcal{I}$f you agree to tie the knot—a good phrase for it—ask him first how he feels about money. Then ask how he feels about a husband who cheats. Finally, ask him how he feels about a wife who cheats. His answers to those three questions will tell you most of what you need to know.   **—FOUR-TIMES-MARRIED VIVIAN VANCE OF** *I LOVE LUCY*

$\mathcal{T}$he most exciting relationship of all is equality, in any relationship, legal or not.   **—NOVELIST JACKIE COLLINS**

$\mathcal{I}$t's worth remembering that marriage is the only contract that cannot be mutually dissolved by the two parties involved. They have to get governmental permission to split up. In some ways it's quite medieval.   **—ELIZABETH MONTGOMERY** *(BEWITCHED)*

$\mathcal{A}$ll this talk about trophy wives is demeaning. It's pathetic. A man who wants a trophy wife is sexist and insecure. What anybody, a man or a woman, should want, is a trophy marriage.

   **—SARAH JESSICA PARKER OF** *SEX AND THE CITY*

$\mathcal{M}$y father did not treat my mother very well. Naturally that made me wary of marriage. I saw housewifedom as sort of an imprisonment for girls not clever or brave enough to create a career and success for themselves. I only wanted marriage if the husband was wonderful and worthwhile, not marriage for its own sake.

   But I found out that future husbands are very good actors indeed.   **—BETTE DAVIS**

Even in modern, wealthier countries, most people marry due to expectations. Or else they have nothing more exciting to do. But tradition or routine is a lousy reason to wed—or to do anything. Be passionate about what you do! Want that marriage! Don't just follow others'' footsteps. Do what you want and love to do. Live your own life.

—CYBILL SHEPHERD

My parents were rather thwarted people who gave up their dreams to marry and have us two kids. They had a very structured marriage, and as a result, I wanted, if I married, a very different kind of marriage.

—SHIRLEY MACLAINE, WHOSE SOLE HUSBAND SPENT MOST OF HIS TIME IN JAPAN

Things are more materialistic than ever. Girls are so easily impressed by cash and flash. But you know what? Most successful men are not that successful as husbands. Marry the man, don't marry the wallet or the wardrobe.

—MODEL NAOMI CAMPBELL

A successful man is one who makes more money than his wife can spend. A successful woman is one who can find such a man.

—THE MUCH-MARRIED, BIG-EARNING LANA TURNER

Aim high, but marry money.

—JOAN RIVERS, WHOSE DAUGHTER DID

If you marry for love and then divorce, where's the love? But if you marry a rich man—and statistics say you're more likely to wind up in divorce than living happily ever after—at least you'll end up with wealth, which helps dull the pain, honey.

—SINGER CARMEN MCRAE

$\mathcal{I}$ want a man who's kind and understanding. Is that too much to ask of a millionaire?              —ZSA ZSA GABOR

$\mathcal{M}$y mother always told me never to accept candy from strange men. Get real estate instead.              —EVA GABOR

$\mathcal{M}$arrying a man is like buying something you've been admiring for a long time in a shop window. You may love it when you get it home, but it doesn't always go with everything else in the house.
—PLAYWRIGHT JEAN KERR

$\mathcal{M}$ost women give more thought to selecting makeup or décor than a husband. If he hasn't got either great heart, great humor, great looks, or a great fortune, pass.
—NATALIE SCHAFER (LOVEY ON *GILLIGAN'S ISLAND*)

$\mathcal{C}$hoose a guy who enjoys life in general . . . a man should be married to his wife, not his career.              —WHOOPI GOLDBERG

$\mathcal{I}$ married because I was lonely. I was lonelier after I got married.
—SCREENWRITER ELEANOR PERRY, WHO WED A DIRECTOR

$\mathcal{I}$t was so cold the other day, I almost got married.   —SHELLEY WINTERS

$\mathcal{I}$ was a virgin when I got married. I married partly in order to learn about sex. I was an idiot.              —BETTE DAVIS

Personally, I know nothing about sex, because I've always been married.
— ZSA ZSA GABOR

I don't think anyone really marries beneath himself. Or herself. I think when people get married, they get just what they deserve.
— EVA GABOR

Yeah, I married beneath me. Doesn't every woman?
— ROSEANNE, POST-TOM ARNOLD

A man in my life, I wouldn't mind so much, but a man in my home, that's a horse of a different color—sometimes even an ass.
— AUTHOR HELENE HANFF

I have to say it, but lots of men are like dogs . . . cute and playful, good at protecting you, and their needs are simple and repetitive. But do you really want to spend twenty-four or even sixteen hours a day with them?
— JENNIFER SAUNDERS, CREATOR-STAR OF *ABSOLUTELY FABULOUS*

The male is a domestic animal which, if treated with firmness and kindness, can be trained to do most things.
— JILLY COOPER, UK AUTHOR

Most men think they're little gods, especially in a household. So why can't they accept that we're, in that case, goddesses?
— UMA THURMAN, WHO WAS NAMED AFTER A HINDU GODDESS

Men do not like to admit to even momentary imperfection. My husband forgot the code to turn off the alarm. When the police came, he wouldn't admit he'd forgotten the code . . . he turned himself in.

—COMEDIAN RITA RUDNER

Sometimes I wonder if men and women really suit each other. Perhaps they should live next door and just visit now and then.

—KATHARINE HEPBURN

If they can put a man on the moon, why can't they put them all?

—ROSEANNE, BETWEEN DIVORCE (TOM ARNOLD) AND REMARRIAGE

Young men are the most selfish. Mature ones make better husbands because they've suffered and are familiar with compromise. Which is all marriage is.   —ANGELINA JOLIE, WHILE MARRIED TO BILLY BOB THORNTON

Young men treat their wives or girlfriends the way they've treated their sisters—with supreme, sometimes amused condescension. They're still too immature to appreciate or respect femininity.

—BRETT BUTLER (*AMAZING GRACE*)

Dr. Ruth says we women should tell our lovers how to make love to us. My boyfriend goes nuts if I tell him how to drive!

—COMEDIAN PAM STONE

My ancestors wandered lost in the wilderness for forty years because even in biblical times, men would not stop to ask for directions.   —COMEDIAN ELAYNE BOOSLER

Men don't live well by themselves. They don't even live like people. They live like bears with furniture.   —COMEDIAN RITA RUDNER

Since women live longer and reach their sexual peaks much later, it makes sense that the wife should be the older one. That whole older-husband thing was originally about giving the man extra leverage over the "girl."   —JENNIFER SAUNDERS

Mother always says that after a certain age a woman should marry a man who is younger than she is, otherwise she will end up nursing an old man.   —ZSA ZSA GABOR, CURRENTLY MARRIED
TO A YOUNGER GERMAN "PRINCE"

Marrying an older man is a throwback. It usually amounts to his mind being closed, his opinions hardened. He'll also look on you as a daughter, but in an incestuous way.   —WINONA RYDER

Audrey [Hepburn] gave up her career because she thought it would make her second marriage more harmonious than her first [to an actor who wasn't as big a star]. She purposely married a nonactor. Of course in time he left her for a younger woman. Then, when Audrey returned to work, it was too late—a whole new generation of younger actresses was getting the good roles.
  —HOLLYWOOD HOSTESS AND PHOTOGRAPHER JEAN HOWARD

The only time a woman really succeeds in changing a man is when he's a baby.   —NATALIE WOOD

Men often marry their mothers.   **—NOVELIST EDNA FERBER** *(GIANT)*

When a man of forty falls in love with a girl of twenty, it isn't her youth he is seeking, but his own.   **—SCREENWRITER LENORE COFFEE**

Seek out a husband who didn't have an overindulgent mother. Why should a woman spend a big chunk of her married life picking up after him? People, men included, should have enough self-respect— and respect for their spouses—to clean up their own mess.

**—ACTRESS TURNED POLITICIAN GLENDA JACKSON**

It's okay for a husband to ask occasional favors and chores from his wife. So long as it works both ways.   **—MELANIE GRIFFITH**

Men complain about their wives' clutter. But most husbands are messy. Some are outright pigs. I think a mess is worse than a comfortable clutter any day.   **—ROSEANNE, THE ERSTWHILE "DOMESTIC GODDESS"**

I'd say that if you discuss one single topic before saying "I do," it should be kids. To be childless or child-free? How does he feel? Or when, and how many kids? This topic must be broached, not just for the sake of the two adults.   **—PIONEERING TALK SHOW HOST VIRGINIA GRAHAM**

After I married I could afford all the nice things I couldn't as a single woman. Now that we have children—a whole parcel of the little darlings—I can't afford the nice things again.

**—PHYLLIS DILLER, PRESTARDOM**

$\mathcal{D}$on't marry a man with kids of his own unless he's rich. Boarding schools are expensive. —HERMIONE GINGOLD

$\mathcal{I}$ wed Nick because I loved him . . . [and] he asked me. He had a lot of ladies in his life, but he wasn't all that matrimonially inclined. . . . Naturally when I married Tony I was also in love . . . [and] any kind of publicity was the furthest thing from my mind.
—OSCAR-WINNING ACTRESS GLORIA GRAHAME, WHOSE CAREER
SUFFERED BECAUSE SHE LATER WED DIRECTOR NICHOLAS RAY'S SON TONY
(THE MEDIA IMPLIED INCEST)

$\mathcal{D}$on't marry the first man who asks you. At least, don't say yes the first time he asks. Esteem yourself. Give yourself time to think and choose. Life is too short for a long marriage of servitude and regret.
—OSCAR-WINNING DAME MARGARET RUTHERFORD, WHO AFTER FIFTEEN YEARS
OF PLATONIC FRIENDSHIP MARRIED A MAN SEVEN YEARS HER JUNIOR

$\mathcal{Y}$ou know that it's still a man's world when they alone can talk about trophy wives. If a woman wants a trophy husband and actually says so, she's deemed grotesque or a user. Or a "ball-buster," which is not bad but is meant to be derogatory. Men, after all, are ovary-busters, yet nobody notices or calls them on it.
—AUSTRALIAN WRITER AND ACTIVIST GERMAINE GREER

$\mathcal{I}$ lost admiration for Jane Fonda when she married Ted Turner and gave up her profession. And then, pretty much, her voice. She became this buff glamourpuss on Turner's arm, his prize possession, just a billionaire's trophy wife.
—MADELINE KAHN *(WHAT'S UP, DOC? PAPER MOON)*

Most women are willing and indeed conditioned to make a go of marriage. They'll put up with more than a man would. So in the long run, the success of a marriage depends more on the husband than the wife. Unfortunately for the institution of marriage.
—**NANCY DICKERSON, FIRST FEMALE NEWS CORRESPONDENT ON TV**

It's so archaic! When the church guy says, "I now pronounce you man and wife." Like it's only changed for the woman. Now she's a wife. He's still a man and not a husband yet?   —**DREW BARRYMORE**

After women marry, for most of them that's their whole life. After a man marries, well, let's just say sometimes he forgets that he is.
—**JOAN COLLINS**

If he isn't willing to wear a wedding ring but expects you to, head for Reno. Better yet, talk all this stuff out before you sign on. Less lust and more talk.   —**MADONNA**

Marry in haste, repent in Reno.   —**HEDDA HOPPER**

Marry in haste, but repent among the leisure classes. In other words, marry rich.   —**ANITA LOOS, AUTHOR OF** *GENTLEMEN PREFER BLONDES*

Who wouldn't want a wife? Even women, people like Gloria Steinem and Shirley MacLaine have said so. You get someone to live in and give you free sex, cleaning, cooking, housekeeping, hostessing and, eventually, babysitting. It's a terrific deal—for the one who isn't the wife.   —**CYBILL SHEPHERD**

Females are trained to be wives almost from birth. Men take a long time to grow into the role of husband. Don't pick a young man. Marry a more mature fellow. Most men are overgrown sons until thirty or more.                                            **—ELIZABETH HURLEY**

There's this myth that there aren't enough men to go around. A complete lie. The world is crawling with men. Sometimes literally. I think the myth is so that girls will be willing to settle for less. So that they'll be flattered that any man is willing to marry them.   **—MADONNA**

How often do they say that all the good men are already married or gay? Like the fact that there's all these gay men in the world means future wives have less to choose from! What they ignore is that there's also a lot of lesbians out there, who aren't looking for husbands. So it balances out.            **—MADONNA'S FORMER GAL PAL SANDRA BERNHARD**

The trouble with some women is that they get all excited about nothing, and then marry him.                    **—CHER, POST–SONNY BONO**

You date a guy, he treats you nice and says nice things. Maybe he even brings flowers. So you think, Isn't he romantic? Wake up and smell the decaf. Only gay men are romantic, and all men are sex maniacs. Dating equals best behavior, and marriage equals real life. So decide how much real life you want.

**—MELANIE CHISHOLM, A.K.A. "SPORTY" SPICE OF THE SPICE GIRLS**

*P*arents frown so on young people living together before, or in place of, marriage. It's just that they prefer tradition to practicality. Too often, the fiancé is Dr. Jekyll and the husband is Mr. Hyde. Better to find out beforehand. Obviously. **—NATASHA RICHARDSON, MARRIED TO ACTOR LIAM NEESON AND DAUGHTER OF VANESSA REDGRAVE, WHO HAD A SON OUT OF WEDLOCK**

*L*iving together kills the romance, but so does marriage. Neither kills the sex—not for a while, depending. But you learn a lot about a man when dishwashing, laundry, and bathrooms are involved.
**—PRACTICAL HUMORIST ERMA BOMBECK**

*I* dated a guy who was tall, dark, and handsome. Also, he was the strong and silent type. I'll tell you, conversation is an eventual must. . . . Silence sometimes covers a lack of interest or a lack of brains.
**—WRITER HELENE HANFF**

*W*henever I date a guy, I think, Is this the man I want my children to spend their weekends with? **—RITA RUDNER**

*D*on't marry the man you're attracted to. Marry the man you like. Like lasts longer. **—FANNY BRICE**

*O*pposites attract. Sometimes. But similarities tend to last. You need common ground and interests to endure as a pair. **—DR. JOYCE BROTHERS**

*M*arry a man who will become your best friend. Then you've got it made. **—MICHELLE PFEIFFER**

$\mathcal{M}$ost heterosexual men are also homosocial. Some very much so. If he wants to spend all his spare time with the boys after he's had sex with you, or before, that's not a marriage, it's an arrangement.

—KIM CATTRALL

$\mathcal{T}$he main problem in marriage is that for a man sex is a hunger, like eating. If he can't get to a fancy restaurant, he'll make for the hot dog stand. —JOAN FONTAINE *(REBECCA, SUSPICION)*

$\mathcal{I}$ did consider marrying Tyrone Power. But I decided he was too fond of the boys for it to work out. —ALICE FAYE

$\mathcal{M}$en cheat. Period. On a beautiful wife, on a plain wife. . . . Wasn't it Eleanor Roosevelt who said, when she found out FDR was keeping a woman in the White House, "If Franklin can have a mistress, so can I!" Or was that Marlene Dietrich? Of course it helps that both those women were bisexual.

—DELPHINE ROSAY, MONTE CARLO COLUMNIST AND RADIO PERSONALITY

$\mathcal{B}$urgess [Meredith] and I had a lot in common when we got married. I loved him and he loved him. —MOVIE STAR PAULETTE GODDARD

$\mathcal{I}$ nevah found a man strong enough to stay married to Bette Davis.

—BETTE DAVIS

Men are reared to be top dog, and if they don't go very high professionally, they at least want to be Numero Uno at home. Thus, a man whose wife is more successful or famous quickly becomes a very unhappy, even abusive husband. —MYRNA LOY, WHO WAS VOTED
QUEEN OF HOLLYWOOD WHEN CLARK GABLE WAS VOTED KING

Our mother used to tell us, "She who marries for money earns it." She believes you should fall in love with a rich man first, then marry him. —MAGDA GABOR, WHO MARRIED SISTER ZSA ZSA'S EX, GEORGE SANDERS

If you want to spend more time with your husband, marry someone who enjoys shopping. That's a big plus. —CANDICE BERGEN

My husband loves to shop, but if I go out with him he always manages to lose me and go off on his own. He doesn't like [my] picking out his clothes. But he likes to pick out mine.
—CAROLYN BESSETTE KENNEDY, ON JFK JR.

It's such a feat that I actually married someone who is heterosexual.
—TALK SHOW HOST RICKI LAKE

A nonheterosexual man can be a fine father and a great friend, but not usually—not in the long run—an ideal husband.
—TV PERSONALITY LEEZA GIBBONS, WHO'D MARRIED A GAY OR BISEXUAL MAN

A lot of women have had bisexual husbands. But as far as I'm concerned, that means he's gay and trying to pass for straight. And marriages like that don't last. Well, they can—if the wife is frigid!
—JOAN COLLINS, WHOSE FIRST HUSBAND MAY HAVE BEEN GAY OR BI

It wouldn't happen if society didn't insist on every man getting married. Let gay men marry each other instead of your daughters, for goodness' sake!  **—KATHY NAJIMY *(SISTER ACT, VERONICA'S CLOSET)***

Hollywood tells us to trust in romance. To marry the romantic stranger. Hollywood is wrong.  **—SCREENWRITER ELEANOR PERRY**

Poor Princess Grace and poor Princess Diana. Every girl's waiting for her prince to come, but why do they always have to look like Prince Rainier or Prince Charles?  **—CAROL CHANNING**

It's difficult to comprehend why he has never once taken the time or the minimal trouble to visit Diana's grave.
**—WRITER-ACTOR EMMA THOMPSON IN 2002, ON PRINCE CHARLES**

Some women, marriage diminishes. You see it in their sloped shoulders, the dying of former laughter, the increased guardedness, the look in the eyes that realizes the best, most carefree times are in the past.  **—NOVELIST JACQUELINE SUSANN**

Married women are a more varied lot, a more diverse matrimonial army, than husbands are. I think marriage standardizes men, overall.
**—FEMINIST AUTHOR GERMAINE GREER**

Wives react to marriage in a bigger variety of ways. You know why? Because women react to men in more varied ways. The average man basically reacts to men in more varied ways. The average man basically reacts or relates to his so-called "opposite sex" in one way.
**—TALK SHOW HOST VIRGINIA GRAHAM**

Ninety-five percent of men's and women's bodies is the same, yet the male establishment has made a cult out of mystifying and exoticizing women, then trying to explain us. Do you realize that the definition and standards of femininity are all created by men? Even the kinds of shoes we wear, over the millennia, from New York to Paris to China with the women's bound feet, have been created by men, for men's esthetic and sexual satisfaction. —CONGRESSWOMAN BELLA ABZUG

I think the best thing I can do is to be a distraction.
—JACQUELINE KENNEDY IN 1957, ASSESSING HER ROLE AS A U.S. SENATOR'S WIFE

Among the other things she may or may not be, a wife, among the middle and upper classes, is a publicist and billboard for her husband's success. She advertises his financial and social status by the way she dresses, lunches, entertains, drives, behaves, and shops.
—PUPPETEER AND AUTHOR SHARI LEWIS

Marriage should still include room for each partner to look forward to tomorrow and to enjoy self-expression and spontaneous happiness, both together and individually. —CYBILL SHEPHERD

If love . . . means that one person absorbs the other, then no real relationship exists any more. Love evaporates; there is nothing left to love. The integrity of self is gone.
—FEMINIST FRONTIERSWOMAN ANNIE OAKLEY

Some of us are becoming the men we wanted to marry.
—GLORIA STEINEM, ON SELF-RELIANCE

*I* used to get married so someone would take care of me. Too many men take a girl, instead of taking care of her. Now I try and marry for companionship. **—JUDY GARLAND**

*I*n the old days, a living husband was a necessity for a woman, and a dead one was a luxury. **—COMEDIAN TOTIE FIELDS**

*A* man in love is incomplete until he is married. Then he's finished. **—ZSA ZSA GABOR**

*I*t's still a double standard. An actress who did what Woody Allen did, her career would be finished. Or severely hampered. With him, the media decides, We'll separate his private life from his work. Which they never did with Ingrid Bergman, to name one. Men— straight men—can get away with anything.
**—ESTELLE GETTY *(THE GOLDEN GIRLS)***

*I*f Woody Allen ever married Soon-Yi, Mia Farrow would be his mother-in-law! **—COLUMNIST CINDY ADAMS**

*I*'ve been badgering him for more than a year to marry me. My heart leaped with joy when he agreed—but sank when he listed all the conditions. **—SOON-YI PREVIN (ADOPTED DAUGHTER OF MIA FARROW AND ANDRÉ PREVIN) ON THE EVE OF HER MARRIAGE TO WOODY ALLEN (THE CONDITIONS, ACCORDING TO *TIME OUT* MAGAZINE, INCLUDED THAT SHE DWELL IN HER OWN HOME, VISIT ALLEN JUST TWICE A WEEK, SIGN AWAY ALL RIGHTS TO HIS MONEY, AND NOT SPEAK TO HER MOTHER, MIA FARROW, WITHOUT THE DIRECTOR'S PERMISSION)**

Jack [Nicholson] was so angry when I let it be known that our son was ours [conceived while the parents made *Five Easy Pieces,* 1970] . . . but we're on good terms now.

—SUSAN ANSPACH, WHO MADE THE REVELATION IN THE MID-1990S

If you want to sacrifice the admiration of many men for the criticism of one, go ahead, get married.    —SUFFRAGIST KATHARINE HOUGHTON HEPBURN, TO DAUGHTER KATE

Any intelligent woman who reads the marriage contract and then goes into it deserves all the consequences.    —ISADORA DUNCAN

I'm human. I am an artist. I'm a fledgling star. I have moods. My first husband once criticized me for my what he called inconsistency. I said, "You want consistency, marry a corpse."

—GILDA RADNER *(SATURDAY NIGHT LIVE)*

If a woman wants to have it all, she should expect eventually to wind up alone. . . . I always knew I would end up alone.   —BETTE DAVIS

Someone once asked me why women don't gamble as much as men do, and I gave the reply that we don't have as much money. That was a true but incomplete answer. In fact, women's total instinct for gambling is satisfied by marriage.    —GLORIA STEINEM

Oh, God, don't get involved with a jealous man. Some jealousy's unavoidable, especially till he's become secure with you. But there's men out there, jealousy is like a passion with them, a fuel. And it can fuel violence. —HALLE BERRY, WHO LOST MOST OF THE HEARING IN ONE EAR WHEN A BOYFRIEND SLUGGED HER

It's frightening that nine of ten females murdered in this country are killed not by strangers or criminals. They're killed by a husband or an ex-husband, or a boyfriend, an ex-boyfriend. . . . —DOROTHY KINGSLEY, SCREENWRITER *(VALLEY OF THE DOLLS)*

When I was young, I thought jealousy was flattering. Then I thought it couldn't be helped. Now I stay the hell away from it. —CHER

Females accept jealousy because we care too much what the male thinks about us. —JENNIFER LOPEZ, WHOSE FIRST MARRIAGE ENDED PARTLY BECAUSE OF HIS JEALOUSY

Jealousy is the fun he thinks you had, and men, especially husbands, are very possessive about a woman's fun, real or imagined. —NOVELIST ERICA JONG *(FEAR OF FLYING)*

Jealousy is never satisfied with anything short of an omniscience that would detect the subtlest fold of the heart. —NOVELIST GEORGE ELIOT (BORN MARY ANN EVANS) IN *THE MILL ON THE FLOSS* (1860)

As a young woman, I cared desperately what men thought about me. As a wife, I wanted to please. Now I like to be pleased too. And with hindsight and valuing myself more realistically, I care more about what I think of others.  —BETTE DAVIS

In all those old movies, they talk about the girl or bride trying to make him a good wife. I kept waiting for them to say how the guy would make her a good husband. . . .  —WINONA RYDER

It used to be that when an actress reached thirty she was considered almost washed up. We started by playing girls who only married at the end of the picture. We didn't play wives. That came later. But the most dreaded thing was when a star had to play a mother. That was the beginning of her professional end.  —LANA TURNER

For an actress, the important thing is not to look married. You can be married, but if you look it, there goes half your star value.  —SCREEN AND STAGE STAR ALEXIS SMITH

Husbands: a necessary, very obtainable, but very costly accessory for the actress at or near the top.  —TINSELTOWN COLUMNIST SHEILAH GRAHAM

My girlfriend met her fiancé online, the worst place to find a mate. Talk about buying a pig in a poke! Thank goodness it never reached the marital stage.  —DAWN STEEL, FORMER HEAD OF COLUMBIA PICTURES

The people who like going online best are people who can't sustain a relationship for more than five minutes.  —MADONNA

Most of the fellows who go online looking for women are sex maniacs or losers. Or is that redundant? Some men actually pretend they're women so they can join a lesbian chat room. . . . I heard about one charmer who sent his unseen cutie an expensive gift, then after they finally met he wanted it back because she didn't measure up to his physical standards. Heaven knows what, if anything, he measured up to.  **—BEA ARTHUR** *(THE GOLDEN GIRLS)*

I have never hated a man enough to give his diamonds back.
**—ZSA ZSA GABOR**

When a man gives you a gift, honey, you will pay for it. . . .
**—PEARL BAILEY**

Blessed are those who can give without remembering, and take without forgetting.  **—WRITER ELIZABETH BIBESCO IN** *BALLOONS* **(1922)**

Almost every celebrity wants to have a reputation for being generous, and wants to buy that reputation as cheaply as possible.
**—MARILU HENNER** *(TAXI)*

But you cannot give to people what they are incapable of receiving.
**—AGATHA CHRISTIE IN** *FUNERALS ARE FATAL* **(1953)**

When I received the script [for *Muriel's Wedding*], it really spoke to me. It was funny and unique, but so rooted in reality. This girl is dying to have a wedding, with all the trimmings . . . with or without the groom.  **—AUSTRALIAN STAR TONI COLLETTE**

What interests me is why and how friendship between a woman and a man changes so, after they've had sex. Don't you think people think a little less of each other after they've seen each other naked? I think men, once sex has occurred, suddenly become very proprietary and presume all kinds of things. After he's had you, in that way, he thinks somehow your body and life partly belong to him.

—ACTOR-DIRECTOR LIV ULLMANN

After you have sex with a man, he thinks he has a hold on you— and a husband knows he has. But with a woman and her boyfriend, after sex, she thinks no such thing; she's just hoping it'll happen again, that he'll come back for more!   —RACHEL GRIFFITHS *(SIX FEET UNDER)*

Not every girl is mad for sex, so if you aren't, don't pick a young guy. Marry an older, calm type who thinks Viagra is a waterfall.

—EMMA BUNTON, A.K.A. "BABY SPICE" OF THE SPICE GIRLS

My husband will never chase another woman. He's too fine, too decent, too old.                        —GRACIE ALLEN, ON GEORGE BURNS

It's a matter of opinion.            —BRITISH ACTRESS HERMIONE GINGOLD,
WHEN ASKED IF HER EX-HUSBAND WAS STILL LIVING

I never married because there was no need. I have three pets at home which answer the same purpose as a husband. I have a dog which growls every morning, a parrot which swears all afternoon, and a cat that comes home late at night.   —BRITISH NOVELIST MARIE CORELLI

One face to the world, another at home makes for misery.
—AMY VANDERBILT IN HER *NEW COMPLETE BOOK OF ETIQUETTE* IN 1963

We were about the same age when we married, but when we split he was a lot older than me. Youthfulness is a state of mind, and he chose to move out of state. —SCREEN AND TV STAR ANN SOTHERN,
ON EX ROBERT STERLING (OF TV'S *TOPPER*)

Yes, it is, it's absolutely true. And it couldn't be less significant if I tried. What's the opposite of "earth-shattering"? —ANN SOTHERN IN 1999,
WHEN THE TABLOIDS BLARED THAT SHE HAD BEEN WITHOUT A MAN
(A HUSBAND) FOR FIFTY YEARS

Eleven percent of women between twenty-five and twenty-nine were single in 1970. By 1987 the percentage had increased to twenty-seven percent. —STATISTICS FROM THE CENTER FOR HEALTH

It's not easy in show business, but I'm holding out for an old-fashioned guy. One who thinks "to have and to hold" means a wife's love and trust, not her body. —BRITNEY SPEARS

Let's face it. A man could not earn what he does if he didn't have a wife. For free, she does all kinds of services he'd have to pay out a lot for, and this is even before having kids. So how come so many men figure all the money is theirs, and that if they give the "little woman" an allowance they're being so nice and generous? Ridiculous. Marriage is a joint venture, and that includes financially. Get real! Housewives are valuable. —UMA THURMAN

$\mathcal{A}$ husband's devotion, like lace, is highly prized—even though it's full of holes.   **—WOOLWORTH'S HEIRESS BARBARA HUTTON,**
**"THE RICHEST GIRL IN THE WORLD"**

$\mathcal{I}$ don't mind housework now and then. If you don't have to do it, it can be sort of fun. But to be a full-time housewife, what could be duller or deadlier?   **—NATALIE WOOD**

$\mathcal{S}$ omething happens when a man sees a woman performing household chores . . . she starts losing her glamour. In the end, she becomes a role rather than an individual.   **—MARLENE DIETRICH,**
**REPORTEDLY A BIG FAN OF HOUSEWORK**

$\mathcal{B}$ y and large, husbands are not very romantic about the unfamiliar, let alone the familiar. The romance of familiarity is a feminine cult.
**—DR. JOYCE BROTHERS**

$\mathcal{T}$ he fact that husbands don't live as long as wives might be seen as nature trying to rectify the inequalities of sexism. For some widows are bereaved, but many others are just relieved.   **—RACHEL ROBERTS,**
**WHO TIMED HER SUICIDE TO GET BACK AT EX-HUSBAND REX HARRISON**

$\mathcal{I}$ saw this documentary on television, where this man in Bali was on the verge of tears over how much his brother's widow loved her late husband. She had gone and jumped on his funeral pyre and immolated herself! And this man found it all so touching. He was touched, all right.   **—JULIE CHRISTIE**

$\mathcal{I}$t's surprising how many girls marry because they're in love with love. With the ritual and concept of marriage, the way it's depicted in movies. Do you know how many girls in the 1960s got married after seeing Julie Andrews's spectacular wedding in *The Sound of Music*? Or in the '80s after seeing Princess Diana get married in St. Paul's Cathedral? Romance and illusion can blind young women to what follows "I do." **—MARY RODGERS, DAUGHTER OF RICHARD RODGERS, COMPOSER OF *THE SOUND OF MUSIC***

$\mathcal{W}$ho wouldn't want to be a bride? Getting to be the total star of your own private show . . . a demure diva . . . everyone wishing you well, being admired, respected—at least so far, and until you become a mother. . . . But being a wife, that's the difference between attending a feast and having to prepare one three times a day for the rest of your life. **—KATE WINSLET *(TITANIC)***

$\mathcal{B}$eing a bride is like being a model. Without any competition. Especially if you make your bridesmaids wear ugly dresses. **—COMEDIAN JUDY TENUTA**

$\mathcal{T}$he role of bride is a piece of cake. Luscious white cake. The role of wife, that's scary! **—GILDA RADNER**

$\mathcal{I}$ called it a bridal gown. I still have it, in plastic in my closet. But now I more accurately refer to it as my slave dress. **—COMEDIAN MOMS MABLEY**

$\mathcal{H}$ousework is the hardest work in the world. That's why men won't do it. **—NOVELIST EDNA FERBER *(SO BIG)***

$\mathcal{I}$ buried a lot of my ironing in the back yard.

—HOUSEWIFE TURNED COMEDIAN PHYLLIS DILLER

$\mathcal{B}$ride is the past tense of domestic helper.

—ROSIE O'DONNELL

$\mathcal{Y}$ou're a bride until you're a mother. You're a mother till your teenagers pretend you're a distant relation. And you're a wife again after the kids leave home. . . . The main difference between a bride and a wife is about two hours" sleep.

—HOUSEWIFE HUMORIST ERMA BOMBECK

$\mathcal{G}$et everything in your own name. Ask him pretty, pretty please— with sex on top, if he insists. Do it while the marriage is still hot— if possible, during the honeymoon.

—JOAN RIVERS

$\mathcal{P}$hase one of marriage, he gives you love. Phase two, he gives you money. Phase three, he gives you short shrift. Phase three lasts the longest.

—NELL CARTER

$\mathcal{T}$here are three stages of yuletide man: He believes in Santa Claus. He doesn't believe in Santa Claus. He is Santa Claus. Marry the third one.

—IMOGENE COCA *(YOUR SHOW OF SHOWS)*

$\mathcal{W}$e are not planning to need [a prenuptial agreement] because of our unique compatibility which will keep us together.

—SHAWN SOUTHWICK, LARRY KING'S LATEST WIFE, IN 1997

*I* changed that line in our ceremony to something more realistic and ethnic. To my bridegroom I said "Love, honor, and oy vey."
— **COMEDIAN AND IMPRESSIONIST MARILYN MICHAELS**

*T*he French believe that in every couple, one person loves the other more. The loved one and the lover, they say. Ah, what do they know? The French eat snails, for goodness' sake.
— **NANCY WALKER (*RHODA* AND *THE MARY TYLER MOORE SHOW*)**

*I*n marriage, the biggest compliment is attention. The longer you're married, the bigger a compliment it is.
— **MELINA MERCOURI, ACTRESS TURNED GREEK POLITICIAN**

*T*he advantage of being married to an archaeologist is that the older one gets, the more interesting he finds you.
— **AGATHA CHRISTIE, WHOSE PREVIOUS HUSBAND LEFT HER FOR A YOUNGER WOMAN**

*J*ane Fonda's [second] husband [politician Tom Hayden] was cheating on her with a younger woman. Though ironically, Jane was much better-looking than her. But that didn't keep it from hurting her enough that she chose to end the once very compatible marriage.
— **MILDRED NATWICK, FONDA'S *BAREFOOT IN THE PARK* COSTAR**

*M*y favorite saying is both joyous and a bit depressing, and quite true, I think: "Love is eternal, as long as it lasts."
— **OSCAR-WINNING ACTRESS JUDY HOLLIDAY *(BORN YESTERDAY)***

$\mathcal{B}$eats me how [Prince] Charles can prefer Camilla Parker-Bowles to Diana, who's younger and much more attractive. Maybe he and she have great conversations. Or maybe it's the idea of cheating that's so attractive. Whatever they have at home, men seldom appreciate it enough. I think it's the lure of the extramarital.

—BRITISH ACTRESS BERYL REID *(THE KILLING OF SISTER GEORGE)*

$\mathcal{J}$ane Fonda's taste in husbands is downright pedestrian. First, that Chinese-looking French director [Roger Vadim], then Mr. Potato-Nose politician [Tom Hayden], now that gap-toothed cable-TV person [Ted Turner] who ruins countless films by colorizing them with arbitrary pastels. Miss Fonda always looks splendid and dresses well, but the one accessory she lacks is a good-looking or appealing husband.

—DAME JUDITH ANDERSON

$\mathcal{J}$f I married every guy I had a thing with, I'd have this long list of ex husbands that would be in every biography of me. I don't want that to be the main fact about me, or my most vital statistic.    —CHER

$\mathcal{J}$t's not the men you see me with that counts, it's the men you don't see me with.                                                —MAE WEST

$\mathcal{J}$t's not the men you may see me with that's important, it's the woman you may not see me with.

—OPENLY GAY LILY TOMLIN ON DECADES-LONG COMPANION JANE WAGNER

Marriage within the same sex is a revolutionary idea to many or most people today [the 1990s]. But so was abolishing slavery in the 1800s, or giving women the vote before the 1920s, or allowing marriage between the races, which was illegal in much of the USA until the 1960s. **—CONGRESSWOMAN BELLA ABZUG**

It's straight men who defined marriage as basically the ownership of women. It's gay people who rejected the inequality and chattel aspects of that and have made marriage more about romance, fun, and equality. **—K. D. LANG**

It isn't that I hadn't ever considered [a lesbian relationship]. I'd say, Well, would that be interesting? Would I want to? And I honestly don't think that the thought ever resolved itself. **—JULIE ANDREWS**

If you have one gay experience, does that mean you're gay? If you have one heterosexual experience, does that mean you're straight? Life doesn't work quite so cut and dried. **—TENNIS CHAMP BILLIE JEAN KING (ONCE MARRIED TO A MAN), WHO CAME OUT IN HER FIFTIES**

Love is wonderful, there's not enough of it in this world. A loving relationship doesn't really need a contract. Though you do need it for the kids' sake, or for when one or both of you falls out of love. **—EMMA THOMPSON** *(HOWARDS END)*

If men had to have babies they would only ever have one each. **—PRINCESS DIANA IN 1984**

*I Lost Everything in the Postnatal Depression.* —**ERMA BOMBECK BOOK TITLE**

Kids are the brakes on a happy, carefree, self-indulgent honeymoon kind of lifestyle. Heaven forbid a husband and wife should have no distractions between them.

—**COMEDIAN AND ADOPTIVE MOTHER PAULA POUNDSTONE**

For years we have given scientific attention to the care and rearing of plants and animals, but we have allowed babies to be raised chiefly by tradition.        —**WRITER EDITH BELLE LOWRY IN** *FALSE MODESTY* **(1912)**

Bringing up children is not a real occupation, because children come up just the same, brought or not.        —**AUSTRALIAN WRITER GERMAINE GREER**

**IN** *THE FEMALE EUNUCH* **(1971)**

Nearly everyone wants babies. But not everyone wants children. . . .

—**ACTRESS LEE REMICK** *(THE OMEN)*

I discovered when I had a child of my own that I had become a biased observer of small children. Instead of looking at them with affectionate but nonpartisan eyes, I saw each of them as older or younger, bigger or smaller, more or less graceful, intelligent or skilled than my own child.        —**ANTHROPOLOGIST DR. MARGARET MEAD**

Honeymoon is the way-past tense of motherhood.

—**BRETT BUTLER** *(AMAZING GRACE)*

Women have sons because husbands fade. . . .        —**SUSAN HAYWARD**

The tie is stronger than that between father and son, and father and daughter. . . . The bond is also more complex than the one between mother and daughter. For a woman, a son offers the best chance to know the mysterious male existence.
—**CAROLE KLEIN, WRITER AND PUBLIC RELATIONS EXECUTIVE**

Death and taxes and childbirth! There's never any convenient time for any of them! —**AUTHOR MARGARET MITCHELL** *(GONE WITH THE WIND)*

It's unfortunately all too easy to drive a grown child away. And not easy to drive an unloved husband away.
—**GERMAN ACTRESS HILDEGARD KNEF**

It's far easier to find a husband than to get rid of one.
—**SAPPHIC COMEDIAN AND ACTRESS PATSY KELLY**

In most animal species, the father gets the mother pregnant but isn't around to help rear the offspring. We're talking the majority of nature . . . so why are we so surprised when this sometimes occurs among humans? —**SINGER-ACTRESS ETHEL WATERS**

Most men avoid trouble. Women, however, and wives in particular, consider trouble a feminine stock in trade and a chance to shine and earn praise. —**BEA ARTHUR** *(MAUDE)*

How desperately we wish to maintain our trust in those we love! In the face of everything, we try to find reasons to trust. Because losing faith is worse than falling out of love.
—**HOUSEWIFE-ACTIVIST SONIA JOHNSON**

Where large sums of money are concerned, it is advisable to trust nobody. **—AGATHA CHRISTIE**

After you've been burned, you're a little less trusting. . . . But experience also acts like something of a shield.
**—TATUM O'NEAL, EX-WIFE OF TENNIS ACE JOHN MCENROE AND IN 2002 REPORTEDLY DATING ALSO VOLATILE ACTOR ALEC BALDWIN**

Women know the truth about men. Wives know it but are publicly silent. Men prefer the heroic, good-natured fiction about themselves, and never stop telling it, publicly or privately. **—BETTE MIDLER**

A lot of men think if they avoid the truth, it may change to something better before they hear it.
**—PLAYWRIGHT MARSHA NORMAN (*'NIGHT, MOTHER*)**

Most men are boys at heart. Husbands can dominate wives because they're usually older, plus society tells them to. I think age and experience should take precedence. . . . My husband [Percy Gibson] is younger than me, so I wear the trousers in our relationship, although there must be a better way of putting it. Let's say I'm the guide. . . .
**—NEWLYWED JOAN COLLINS (FIFTH TIME) IN 2002**

Women never have young minds. They are born 3,000 years old.
**—BRITISH PLAYWRIGHT SHELAGH DELANEY (*A TASTE OF HONEY*)**

Each suburban wife struggled with it alone. As she made the beds, shopped for groceries, matched slipcover material, ate peanut butter sandwiches with her children, chauffeured Cub Scouts and Brownies, lay beside her husband at night—she was afraid to ask even of herself the silent question—"Is this all?"

—BETTY FRIEDAN IN *THE FEMININE MYSTIQUE* (1963)

I am not impressed by external devices for the preservation of virtue in men or women. Marriage laws, the police, armies, and navies are the mark of human incompetence.

—DORA RUSSELL, COUNTESS, WRITER, AND ACTIVIST

By and large, mothers and housewives are the only workers who do not have regular time off. They are the great vacationless class.

—AVIATOR AND AUTHOR ANNE MORROW LINDBERGH
(WIFE OF AVIATOR CHARLES LINDBERGH)

But there is a natural tribal hostility between the married and the unmarried. I cannot stand the shows so often quite instinctively put on by married people to insinuate that they are not only more fortunate but in some way more moral than you are.

—NOVELIST AND PHILOSOPHER IRIS MURDOCH

Happiness in marriage is entirely a matter of chance.

—JANE AUSTEN IN *PRIDE AND PREJUDICE* (1813)

One advantage of marriage, it seems to me, is that when you fall out of love with him, or he falls out of love with you, it keeps you together until you maybe fall in again. —WRITER-POET JUDITH VIORST

All that is good and commendable now existing would continue to exist if all marriage laws were repealed tomorrow. . . . I have an inalienable, constitutional, and natural right to love whom I may, to love as long or as short a period as I can, to change that love every day if I please! **—WRITER, REFORMER, AND THE FIRST AMERICAN WOMAN TO RUN FOR PRESIDENT, VICTORIA WOODHULL, IN 1871**

Whatever women do, they must do twice as well as men to be thought half as good. Luckily, this is not difficult.
**—CHARLOTTE WHITTON, CANADIAN POLITICIAN**

Women have been called queens for a long time—but the kingdom given them isn't worth ruling. **—LOUISA MAY ALCOTT *(LITTLE WOMEN)***

I am a woman, I am a mother . . . I want to remain a woman but I want a man's life. **—DESIGNER DIANE VON FURSTENBERG, WHOSE EX-HUSBAND EGON VON FURSTENBERG WAS OPENLY BISEXUAL AND WHO IN 2001 SHOCKED MANY BY WEDDING CONFIRMED BACHELOR AND MEDIA MOGUL BARRY DILLER**

Why does a woman work ten years to change a man's habits and then complain that he's the not the man she married?
**—BARBRA STREISAND**

He looked homemade, as though his wife had self-consciously knitted or somehow contrived a husband when she sat alone at night.
**—WRITER EUDORA WELTY**

. . . many [married women] have to go about creating their husbands. They have to start ascribing preferences, opinions, dictatorial ways. Oh, yes, they say, my husband is very particular. He won't touch turnips. He won't eat fried meat. [Or he will only eat fried meat.] He likes me to wear blue [brown] all the time. He can't stand organ music. He hates to see a woman go out bareheaded. He would kill me if I took one puff of tobacco. This way, bewildered, sidelong-looking men are made over, made into husbands, heads of households.                                    **—CANADIAN WRITER ALICE MUNRO**

Outside of the drastic step of becoming an actress, the best way a woman can dramatize herself is by becoming a wife.

**—PUBLISHER KATHARINE GRAHAM**

Women have a bigger, deeper interior life than men do. They can inject more meaning, symbolism, romance, passion, martyrdom, and universal significance into a humdrum marriage than anyone but the best male playwrights.            **—BROADWAY PRODUCER CHERYL CRAWFORD**

Some women would be less content in their marriages if they didn't get to reembroider or fabricate them for the benefit of their feminine relatives and friends and, of course, themselves.

**—WRITER-PRODUCER VIRGINIA VAN UPP *(GILDA)***

One loves in the mind and in the heart. The body is a thing apart. A female's body can definitely belong to one person but her heart to another.                                    **—JOURNALIST JANET FLANNER**

It was a perceptive Roman emperor who said that a man's life is what his thoughts make it. The same holds for a woman's marriage.
—CHOREOGRAPHER MARTHA GRAHAM

The greater part of our happiness or misery depends on our disposition and not on our circumstances. —FIRST FIRST LADY MARTHA WASHINGTON

The best thing in marriage—in life, really—is self-confidence. Women aren't instilled with it; we mostly have to breed it in ourselves. But when you're a self-confident person, wife, whatever, there's less strain and stress, and one can do things better and thus be prouder of the result. —PLAYWRIGHT LILLIAN HELLMAN

You have to take yourself at your own estimation. Even the best of husbands will sometimes see you chiefly in the role that he thinks marriage or biology has assigned you. Value yourself!
—ROSALIND RUSSELL *(AUNTIE MAME)*

Remember, no one can make you feel inferior without your consent.
—STATESWOMAN AND FIRST LADY ELEANOR ROOSEVELT

It's an important Hollywood rule that also goes for the other roles that most women fulfill in everyday life: The more you value yourself, the more others will value you. —BARBRA STREISAND

Women should correctly value their work, because in our male-defined society, "women's work" is undervalued. Being a wife and mother is the hardest, most full-time, least-paid work on earth.

—GLORIA STEINEM

I must say, men in Europe and the United States work pretty hard, but when you visit Third World countries, where men are much more in charge of everything, you see the women doing all kinds of work besides child-rearing, including most of the farming. Meanwhile, the men lie around smoking and chatting, in between waiting for the next meal to be served to them.      —KATE WINSLET *(IRIS)*

It's the rooster that does all the crowing, but it's the hen that delivers the goods.      —FORMER TEXAS GOVERNOR ANN RICHARDS

When it comes to women, men expect the moon—doubly high standards. A woman should be beautiful and talented but not too intelligent or intimidating. She should be virginal but sexy, accomplished but needy. Vulnerable yet semi-independent. Ambitious, but not for herself. Innocent yet knowing, spirited yet submissive. Enough said?      —STEVIE SMITH, UK POET AND WRITER

It seems the only sort of female men can truly respect is a woman who is at once a virgin and a mother. It's no coincidence that in several male-created religions, the founder's mother is both virginal and maternal.      —SCHOLAR AND NOVELIST MARY RENAULT *(THE PERSIAN BOY)*

You know the romance is gone when instead of calling you "Sweetie" or by your first name, he calls you "Ma" or "Mother."
—BARBARA BILLINGSLEY *(LEAVE IT TO BEAVER)*

When I've been on dates with men, some of them still make a slip and before we get to first names call me Mrs. Brady.
—FLORENCE HENDERSON, MATRIARCH OF *THE BRADY BUNCH*

It's nicer when you have a husband who lets you discover his good qualities rather than announcing them himself.
—LONI ANDERSON, FORMER WIFE OF BURT REYNOLDS

My husband was interested in horses and racing, women, and movies. I did learn two things from him—on horses, people look better than they really are, and they look worse than they are in cars.
—ACTRESS URSULA ANDRESS, FORMER WIFE OF ACTOR TURNED DIRECTOR JOHN DEREK (WHO WAS ALSO MARRIED TO LINDA EVANS AND BO DEREK)

Love means being stupid together.   —BRIDGET FONDA

Men are creatures with two legs and eight hands.   —JAYNE MANSFIELD

In a great romance, each person basically plays a part that the other really likes.   —ACTRESS ELIZABETH ASHLEY *(EVENING SHADE)*

My ex-husband was so generous, he'd give you the hair off his back.
—ROSEANNE, PRE–TOM ARNOLD

Anna Nicole Smith's late husband was so old, he knew Burger King when he was a prince.  **—WHOOPI GOLDBERG**

Not every man I've dated has been intelligent, though most have been successful. I remember one who would have dialed information to get the number for 911.  **—MORGAN FAIRCHILD**

And if the rascal overspends his per diem, he doesn't get any the next day.  **—CELINE DION IN 2002, HALF-JOKING ABOUT THE DAILY GAMBLING ALLOWANCE SHE GIVES HER TWENTY-SIX-YEARS-OLDER MANAGER-HUSBAND**

What is sad for women of my generation is that they weren't supposed to work if they had families. What were they to do when the children were grown—watch the raindrops coming down the windowpane?  **—JACKIE KENNEDY ONASSIS, WHO RESUMED OUTSIDE WORK AFTER BOTH HER HUSBANDS DIED**

No matter what your fight, don't be ladylike! [Nature] made women, and [male industrialists] made the ladies.  **—"MOTHER" MARY JONES (1830–1930), U.S. LABOR LEADER**

The world has been busy for some centuries in shutting and locking every door through which a woman could step into wealth, except the door of marriage.  **—NINETEENTH-CENTURY WRITER AND REFORMER HARRIET BEECHER STOWE**

Marriage can either keep the world out, or keep you in, depending how you look at it. Same thing, either way. What's unnerving is the number of females who don't mind living in a cage, imagining that it or a strong, domineering husband will keep bad things away. By middle age, such fantasies have usually been blown away.
—MARGARET HAMILTON, THE WICKED WITCH IN *THE WIZARD OF OZ*

If you want to get at the core of how your potential husband relates to women, go back to the source, to the original relationship. How does he feel about, and how does he treat, his mother? That will speak volumes, especially as most wives eventually become mothers.                           —DORIS ROBERTS *(EVERYBODY LOVES RAYMOND)*

It's changing. It changes slowly. Our society encourages the imbalance of power and of redress between husbands and wives. . . . Lack of fairness to an opponent is essentially a sign of weakness.
—EMMA GOLDMAN, WRITER-ACTIVIST (1869–1940)

There's this older couple, both actors, famous for saying in interviews that they're so happy together they've never had one fight. After all, actors act off the screen too. . . . Obviously, they've fought. If somehow they truly never have, then all it means is: they've never communicated.                           —DEBRA MESSING *(WILL AND GRACE)*

People are often ashamed to admit they quarrel. But any two people living together will, at some time. In fact, a marriage minus any arguments would be one that's dead or perishing from emotional undernourishment. The opposite of love, of being in touch, is indifference. There's nothing colder than indifference.           —DR. JOYCE BROTHERS

$\mathcal{I}$ like a good, involved, passionate fight . . . and the making up afterwards.
— BARBRA STREISAND

$\mathcal{I}$f I met a man I wanted to be married to my whole life, he'd have to let me be me. In fact, I shouldn't need permission for honesty. You can't be happy or confident if you aren't yourself. . . . At first, I wished I was more Anglo, but with time and with truth, I'm glad I'm of Mexican origin and proud of it. . . . A husband should praise his wife for what she is, not try and remake her in his image or fantasy.
— SLAIN SINGER SELENA IN 1994, THE YEAR BEFORE HER MURDER

$\mathcal{E}$ven if we don't do Shakespeare, dearie, acting is supposed to come from truth. In the 1930s when I was riding high, boy, the pressure they put on me to get married, to pass for a lady who liked gentlemen in the boudoir! I said no. It wouldn't be worth it. Even if it made me some kind of a star, my life and my integrity's more important than living a lie just to fit in or make more dough.
— COMEDIC ACTRESS PATSY KELLY, WHO CAME OUT IN THE BOOK *HOLLYWOOD LESBIANS*

$\mathcal{I}$f you start by lying to your new husband, you end by lying to the world and even yourself.
— LUCILLE BALL IN 1963

$\mathcal{I}$f you feel you must lie to your husband, you're afraid of him. Or, which is the same result, he's not the man for you.
— AUSTRALIAN ACTRESS DIANE CILENTO, FORMER WIFE OF SEAN CONNERY

$\mathcal{I}$n marriage, it's all right for either spouse to lie about their past. But if you prevaricate about the present, then what's the marriage for? There should be, in your life, one nonparental person, a peer, to whom you can admit anything and still be loved.

—EVE ARDEN *(OUR MISS BROOKS)*

$\mathcal{A}$ good psychiatrist listens, and listens well, because he's a professional and he's paid. A good husband listens because he cares. Marry a listener, it'll last longer and you'll be happier. Too many men don't give a damn what a woman says if it isn't "yes"; they care more about how she looks.   —VIVIAN VANCE *(I LOVE LUCY)*, A LONGTIME FAN OF PSYCHIATRY

$\mathcal{I}$ like a man who has questions. . . . Avoid a man who thinks he has all the answers.   —WINONA RYDER

$\mathcal{M}$en joke about how women talk too much. But notice how in a mixed group it's the men dominating the conversation with opinions and declarations . . . the women listening, maybe nodding their heads. . . . If I want a man to do my talking for me in public, I'll marry a ventriloquist. If I married one who felt it's manly to lecture and feminine to listen, I'd be the dummy.   —CANDICE BERGEN IN 1974
(HER FATHER WAS VENTRILOQUIST EDGAR BERGEN)

$\mathcal{I}$f you flub the first two acts (of your life), you have a chance to fix it in the third act. . . . In your final act, you may or may not have a man around permanently, but you're less likely to be lonely than you have been before, single or married.   —JANE FONDA AT SIXTY-FOUR

We've all been single, if only while living at home. But not everyone's been married, and today less and less, later and later. What I resent is when somebody single says you're screwed up because you're married. What do they know? It could be because you've got a louse of a spouse. Don't condemn marriage just because of some bad examples. **—SANDRA GOULD (THE SECOND MRS. KRAVITZ ON** *BEWITCHED*)

You notice how when someone else is single, most wives will try and fix her up, bring her into the club, as it were? While most men will more or less admire the bachelor—or even resent him for living freely. I'm afraid these reactions do mirror how men and women really feel about marriage as a whole. **—VANESSA REDGRAVE**

Older people had different marriages than we do. Their standards do not apply. Thank goodness. And unmarried people can't relate. It's like that saying that nothing makes you more tolerant of a neighbor's party than being there. **—MELISSA GILBERT**

Marriage doesn't change, but husbands do. **—LENA HORNE**

What men have always wanted is a virgin who's a whore in bed. **—MADONNA**

We should like men more and admire them less. **—SUSAN SARANDON**

The intense admiration of a man by a woman is a form of bondage. Besides, how many women do men actually admire? **—SHARON GLESS (CAGNEY AND LACEY)**

$\mathcal{W}$omen are social creatures. More so than men. Cats may be more popularly associated with women, dogs with men, yet the opposite is true. Women crave company and affection. But the only time men classify us with "dogs" is when they think us unattractive.

—CANINE EXPERT BARBARA WOODHOUSE

$\mathcal{E}$very serial killer but one or two has been a man. Serial killers are strict loners who keep everything to themselves. A woman serial killer wouldn't have a chance—too many friends, get-togethers, secrets to share . . . including what's in our icebox!   —PHYLLIS DILLER

$\mathcal{S}$ome dreadfully perceptive person, probably French or English, once said that good manners are the extra effort we make toward people we dislike. Be that as it may, I am rather suspicious of chivalry, because I've noticed the more of it there is, the more of a cover-up for inequality. Like men in the South who insist on opening the door for you, almost like a reminder: We're bigger, we're stronger, you need us. You need us, or else.   —BRETT BUTLER

$\mathcal{P}$oliteness is charming . . . unlike petrified rituals and hard-and-fast attitudes about men's behavior toward "the fair sex"—and yes, we are fairer than men—so here's a good tip-off to what you might be getting stuck with. Just see if your beau refuses to let you hold the door for him. . . .   —ELAYNE BOOSLER

$\mathcal{I}$ have a friend whose husband married her on February 29 so he would only forget their anniversary every four years.

—ANN B. DAVIS OF *THE BRADY BUNCH*

So some husbands forget to give their wives an anniversary gift. Don't fret or stew. Just tell him you've forgotten which were the store-bought mushrooms and which ones you picked yourself.

—VIVIAN VANCE OF *I LOVE LUCY*

When my father, for one very special anniversary, gave my mother a small piece of cheap costume jewelry, she gave him a big piece of her mind. —DIVA MARIA CALLAS

I always heard two can live as cheaply as one—this was an actual inducement to marriage. Not true. Not on a honeymoon—not if you order room service. —GILDA RADNER

He tricked me into marrying him. He told me I was pregnant.

—COMEDIAN CAROL LEIFER

Have a good long look at the face of the man you choose. You're going to have to wake up to that face every day for the rest of your mutually aging life. . . . —ANDREA MARTIN *(SCTV)*

For the first four months of our marriage, I never took my wig off. Little did he know the hair he loved to touch he could take with him to the office. —JOAN RIVERS

I don't think I'm capable right now of knowing what love is, except toward my son. I think I've put up so many walls. . . . It's day-to-day. —JOAN'S DAUGHTER MELISSA RIVERS ON HER THREE-YEAR MARRIAGE BREAKING DOWN

$\mathcal{R}$omance is the icing but love is the cake.

**—CHEF JULIA CHILD'S PHILOSOPHY**

$\mathcal{L}$ove is a great beautifier.  **—LOUISA MAY ALCOTT *(LITTLE WOMEN)***

$\mathcal{T}$rue story. My daughter, a boyfriend of hers, and I were going to go to the movies one day. Long ago. "What's playing?" he asks. She reads the titles, then there's one she'd like to see: "How about *Little Women?*" she asks. He declines graciously. "Who the hell wants to see a movie about midgets?" Later that night I advised her, "Lose him."

**—EVE ARDEN, THE PRINCIPAL IN *GREASE***

$\mathcal{I}$ thought it was only in the movies, but I know a few girls married to older men who call them "the little woman." Can you believe it? I'm on the short side, so I'd be self-conscious and think he was referring to my height. But what it really is, is a put-down, it makes your status little. And besides, "little man" is more appropriate—or it is for some of the big-acting but short-cheated guys who swagger around Hollywood and the rest of the world, no doubt.

**—JULIETTE LEWIS *(NATURAL BORN KILLERS)***

$\mathcal{I}$n acting, actresses routinely pad their bras. Or the studios did it for them, mostly from the '50s on, when mammaries came to the forefront. Actors, or men, don't have that prerogative, yet I dated two producers who used socks in the crotch, and also an actor whom I briefly—pardon the expression—considered marrying.

**—CAROLYN JONES *(THE ADDAMS FAMILY)***

We did argue. But one of the more hurtful things [third husband] John Huston said to me, he said completely calmly. Said he preferred horses to women. Not sexually, but as people.
—EVELYN KEYES *(THE SEVEN YEAR ITCH)*

The labor of women in the house, certainly, enables men to produce more wealth than they otherwise could; and in this way women are economic factors in society. But so are horses.
—AMERICAN ACTIVIST-WRITER CHARLOTTE PERKINS GILMAN IN 1900

Marriage is like twirling a baton, turning a handspring, or eating with chopsticks; it looks so easy until you try it.
—HUMORIST HELEN ROWLAND IN *REFLECTIONS OF A BACHELOR GIRL* (1909)

We Germans have a saying: Fire in the heart sends smoke into the head. It's fine, it's marvelous, to be in love—as often as you like—and somewhat lose your mind in the process. It's temporary, after all, like a splendid holiday or eating an entire chocolate cake by yourself. But marriage . . . ladies, that is not temporary, and it is so important. Before you decide about that, use your head, not just your heart— and keep your head smoke-free! Good luck.
—ACTOR-AUTHOR HILDEGARD KNEF

# Men on Marriage

Ꙭ

Marriage: the only sport in which the trapped animal has to buy the license.
                                                            —ANONYMOUS

The only really happy folk are married women and single men.
                                                —WRITER H. L. MENCKEN

It is a woman's business to get married as soon as possible, and a man's to keep unmarried as long as he can.   —GEORGE BERNARD SHAW

I waited so long [to marry] because I didn't want to make the same mistake twice.                    —HAPPILY MARRIED WARREN BEATTY

Some studies say that married people live longer. Not really. It only seems longer.
                                                        —JERRY SEINFELD

Still I can't contradict what so oft has been said, "Though women are angels, yet wedlock's the devil."
                                                    —POET LORD BYRON

Yeah, I've occasionally thought about getting married. And then I thought again. **—FORTY-PLUS BACHELOR GEORGE CLOONEY**

The music at a wedding procession always reminds me of the music which leads soldiers into battle. **—POET HEINRICH HEINE**

I started having doubts when I thought I heard the minister say, "Do you take this woman to be your awful wedded wife?" **—TOM ARNOLD, POST-ROSEANNE**

It doesn't really matter who you marry. Next morning she'll turn into someone else. **—REDD FOXX *(SANFORD AND SON)***

A male can live fairly happily with his mother for the first twelve years or so. If he's lucky, he can live fairly happily with his wife for about twelve months. **—WILLIAM FRAWLEY *(I LOVE LUCY)*, WHOSE SOLE MARRIAGE, EARLY ON, WAS AN UNHAPPY ONE**

I belong to Bridegrooms Anonymous. Whenever I feel like getting married, they send over a lady in a housecoat and hair curlers to burn my toast for me. **—DICK MARTIN *(ROWAN AND MARTIN'S LAUGH-IN)***

Marriage vows should be written like a dog license that has to be renewed every year. **—ROCKER ROD STEWART**

A man and woman marry because both of them don't know what to do with themselves. **—RUSSIAN PLAYWRIGHT ANTON CHEKHOV**

Men marry because they are tired. Women because they are curious. Both are disappointed.    —OSCAR WILDE

We want playmates we can own.
—CARTOONIST JULES FEIFFER ON WHY MEN MARRY

Ladies, stick around. Work if you must, but don't take a night job. Absence makes the heart go yonder.
—CHER'S EX, CONGRESSMAN SONNY BONO

Without question it's a tough business on relationships. You really have to think seriously about what it means to be a "husband." You have to go the extra mile. It's not so much that temptation is all around you, because as far as I'm concerned, that's not an issue. It's absence. Absence is difficult.    —ACTOR SAM NEILL *(THE PIANO, JURASSIC PARK)*

Marriage has a calming effect and makes things easier for a man, as it offers moderate temptation with the maximum opportunity and minimal fuss.    —MICHAEL CAINE

Marriage is so widespread because it's endorsed by the powers that be and because dating is so demanding.    —DREW CAREY

I think a man can have two, maybe three affairs while he is married. Three is the absolute maximum. After that, you are cheating.
—FRENCH STAR YVES MONTAND, ONE OF WHOSE AFFAIRS (WHILE MARRIED TO SIMONE SIGNORET, UNTIL HER DEATH) WAS WITH *LET'S MAKE LOVE* COSTAR MARILYN MONROE

$I$ like women sexually and for dates, sometimes even vacations together. But how can you stay passionate about someone you have to live and plan and scheme and budget with?
—*POLITICALLY INCORRECT* **HOST BILL MAHER**

$B$eing married to a beautiful girl is expensive. Because you also have to hire a cook.
—**SAMMY DAVIS JR.**

$I$ ought to—I married one.
—**GROUCHO MARX, WHEN ASKED IF HE KNEW THE DEFINITION OF AN EXTRAVAGANCE**

$I$t's better to marry before you're rich. That way the wife won't spend like a shopaholic, and she'll even help you save. God help you once you're rich. Then she expects to spend a fortune, and it might even be her main motivation for getting hitched to you.
—**CHARLIE SHEEN**

$P$ossibly the worst thing about being a celebrity is not knowing for a certainty if people like you for you . . . [and] if a girl wants you for a mate or a prize. On the other hand, one of the bonuses of fame is how many birds will sleep with you just because you're Somebody. So unless romance and sincerity are your priorities, it's not exactly a bad trade-off.
—**MICK JAGGER**

$I$ was digging her, but there was a desperate neediness about her, an impatience to get married.
—**VANILLA ICE ON WHY HIS RELATIONSHIP WITH MADONNA ENDED**

Women are lucky. If a woman has a happy marriage, she can be counted as a success. If a man has a happy marriage, it's like, so what? What about his career? How much does he earn? Is that a good way to measure success? Life is about so much more than a career.
**LONGTIME MARRIED ALAN ALDA**

There's nothing in the world like the devotion of a married woman. It's a thing no married man knows anything about.    **—OSCAR WILDE**

I like my cigar too, but I take it out once in a while.
**—GROUCHO MARX, TO A FEMALE CONTESTANT ON HIS QUIZ SHOW WHO EXPLAINED THAT SHE'D BORNE TWENTY-TWO CHILDREN BECAUSE "I LOVE MY HUSBAND"**

*How To Be Happy Though Married*
**—THE TITLE OF AN 1885 BOOK BY IRISH ARMY CHAPLAIN E. J. HARDY**

Marriage has many pains, but celibacy has no pleasures.
**—BRITISH WRITER DR. SAMUEL JOHNSON**

[Marriage] resembles a pair of shears, so joined that they cannot be separated; often moving in opposite directions, yet always punishing anyone who comes between them.
**—ENGLISH CLERGYMAN SYDNEY SMITH (1771–1845)**

I love Mickey Mouse more than any woman I've ever known.
**—WALT DISNEY, MARRIED FATHER OF TWO DAUGHTERS**

See that fish mounted on the wall with its mouth open? Please read the inscription on the plaque below it: "If I'd kept my mouth shut, I wouldn't be here." **—TV SPORTSCASTER HOWARD COSELL TO A FEMALE REPORTER WHO ASKED HIM HOW HE MET AND COURTED HIS WIFE**

The more you talk, the more you give a girl a matrimonial in.
**—GEORGE CLOONEY**

Wives are people who feel they don't dance enough. **—GROUCHO MARX**

The first few years of marriage are a time of much promise— broken promises. **—MUSICIAN CAB CALLOWAY**

Marry an outdoors woman. Then if you throw her out into the yard for a night, she can still survive. **—W. C. FIELDS**

A bachelor is a man who never made the same mistake once.
**—ED WYNN, WHO WAS JEWISH AND MARRIED AN ANTI-SEMITE**

Do not marry the enemy of your excitement.
**—WRITER NATHANIEL BRANDEN**

Ah, yes, marriage—a great institution. But who wants to live in an institution? **—W. C. FIELDS**

All men are born free, but some get married.
**—ANONYMOUS (PROBABLY A MALE)**

Marriage: the state of condition of a community consisting of a master, a mistress, and two slaves, making, in all, two.
**—AMERICAN JOURNALIST AMBROSE BIERCE**

I have always thought that every woman should marry, and no man.
**—NINETEENTH-CENTURY PRIME MINISTER BENJAMIN DISRAELI**

Alas, beyond a certain point, there is no romance in familiarity.
**—FORMER JAMES BOND TIMOTHY DALTON**

Marriage is a wonderful invention. But then again, so is a bicycle repair kit.   **—SCOTTISH COMEDIAN BILLY CONNOLLY**

Nowadays everyone thinks if you're over forty and not married, you're gay. But some guys are just plain lucky.   **—WARREN BEATTY IN 1983**

This is one profession where most of the lesbians get married, because of their screen image, and where a lot of the straight women don't have kids, so they can keep looking good on screen and not interrupt their careers. In Hollywood it's all topsy-turvy.
**—WILLIAM DEMAREST (UNCLE CHARLIE ON *MY THREE SONS*)**

Whatever happened to John Travolta? I heard he either joined some cult [Scientology] and got fat. Or married and had a child. Which amounts to the same thing.   **—FRENCH STAR GÉRARD DEPARDIEU IN THE 1980S**

Show me a great actor, and I'll show you a lousy husband; show me a great actress, and you've seen the devil.   **—W. C. FIELDS**

$\mathcal{I}$ try to conduct my life with a certain amount of dignity and discretion. But marriage is a hard, hard gig. **—KEVIN COSTNER, DIVORCED AFTER HIS "CHILDHOOD SWEETHEART" WIFE FOUND OUT HE'D BEEN INTIMATELY INVOLVED WITH MODELS, ACTRESSES, A PUBLICIST, A HATCHECK GIRL, AND A HULA DANCER**

$\mathcal{S}$omewhere I read that the average guy thinks about sex every eight minutes. And women talk about marriage more than any other topic. Men don't talk about marriage, unless a gal brings it up, or unless they're celebrities talking about it for interviews that mostly women read anyway. **—JAMES GARNER**

$\mathcal{A}$ mistress, you have fun with. But a wife you have to more or less respect. It's too bad that wives probably get the short end of the stick, but does a guy have to give up having fun because he's married? **—ANDREW DICE CLAY**

$\mathcal{F}$or the first year of marriage I had a basically bad attitude. I tended to place my wife underneath a pedestal. **—WOODY ALLEN**

$\mathcal{B}$efore I met Nicoletta, I was not in a good time. I had a smiling face, but inside I was not happy. I was surrounded by people, but I was lonely, and the worst loneliness of all is in the crowd. **—LUCIANNO PAVAROTTI, SIXTY-TWO, AFTER LEAVING HIS WIFE OF THIRTY-FIVE YEARS (MOTHER OF THEIR THREE CHILDREN) FOR HIS TWENTY-EIGHT-YEAR-OLD ASSISTANT**

$\mathcal{I}$ find a way to flee . . . I experience a sense of drowning. I suppose that's why some of my most momentarily successful romances have been with married people. With them I have the unspoken safety-net line, "But you're married," thus keeping me from being swallowed up in a sea of intimacy. . . . I really want a marriage and I really don't, I reckon, because surely by this time—fifty-seven as I write this—I could have had it.              **—DANCER-DIRECTOR TOMMY TUNE**

$\mathcal{W}$asn't it Descartes who said, "I think, therefore I am"? Well, I think, therefore I'm single.              **—CESAR ROMERO**

[$\mathcal{E}$vita Peron] told me and Tyrone [Power] over dinner [in Buenos Aires, Argentina], "You're fortunate, because in America they treat movie stars right. Here they spit at them. I should know. I was an artist." I'm sure that if Darryl F. Zanuck [head of Fox] had offered her a contract she would have left Juan [Peron]. **—CESAR ROMERO IN 1991,**
**RECALLING A GOODWILL TOUR OF LATIN AMERICA**

$\mathcal{W}$ell, when you're costars you get to hang out . . . you can get to know each other very well. Sometimes it clicks, sometimes it ends in marriage, other times it's all manufactured publicity.              **—TED *CHEERS***
**DANSON ON WHOOPI GOLDBERG**

Some men have been made, or elevated, by marrying or cohabiting with very famous women who then made them into celebrities in their own right. Look at Jon Peters [via Barbra Streisand] or Tom Arnold [via Roseanne]. Or more recently, actor Benjamin Bratt and director Guy Ritchie—who noticed them very much until they took up with Julia Roberts and Madonna?

Those men don't get criticized—well, not so much—for moving up socially and professionally through women. But in this town, if a wife is ambitious and wants to be known as more than just Mrs. Him, she's called ambitious, aggressive, a bitch. But guess what? Most of the bitches in Hollywood are men!  **—SHOW-BIZ WRITER LANCE LOUD**

Inside sources reveal that what prevented Benjamin Bratt marrying his adoring Julia Roberts was the intimidation factor of her $20-million-a-movie fee, the worry that his career might not ascend while hers continues to soar, and pressure to make a movie together—which if it flopped would be attributed primarily to him.

But the straw factor which broke the relationship's back is a reportedly very heated disagreement over whether Julia's niece, a minor, should go into acting now; Julia's all for it, giving her considerable encouragement, while Ben's deadset against it. . . . At least Bratt will no longer find that nine out of ten questions interviewers ask him are about J.R.  **—LONDON COLUMNIST COLIN DAVIES**

Many if not most stars are more interesting solo. For some, being half of a couple or part of an entity seems to diminish them. . . . Every one of the films that Tom Cruise and Nicole Kidman made together was a flop, which is one of the publicly mentioned reasons that they broke up.  **—ACTOR-WRITER DALE REYNOLDS**

The marital knot is the lock in the bolt to the room at the top.
—LEADING (GAY) HOLLYWOOD AGENT HENRY WILLSON, WHO ENGINEERED THE
MARRIAGE OF PRIZE CLIENT ROCK HUDSON TO WILLSON'S FEMALE SECRETARY

What happens is that agencies like CAA control the industry. They package people together. They go to some woman . . . and say, "Look, if you marry X and participate in this PR scam, we'll package you into movies with directors and actors that we represent as well." So she gets something out of it, (he) is covered, and everybody's happy.
—OPENLY GAY ACTOR CRAIG CHESTER ON HIGH-LEVEL CLOSETING
OF MALE SUPERSTARS

Though unmarried, I have had six children.
—SECRETLY GAY POET WALT WHITMAN, NONE OF WHOSE
PURPORTED OFFSPRING WERE EVER TRACED

Well, Cary Grant was said to be a matrimaniac, marrying so many times. Had the truth been known, he was trying to convince the public he was heterosexual. When in his sixties he finally had a child, the press automatically cooed and aahed; no one dared ask out loud why he'd never become a father via any of his previous wives.
—HOLLYWOOD AUTHOR PAUL ROSENFIELD

I like kids. I don't know why you have to get married to have kids. Kids, you can get along with . . . a wife ain't so easy.   —SAMMY DAVIS JR.

*I* was seeing this girl who said she hadn't dated in a long time. At her apartment, she introduced me to her cat. And she said on Valentine's Day she gave her cat a card and a gift. . . . It must have been a very long time.  **—*POLITICALLY INCORRECT* HOST BILL MAHER**

*W*hat's with women and cats? Most girls love everything about a cat. Like, a cat's independent, a cat sleeps way too often, cats don't come when you call, they stay out a lot at night, and when they are home they want to be left alone. So, what women don't like about men, they love about cats.  **—ARSENIO HALL**

*D*on't marry a beautiful woman. They lie like cats. . . . Half of beauty is a lie.  **—ROBERT REED *(THE BRADY BUNCH)***

*L*ana Turner's not an outstanding actress, but a man is better off with a woman who can't lie too well. I'd be uncomfortable married to, say, [First Lady of the American Stage] Katharine Cornell.  **—LEX BARKER, JOHNNY WEISSMULLER'S SUCCESSOR AS TARZAN**

*T*he one charm of marriage is that it makes a life of deception absolutely necessary for both parties.  **—OSCAR WILDE**

*I*t is charming that everyone applauds newlyweds . . . and those who remain wed. It's not fair, however, that no one applauds or roots for the single individual who is perfectly content to remain so.  **—ALBERT FINNEY *(TOM JONES, MURDER ON THE ORIENT EXPRESS)***

*A*fter he got married, Michael J. Fox received five thousand threatening letters, almost all from female fans.  **—*PREMIERE* MAGAZINE**

Congratulations on getting the other 90 percent.

—TELEGRAM SENT BY A FRIEND TO LEADING TALENT AGENT LELAND HAYWARD
WHEN HE WED HIS STAR CLIENT, ACTRESS MARGARET SULLAVAN

Grace Kelly thought that by leaving Hollywood to become the wife of a fat prince of a tiny country owned by France, she would find some greater destiny or happier status. Instead, it was the beginning of her end, and it didn't keep her from becoming an alcoholic.

She wanted to get back into the movies, but it was forbidden. In the 1960s, Hitchcock made her a fantastic offer, but the Grimaldis of Monaco were still in the nineteenth century, and Grace was stuck living inside a social refrigerator.      —BRITISH STAR TREVOR HOWARD

American women expect to find in their husbands the perfection that Englishwomen only hope to find in their butlers.

—W. SOMERSET MAUGHAM

There are two kinds of women who are only too happy to point out your imperfections: mothers and wives. You can't help the first few decades of your life, but why get stuck for the whole rest of it?

—COMEDIAN TOM GREEN, EX-HUSBAND OF DREW BARRYMORE

The reason I live alone is that I cannot conceive of trying to bravely face each new day when after you turn over in bed the first words you hear are, "And another thing. . . ."      —UK AUTHOR QUENTIN CRISP

Women are divided into those who think they're always right.

—DANNY DEVITO

There's very little advice in men's magazines, because men don't think there's a lot they don't know. Women do. Women want to learn. Men think, "I know what I'm doing. Just show me somebody naked."

—JERRY SEINFELD

Marriage is divine. But only during the wedding ceremony.

—FRANK SINATRA

Marriage is a feast where the grace is sometimes better than the dinner. —ENGLISH CLERGYMAN CHARLES CALEB COLTON (1780–1832)

What they do in heaven we are ignorant of; what they do not we are told expressly: that they neither marry, nor are given in marriage.

—JONATHAN SWIFT, CLERGYMAN AND AUTHOR *(GULLIVER'S TRAVELS)*

Marriage is distinctly and repeatedly excluded from heaven. Is this because it is thought likely to mar the general felicity?

—SAMUEL BUTLER

Marriage is about roughage, bills, garbage disposal, and noise. There is something vulgar, almost absurd, in the notion of a Mrs. Plato or a Mme. Descartes, or of Wittgenstein on a honeymoon. Perhaps Louis Althusser was enacting a necessary axiom or lyrical proof when on the morning of November 16, 1980, he throttled his wife.

—WRITER GEORGE STEINER

The true artist will let his wife starve, his children go barefoot, his mother drudge for his living at seventy, sooner than work at anything but his art. —GEORGE BERNARD SHAW

$\mathcal{M}$an is the only animal that blushes. Or needs to.  **—MARK TWAIN**

$\mathcal{D}$idn't some wise man or philosopher once say that, like, adultery is the application of democracy to love?

**—*THE DAILY SHOW* HOST JON STEWART**

$\mathcal{S}$ome people claim that marriage interferes with romance. There's no doubt about it. Anytime you have a romance, your wife is bound to interfere.  **—GROUCHO MARX**

$\mathcal{I}$'ve heard it said that a pessimist is a man who believes all women are bad, and an optimist is a man who hopes they are.  **—JACKIE GLEASON**

$\mathcal{I}$ guess it is a man's world, really. When a woman works, she earns about two-thirds what a man does. But when she, uh, sins, she earns a man's wage and then some.  **—TIM ALLEN**

$\mathcal{T}$he dream of the American male is . . . a beautiful, but comprehensible, creature who does not destroy a perfect situation by forming a complete sentence.  **—WRITER E. B. WHITE**

$\mathcal{I}$n the East, women religiously conceal that they have faces; in the West, that they have legs. In both cases they make it evident that they have but little brains.  **—HENRY DAVID THOREAU IN 1852 (THE SKIRT HAS SINCE RISEN, BUT IN MANY LANDS THE VEIL STILL HASN'T FALLEN)**

$\mathcal{I}$t's women depending on men for money that can really keep them enslaved. . . . I can remember here in America when the establishment attitude was, Oh, it's too bad that more and more wives have to work outside the home. I think it's excellent. So does my wife—I'm a fairly successful actor, but she's a wonderful photographer. Why should she stay home getting bored, sitting on my laurels?

—ALAN ALDA *(M\*A\*S\*H)*

$\mathcal{W}$e've seen people who had decent marriages who came into money and it destroyed the marriage. Bringing a huge amount of money into the scene is a life-changing event. It's incredibly stressful.

—PSYCHOLOGIST STEPHEN GOLDBART, CODIRECTOR OF THE MONEY, MEANING, AND CHOICES INSTITUTE IN KENTFIELD, CALIFORNIA, WHICH ADVISES PEOPLE WHO COME INTO FINANCIAL WINDFALLS, PARTICULARLY LOTTERY WINNERS

$\mathcal{M}$y wife didn't marry me for my money. She married me for my father's money. No, no, just kidding.

—NICKY HILTON, SON OF CONRAD AND ELIZABETH TAYLOR'S FIRST HUSBAND

$\mathcal{M}$y wife, Anna, says I reveal all our bedroom secrets on my show— they get into the script. But people, the viewers, everyone loves it. She complains about it. I tell her it helps make the show a hit. I say, "Honey, go cry on a bag of money if it gets too hard."

—RAY ROMANO OF *EVERYBODY LOVES RAYMOND*

$\mathcal{M}$y wife berates me for being too outspoken in interviews. I tell her I've a flair for the dramatic . . . [and] besides, as the American car [rental] people say, when you're No. 2 you have to try harder.

—BRITISH ACTOR ROBERT STEPHENS *(THE PRIME OF MISS JEAN BRODIE)*, THEN-HUSBAND OF TWO-TIME OSCAR-WINNER MAGGIE SMITH

$\mathcal{M}$y wife says I play too much golf. She doesn't realize golf is sometimes the secret to a calm and enduring truce—I mean marriage. **—GARY MORTON, LUCILLE BALL'S SECOND HUSBAND**

$\mathcal{M}$y wife would rather sit and listen to me sing in a nightclub than be out making a movie. **—BOBBY DARIN, MONTHS BEFORE HE AND SANDRA DEE DIVORCED**

$\mathcal{I}$'m committed to Laura [Dern]. . . . We have a big future together. **—BILLY BOB THORNTON, WEEKS BEFORE TRADING HIS LONGTIME FIANCÉE FOR ANOTHER ACTRESS, RECENT OSCAR-WINNER ANGELINA JOLIE**

$\mathcal{I}$ keep reading that [Debra Winger] is "difficult." She may, on the set, be a bit demanding or . . . something of a perfectionist. In regular life, she's easier to live with. **—TIMOTHY HUTTON *(ORDINARY PEOPLE)*, MONTHS BEFORE THEY SEPARATED, THEN DIVORCED**

$\mathcal{I}$n marriage, to argue can keep it from becoming boring. But my wife can argue 'round and 'round the same two things, over and over. She should be a tape recorder. About money—"Don't spend so much!"—and we should go out more—"I want to go out more, you don't take me anywhere." Should I take her somewhere that's free? Then I'd get, "You don't spend enough on me!" **—HERVÉ VILLECHAIZE *(FANTASY ISLAND)***

$\mathcal{I}$ met my wife coming out of a department store—in a revolving door—and we've been going around together ever since. This is one dizzy dame. **—COMEDIAN JOE E. LEWIS**

*I* like college girls, sometimes. They're young and smart . . . I think my last wife majored in shopping. **—ROD STEWART**

*My* wife's hobby—headaches!
**—COMEDIAN HENNY "TAKE MY WIFE, PLEASE" YOUNGMAN**

*My* wife reminds me of what's in my drink here: an ice cube with a hole in it.
**—COMEDIAN SHECKY GREENE, DURING HIS LAS VEGAS NIGHTCLUB ACT**

*Most* bachelors are more romantic than married men. Bachelors still have their illusions about women. **—JULIO IGLESIAS**

*Overall*, wouldn't you say women are happier in marriage than men usually are? Which is ironic and kind of touching, because until recent times, because of economics and pressures and all, women had to marry. Usually to guys their parents, or father, chose. Whereas men had the means not to marry, if they were really against it. Yet men, now as then, still complain about marriage far more than the wives do.
**—PHIL DONAHUE**

*I* believe it's only the female sex that fools itself into thinking, Gee, out of everybody in the world, he chose me. **—JERRY SEINFELD**

*Gloria* didn't select me as a husband so much as a potential father. She thought I had material, or should I say, good paternal, qualities. I did my best . . . and when she wanted twins, well, I just, I rose to the occasion and I, I just delivered, that's all. **—JAMES STEWART**

$\mathcal{I}$ remember when my dear friend and discovery Marilyn Monroe wanted more than anything to meet Albert Einstein. Marilyn always wanted to become a mother, but she thought if she got pregnant by Einstein, that would be some baby. She figured it would have Einstein's brains and her looks. Until inevitably somebody pointed out that the baby might end up with her brains and Einstein's looks.

— HOLLYWOOD COLUMNIST SIDNEY SKOLSKY

$\mathcal{T}$he minute a man has a kid, he gets a rival for his wife's time and affection.   — FORMER TALK SHOW HOST MORTON DOWNEY JR.

$\mathcal{I}$ rather like children. But not until they're twenty or twenty-five and are easier to entertain.   — HUGH GRANT

$\mathcal{H}$ollywood has done a lot of damage. It tends to idealize family life, so when problems come up in reality, it's as if it's not working out right. . . . And then the thing where, in the movies, a couple has problems, and the automatic solution is to have a baby. Which, who ends up paying? The kid. A child or children do not solve the parents' problems, and usually add to them, if anything.

— JEREMY BRETT, BRITISH ACTOR (TV'S SHERLOCK HOLMES)

$\mathcal{L}$ove happens way too fast in the movies. Love at first sight is their biggest myth. And from that, you're supposed to assume that marriage is eternal . . . "happily ever after," which is so Santa Claus.

— KEANU REEVES

It's actually to lure the female audience . . . that Hollywood substitutes the word "love" for "sex." So it's "making love," which is less animalistic and implies a relationship. . . . In most cases, the leading lady, who has a supporting role, is essentially there to demonstrate that the hero is heterosexual.

—**PRODUCER JERRY B. WHEELER** *(THE CAROL BURNETT SHOW)*

I know guys who spend more time on picking their next car than consciously deciding what kind of girl they want to marry. When it comes to wives, men aren't that choosy. So long as she's pretty and has standard equipment, and she's not too old, too fat, or too bossy, hey, she's marriage material. —**KURT COBAIN (WHO MARRIED COURTNEY LOVE)**

It sometimes happens that matrimony changes a man's wife into someone akin to his mother or a sister. He then, perhaps understandably, looks elsewhere for a sexy stranger for a mistress.

—**DONALD PLEASENCE** *(HALLOWEEN)*

The opposite sex does not seem to comprehend how or why it would be and is often easier for the male of the species to have workable, enjoyable, or even ecstatic sex with somebody he doesn't know and may not even like, may even detest, than it is with somebody familiar and even beloved. —**BRITISH ACTOR-WRITER PETER COOK**

All too often, for a man, sex is an aggressive act. You don't typically want to do it to someone you esteem highly or venerate. . . . For better or worse, sex and respect are mutually exclusive. At least, they tend to become so with time and detail.

—**ARTHUR C. CLARKE, SCI-FI WRITER** *(2001)*

If a man really loves a woman, of course he wouldn't marry her for the world if he were not quite sure that he was the best person she could by any possibility marry.    **—OLIVER WENDELL HOLMES SR. IN 1858**

My ex-wife [actress Brenda Benet] tried to convince me she was too good for me, and very nearly did. When we were breaking up, I informed her, "By definition, a saint cannot be married."
**—TV STAR BILL BIXBY**

Marriage: a legal or religious ceremony by which two persons of the opposite sex solemnly agree to harass and spy on each other for ninety-nine years, or until death do them join.
**—WRITER ELBERT HUBBARD IN 1923**

Marriage: a ceremony in which rings are put on the finger of the lady and through the nose of the gentleman.
**—ENGLISH PHILOSOPHER HERBERT SPENCER (1820–1903)**

Man has his will—but woman has her way!   **—OLIVER WENDELL HOLMES**

The nags shall inherit the hearth.                 **—LENNY BRUCE**

With marriage, as with cages: the birds outside despair to get in, and those inside despair of getting out.
**—FRENCH ESSAYIST MONTAIGNE (1533–1592)**

*I*s not marriage an open question, when . . . such as are in the institution wish to get out, and such as are out wish to get in?

—RALPH WALDO EMERSON IN 1850

*I*t's a funny thing that when a man hasn't got anything on earth to worry about, he goes off and gets married.     —POET ROBERT FROST

*W*ho are happy in marriage? Those with so little imagination that they cannot picture a better state, and those so shrewd that they prefer quiet slavery to hopeless rebellion.     —WRITER H. L. MENCKEN IN 1920

*I*'m a Jewish New Yorker, a writer, and a comedian. My first marriage was not what I'd been led to expect. I had to get out of it. It was too happy.     —WOODY ALLEN

*W*hen you get too happy in your home life, it dulls the edge of your ambition. Most unambitious people are content just to be happy.     —PETER O'TOOLE

*C*ompromise can kill a marriage. That is, if it's mostly on the side of the one with greater pride, whoever that may be.

—CARROLL O'CONNOR *(ALL IN THE FAMILY)*

*C*ompromise makes a good umbrella but a poor roof.

—JAMES RUSSELL LOWELL IN 1884

Compromise is the cement of matrimony. Without it, you have two roommates, living together but separately.
**—JOHN DENVER, COMPOSER OF "ANNIE'S SONG"**

Every time a man remarries, he compromises himself. But in a hopeful or sweetly masochistic way.   **—PETER FINCH (NETWORK)**

When I've found myself divorced, that's when I've been most optimistic about marriage and finding my ideal mate. Then I get married again, and sooner or later I think, Here I am again—dummy.
**—MICKEY ROONEY**

Any widower who remarries doesn't deserve to be a widower!
**—REDD FOXX**

"Till death do us part." And wouldn't you know, nowadays people are living a lot longer.   **—MICHAEL LANDON**

I was exploring the ways women and men related to me as Dorothy and I'd never been related to that way before in my life—having men meet me, say hello, and immediately start looking over my shoulder trying to find an attractive woman! . . . I would get very hostile: I wanted to get even with them.   **—DUSTIN HOFFMAN OF TOOTSIE**

It's lucky for us that girls aren't as entranced by good looks as we are. I think it has something to do with that old saw: Beggars can't be choosers. But what's starting to spoil it is this cult of male beauty; the gays started it, and now women are starting to think how a guy looks is important or sexy. In the old days, a big wallet was sexy enough. —ROBERT MITCHUM *(FAREWELL, MY LOVELY)*

The American woman's ambitions are too high. In Europe a woman decides early what type she will be—mother, cook, or siren. Women here want to be all of these and also run Wall Street.
—U.S.-BASED BRITISH JOURNALIST ALISTAIR COOKE

I always tell young men there are three rules: They hate us, we hate them; they're stronger, they're smarter; and most important, they don't play fair. —SELDOM-MARRIED JACK NICHOLSON

Girls have an unfair advantage over men: If they can't get what they want by being smart, they can get it by being dumb. —YUL BRYNNER

Love is the delusion that one woman differs from another.
—WRITER H. L. MENCKEN

Henry VII [*sic*] . . . he didn't get divorced, he just had their heads chopped off when he got tired of them. That's a good way to get rid of a woman—no alimony. —TED TURNER, THE MAN BEHIND COLORIZATION

$\mathcal{A}$ woman—the same may be said of the other sex—all beautiful and accomplished will, while her hand and heart are undisposed of, turn the heads and set the circle in which she moves on fire. Let her marry, and what is the consequence? The madness ceases and all is quiet again. Why? Not because there is any diminution in the charms of the lady, but because there is an end of hope.   **—GEORGE WASHINGTON**

$\mathcal{M}$en have a much better time of it than women; for one thing they marry later; for another thing they die earlier.   **—H. L. MENCKEN**

$\mathcal{T}$he most popular labor-saving device today is still a husband with money.   **—COMEDIAN JOEY ADAMS (COLUMNIST CINDY'S LATE HUSBAND)**

$\mathcal{B}$achelors should be heavily taxed. It is not fair that some men should be happier than others.   **—OSCAR WILDE**

$\mathcal{I}$'m looking for an old-fashioned girl. One who powders her nose from the outside.   **—DUDLEY MOORE, AFTER KICKING DRUGS**

$\mathcal{A}$ sufficient measure of civilization is the influence of good women.   **—RALPH WALDO EMERSON IN 1870**

$\mathcal{Y}$ou absolutely can judge the quality of a nation and its people by the way three groups are treated there: women, and wives particularly; homosexual men and women; and animals. . . . For one thing, Australia was the second country to grant women the vote.
**—AUSTRALIAN WRITER PATRICK WHITE (NEW ZEALAND WAS THE FIRST COUNTRY, AND HAS ALREADY HAD TWO FEMALE HEADS OF STATE)**

$\mathcal{D}$avid is 100 percent heterosexual. And Elton John has never met David Gest. —SPOKESPERSON FOR LIZA MINNELLI'S FOURTH HUSBAND, IN 2002 (TWO OF HER PREVIOUS HUSBANDS WERE GAY, AND VARIOUS OF HER MOTHER'S); LONDON'S *MIRROR* NEWSPAPER REPORTED THAT WHEN ASKED WHAT HE WOULD GIVE LIZA AS A WEDDING PRESENT, SIR ELTON DECLARED, "A HETEROSEXUAL HUSBAND"

$\mathcal{O}$ne good Husband is worth two good Wives; for, the scarcer things are, the more they're valued. —BENJAMIN FRANKLIN IN 1742

$\mathcal{B}$ack when he was alive, Leonardo da Vinci was the guy who said, "Impatience is the mother of stupidity." Which surprises the hell out of me. I knew my mother-in-law was old, but I didn't know her real name was Impatience. —COMEDIAN JOE E. LEWIS

$\mathcal{A}$ man may be a fool and not know it, but not if he is married. —WRITER H. L. MENCKEN

$\mathcal{A}$ husband may forget where he went on his honeymoon, but he never forgets why. —BRITISH WRITER BEVERLEY NICHOLS

$\mathcal{A}$ man marries to have a home, but also because he doesn't want to be bothered with sex and all that sort of thing. —BRITISH WRITER W. SOMERSET MAUGHAM

$\mathcal{D}$ora and I are now married, but just as happy as we were before. —LORD BERTRAND RUSSELL, PHILOSOPHER AND WRITER

Today, he admits, he gave his sons just one piece of advice: "Never confuse 'I love you' with 'I want to marry you.'"
—**WRITER CLEVELAND AMORY**

A bachelor is a guy who's right now and then. —**JERRY SEINFELD**

The vow of fidelity is an absurd commitment, but it is the heart of marriage. —**FATHER ROBERT CAPON**

Contraceptives should be used on every conceivable occasion.
—**BRITISH WRITER-ACTOR PETER COOK**

People sweat so that they won't catch on fire when they're having sex.
—**WOODY ALLEN**

After the honeymoon's over and grim reality sets in, you become numbingly aware that the future will be much like the present, only far, far longer. —**DREW CAREY**

A man's mother might be his misfortune, but his wife is his own fault. —**GROUCHO MARX**

Breakfast is the most crucial time in a marriage. Breakfast time is symbolic. . . . —**SCREENWRITER PADDY CHAYEFSKY** *(NETWORK)*

They say more divorces are caused by men breakfasting with their wives than dining with their secretaries. —**WRITER-DIRECTOR BILLY WILDER**

One reason I moved to Japan is the connubial situation. The Japanese have a word, "judo." It stands for the art of conquering by yielding. The American equivalent of "judo" is "Yes, dear."
—**PRODUCER STEVE PARKER (EX-HUSBAND OF SHIRLEY MACLAINE)**

Behind most men's success is a proud wife and a flabbergasted mother-in-law.
—**CONAN O'BRIEN, *LATE NIGHT* HOST**

Marriage, it's like the lottery. What are the odds? Unfortunately, in marriage if you lose, you can't tear up the lottery ticket.
—**DON JOHNSON *(MIAMI VICE)***

The sole cause of divorce is marriage.
—**WALTER CRONKITE**

If love didn't exist, there wouldn't be divorce.
—**BOB HOPE**

Friendships, like marriages, are dependent on avoiding the unforgivable.
—**NOVELIST JOHN D. MACDONALD**

In marriage, as in my game show, the most important things aren't what you say but what you don't say.
—**TOM KENNEDY, HOST OF *YOU DON'T SAY***

Frankness is good in business, not always good in marriage. Women appreciate a little reticence into the bargain.
—**RAUL JULIA *(THE ADDAMS FAMILY)***

When I got upset and said she wasn't a good wife, she took it on the chin. With a defiant, well, a sneer. But when I opined that she wasn't a good mother, she went through the roof.
—ACTOR PHILIP TERRY ON EX-WIFE JOAN CRAWFORD

What does it mean to be a good wife? If you're rich, you hire someone to do the things that the average wife does. To me, the important thing is she should be a good mother. . . . Servants and machines can do the things a wife does, but no one can substitute for the mother.  —OMAR SHARIF *(DR. ZHIVAGO)*

Did you hear? Heather Locklear of *Melrose Place* is taking four whole months off so she can be, she says, "a full-time mom." Isn't that so maternal of her?  —CHRIS FARLEY

My girlfriend said she wants to coparent with someone who's strong and solid, butch yet maternal. I almost panicked—I thought she meant Rosie O'Donnell.  —CONAN O'BRIEN

I don't know if it's marriage or just feminine nature that takes the starch out of someone's libido. I was at the cinema with a relative; I won't give her name. *Women in Love,* which had the first major male nude scene in any major movie. Alan Bates and Oliver Reed, naked, wrestling together on a carpet in front of a blazing fire. The audience was spellbound; I was entranced. You could hear a pin drop until after the scene, when several people sighed or coughed.

And my relative, she turns to me and whispers, "Did you notice what an elegant carpet that was?"
—IAN CHARLESON, THE GAY STAR OF *CHARIOTS OF FIRE*

You stay together long enough, she gets more married to the house than to you. Buying things for it, dusting, cleaning constantly, telling the hubby, "Oh, don't sit there," "Don't put the newspaper there," "Be careful of that." It's like she married you to have an affair with the house. **—MOE HOWARD OF THE THREE STOOGES**

It's hard to find the ideal woman in one package. . . . I think it was Phyllis Diller who said something like Why bother cleaning while the kids are still growing—it's like shoveling snow before it stops snowing. Or was it Roseanne? I'd like to find a wife with that easy-going outlook but who looks like Cindy Crawford.

**—TRUMPETER AL HIRT**

Don't blame me, man. Who else but a housewife's willing to work full-time for room and board and a little affection? I'm supposed to respect that and vote for equal rights?

**—STAND-UP "ANGRY COMIC" SAM KINISON**

If she'd been a fish, I'd have thrown her back in.

**—TONY CURTIS, ON AN EX-WIFE**

A woman is a good substitute, overall, for what some crazy fool decided to call self-abuse. **—REDD FOXX**

Love will find a lay. **—ANDREW DICE CLAY**

Love is an ocean of emotions surrounded by an expanse of expenses.

**—MILTON BERLE**

A man is as old as the girl he feels. —TRADITIONAL

Sex is the biggest nothing of all time. —ANDY WARHOL

One lover, that is love; two lovers, that is passion; three lovers, that is commerce. —FRENCH PROVERB

A woman with one lover is an angel, a woman with two lovers is a monster, a woman with three lovers is a woman. —VICTOR HUGO

When it comes to love, too much is not enough. —FRANK SINATRA

Love is a cloth which imagination embroiders. —VOLTAIRE

We are shaped and fashioned by what we love. —GOETHE

Love is many things. But more than anything it is a disturbance of the digestive system. —GABRIEL GARCIA MARQUEZ

There is no love sincerer than love of food. —GEORGE BERNARD SHAW

Fellatio is the sincerest form of flattery.
—ATTRIBUTED TO WOODY ALLEN, AMONG OTHERS

$\mathcal{F}$ar more than men ever do, the opposite sex use their head when it comes to sex. They have to . . . pregnancy. By comparison, an erection has little brain and no conscience. **—BURT LANCASTER, WHO SHOWED SEX EDUCATION FILMS AT HOME TO HIS FIVE CHILDREN**

$\mathcal{W}$e English have sex on the brain. Not the best place for it, actually. **—ACTOR LAURENCE HARVEY *(BUTTERFIELD 8)***

$\mathcal{S}$plendid couple—slept with both of them. **—SIR MAURICE BOWRA, AT THE WEDDING OF A FAMOUS (MALE-FEMALE) LITERARY COUPLE**

$\mathcal{M}$y mother was engaged to a man, and I had been sleeping with that man's son. My mother said, "Oh, I'm going to get married to this man," and I said, "Oh, good! It can be a double wedding!" **—WRITER EDMUND WHITE**

$\mathcal{I}$ have been with men. I like sex. I like beautiful people, men and women. And I'm not ashamed of it. Besides, a lot of women like that because they like to see a man . . . able to be with men and not embarrassed by it. **—ANDY DICK *(NEWSRADIO)***

$\mathcal{L}$ove is like the measles—it's much worse if you get it later in life. **—UK TV STAR BENNY HILL**

$\mathcal{Y}$ou may not need a doctor for love, but it starts with fever and ends with pain. **—ANDY RICHTER**

Whoever said love is blind [Chaucer] must have been referring to the female point of view. For men—young men, old men, rich men, poor, gay, straight, red, white, black, everything—love not only ain't blind, it's damn critical!    **—COUNTRY SINGER RANDY TRAVIS**

Love built on beauty, soon as beauty dies.    **—JOHN DONNE**

Love is blinding, That is why lovers like to touch.    **—GERMAN PROVERB**

Love is blind, but oy, marriage is a real eye-opener.    **—JACKIE MASON**

Love is like war: you begin when you like and leave off when you can.    **—SPANISH PROVERB**

A good wife is your friend for life. A bad one is a curse on all your days. An ex-wife, if she doesn't disappear from your life, is hell on earth.    **—MICHAEL LANDON**

Hell hath no fury like a woman scorned.    **—CONGREVE**

I once heard it said that the secret of a successful marriage went: If you adore her, adorn her. I thought it meant clothes; buy her what she desires. Eventually I learned it meant to adorn her with love and admiration. Clothe her in your sincerity and devotion.

**—RICHARD BURTON**

The heart that loves is always young.    **—GREEK PROVERB**

Love is general, hate is specific. Love makes everything seem wonderful, while hate is focused on the thing or person hated.
—SEVEN-TIMES-MARRIED FORMER MUSICIAN ARTIE SHAW

We are easily duped by those we love.    —MOLIÈRE

I think models are great. I don't think they're dumb—no dumber than anyone else.
—GOLFER TIGER WOODS ON GIRLFRIEND ELIN NORDEGREN, A SWEDISH MODEL

I'm not one of those guys who thinks if he's seen one model, he's seen them all.    —ED BURNS, WHO DAYS AFTER HIS PLANNED MARRIAGE TO
CHRISTIE TURLINGTON WAS CALLED OFF, TOOK UP WITH ESTHER CANADAS,
A MODEL FOR DONNA KARAN

The wonderful thing about love is that the object of your affection is always, at least during love, beautiful to you, in one or many ways.
—SIMON CALLOW *(FOUR WEDDINGS AND A FUNERAL)*

Even if I don't fancy the person, I always get an inner stirring. In the past, I've had to ask the director to hang on for three because I had to wait for the stirring to subside. There's something so fabulous about two strangers being made to kiss.
—ACTOR HUGH GRANT, ON MOVIE LOVE SCENES

Let's be honest. When a girl looks at some good-looking guy and stares, it's for herself. But half of the time, if a guy is staring at a pretty girl—or a girl, period—it's also for the men he's with.
—TED KNIGHT *(TOO CLOSE FOR COMFORT)*

Elvis Presley confided in me soon after he did *Viva Las Vegas* with Ann-Margret that he was considering marrying her. I'm not implying that anything untoward ever occurred between them, but they had a marvelous chemistry. But soon after that, . . . he heard Ann-Margret described as "a female Elvis," and Elvis reacted negatively. To his mind, it was vaguely homosexual! Whether that's what cooled his feelings for Ann-Margret or not, I don't know.

—SINGER-ACTOR BOBBY DARIN

Yeah, really, I'd like to be true to just one woman. But then I'd be false to all the others.    —WILL SMITH, PRIOR TO MARRYING JADA PINKETT

Your wife is like TV. It's home and it's free.    —COMEDIAN SLAPPY WHITE

My wife has a nice, even disposition—miserable all the time.

—HENNY YOUNGMAN

My wife's an earth sign. I'm a water sign. Together we make mud.

—RODNEY DANGERFIELD

If you want to read a book on love and marriage you've got to buy two separate books.    —ALAN KING

Some couples who get along beautifully really need each other. Some not so much. But I've observed that some couples who argue every day, have the same hates, share the same crabby outlook, would be miserable without each other. They have such a need for that, for each other. Negativity is their daily fix.

—ALLEN LUDDEN, HOST OF *PASSWORD* AND HUSBAND OF BETTY WHITE

Be it ever so vile, there's no place like home. —JON LOVITZ

Shelley Winters has a fondness for Italian men. She married me and Anthony Franciosa. But she doesn't like Italy enough, and to me it was more important to be at home in Italy than to be in America with her. Mamma Italia comes first. —ACTOR VITTORIO GASSMAN

I'm not cynical. Maybe he loves her. But it's a smart move—he caught a prize fish! It's certainly one way for an aging TV star to get back in the spotlight, and it beats the route O.J. took. . . .
—MOREY AMSTERDAM *(THE DICK VAN DYKE SHOW)* ON JAMES BROLIN AND
BARBRA STREISAND

Merv Griffin does claim to have invented *Jeopardy!* In truth, his wife invented it but he got credit and the rewards. . . . He's a better businessman than he lets on. . . . However, he's less of a singer or a creative mind than he likes people to believe.
—GRIFFIN'S TV TALK SHOW SIDEKICK ARTHUR TREACHER

I admired [producer] Hal Wallis. As a man and an executive. . . . An executive: That's a man who can always take refuge in his office after a long, hard day or night at home. —DEAN MARTIN

Frank [Sinatra] once asked an associate his marital status. The guy says, "Married, I've been. Now I simply rent." —DEAN MARTIN

$\mathscr{B}$rigitte Bardot asked me to marry her. I don't know if she was joking, but I said no. I did not explain that I couldn't marry an actress who could never be faithful to me. Or at least try. Like I would at least try, for the first year or two.  —STEPHEN BOYD *(BEN-HUR)*

$\mathcal{J}$oan Crawford thought about marrying Clark Gable and even considered me for a while. But I don't think either Clark or I would have relished playing a supporting part in Miss Crawford's private life. . . . My advice to most any man in this business is, don't marry an actress, and I know whereof I speak.  —HENRY FONDA

$\mathcal{J}$ wanted to be real polite to my Mother-in-law Dearest. So I said, "My house is your house." So she sold it.  —STAND-UP COMIC STEVE MOORE

$\mathcal{W}$ell, because Hollywood's real homophobic, and after we got married we could get credit cards.  —NOW OPENLY GAY COMEDIAN STEVE MOORE, ON WHY HE MARRIED A LESBIAN (FOR FIFTEEN YEARS)

$\mathcal{M}$y mother-in-law has such a big mouth. When she smiles, there's lipstick on her ears.  —REDD FOXX

$\mathcal{W}$hen I got married, my mother-in-law said the bride and I made a perfect couple—except for me.  —GEORGE BURNS

$\mathcal{J}$ never really thought I'd live so long that I wasn't known as Gracie Allen's husband.  —GEORGE BURNS ON HIS 100TH BIRTHDAY

$\mathcal{W}$e had a wisecracker for a minister. When he married us he said, "Soon you two will become one—which is all he can afford on his salary." **—EDDIE CANTOR**

$\mathcal{R}$omeo and Juliet spent one night together and the next day he committed suicide. Then she committed suicide. I'm trying to figure what went on in that bedroom. **—ALAN KING**

$\mathcal{I}$ went to a wedding . . . I couldn't believe the groom was married in rented shoes. You're making a commitment for a lifetime, and your shoes have to be back by 5:30. **—JERRY SEINFELD**

$\mathcal{I}$ found out after I got married that the husband's closet never comes with the apartment. **—RODNEY DANGERFIELD**

$\mathcal{M}$y [Mexican] wife Margo had trouble pronouncing the letter *v*, and she once remarked on a radio interview, "My husband is a slob." She was really saying, "My husband is a Slav." Thereafter, I asked her to refrain from describing my background in public. Also to avoid mention in public of Shakespeare's play *Richard III*. She had pronounced it, luckily at home, as *Richard the Turd*.
**—CZECHOSLOVAKIAN ACTOR FRANCIS LEDERER**

$\mathcal{M}$y wife threatened me with her cooking. Did you know meat loaf could be lethal? She's gotten more subtle since we came home from the honeymoon and she waved a cleaver at me and said, "If you ever let your meat loaf . . ." **—COMEDIAN JOE E. LEWIS**

Last week I told my wife a man is like wine, he gets better with age. She locked me in the cellar.   **—RODNEY DANGERFIELD**

My wife's most ingenious lie: "It wasn't really expensive if you think how much use we'll get out of it."   **—TIM ALLEN**

I overheard my wife's girlfriend telling her about her husband: "I just know he's incompatible, though I haven't caught him at it yet."
**—HUMORIST SAM LEVENSON**

The only person who listens to both sides of a husband–wife argument is the woman in the next apartment.   **—BROOKLYN PROVERB**

For our anniversary, I took the little woman to the corner pub. I hadn't bought her anything, and she said I should buy something for the house. So I did—a round of drinks.
**—UK TV STAR (AND SINGLE MAN) BENNY HILL**

My ball and chain—I mean my lovely wife—hinted that for our next anniversary I should get her something she could use forever. I bought her a diet book.   **—AUSTRALIAN COMEDIAN BARRY HUMPHRIES**
**(SOMETIMES A.K.A. DAME EDNA EVERAGE)**

My wife wondered what I'd like for our anniversary. I said, "How about something to go with my favorite sports coat?" She got me a clown mask.   **—ROBIN WILLIAMS**

Women are a lot like umpires. They make quick decisions, never reverse them, and they don't think you're safe when you're out.

—PETE ROSE

Marriage is a mistake every man should make. —GEORGE JESSEL

The bonds of wedlock are so heavy it takes two to carry them—sometimes three.

—BALZAC

There are a number of mechanical devices which increase sexual arousal, particularly in women. Chief among these is the Mercedes-Benz 380SL convertible.

—P. J. O'ROURKE

Anxiety is the first time you can't do it a second time; panic is the time you can't do it the first time.

—WRITER WILLIAM A. NOLEN IN *ESQUIRE* (NOVEMBER 1981)

No matter how happily a woman may be married, it always pleases her to discover that there is a nice man who wishes she were not.

—H. L. MENCKEN

I have a loved one who decided to become a nun. Among other things, she liked the idea of being married to the church—which is both more and less intimidating than being married to a man, a living spouse. My initial reservations were that she'd be unhappy with her lifelong choice. And when the family would gather and she'd be smiling or making a joke, I'd point out, "Nun too happy?'

—PATRICK DENNIS, AUTHOR OF *AUNTIE MAME*

$\mathcal{M}$y grumpy sometime friend and professional hostess Elsa Maxwell did her memoirs and proclaimed that she'd married the world—"The world is my husband," or some such twaddle. Amazing how many people believed it, for the late Elsa was a very convincing lesbian.

—SIR NOEL COWARD

$\mathcal{M}$arriage in the United States, if not in Europe, is like clubs used to be, where they kept out the Jews and blacks. Now it's heterosexist bigots who claim that gay marriage would somehow weaken straight marriage. Which if it were true would be a pitiful comment on heterosexual relationships.   —SIR IAN MCKELLEN *(THE LORD OF THE RINGS)*

$\mathcal{C}$hurches are in the business of preaching and trying to dictate to people on how to live, love, behave, you name it. But government has no business telling its citizens and taxpayers which lifestyle to adopt and whom to love. The only really queer people are those who hate more than they love.   —SIR ELTON JOHN

$\mathcal{H}$ollywood will use the homosexual character as comedy or scapegoat or villain, but in the 1980s they're still afraid to make a movie showing two men in a committed, loving relationship.

—PAUL NEWMAN, WHO TRIED FOR YEARS TO MAKE A FILM OF
PATRICIA NELL WARREN'S *THE FRONT RUNNER*

$\mathcal{Y}$ou can learn much more about your partner from an embrace than a kiss. Kisses are generic. Hugs are individual.

—IAN CHARLESON *(CHARIOTS OF FIRE)*

Love relationships can't take the place of a full life. But a full life must include love relationships.
**—MAHARISHI MAHESH YOGI, THE BEATLES' GURU**

Don't smother each other. No one can grow in shade.
**—EDUCATOR AND AUTHOR LEO BUSCAGLIA**

Love is an act of endless forgiveness, a tender look which becomes a habit.    **—ACTOR-AUTHOR PETER USTINOV, TWO-TIME OSCAR-WINNER**

Marriage must constantly fight against a monster which devours everything: routine.    **—BALZAC**

To do the same thing over and over again is not only boredom; it is to be controlled by rather than to control what you do.    **—HERACLITUS**

It may be that the contemporary heart courts the happiness and drama of marriage in place of yesteryear's adventures, dangerous travel, unexplored vistas, and wide, open spaces. . . . Our adventures are smaller, but our relationships more intense.
**—FRENCH DIRECTOR FRANÇOIS TRUFFAUT**

The supreme happiness of life is the conviction of being loved for yourself, or, more correctly, of being loved in spite of yourself.
**—AUTHOR VICTOR HUGO *(LES MISERABLES, THE HUNCHBACK OF NOTRE DAME)***

$\mathcal{B}$ored single people look for passion in marriage, and bored marrieds look at single lives as being more exciting and eventful. Wherever you are, it ain't.
—**WRITER-DIRECTOR BILLY WILDER** *(DOUBLE INDEMNITY)*

$\mathcal{I}$n marriage, husbands' and wives' joys are pretty universal. We all have them in common. The regrets are as individual as fingerprints.
—**TELLY SAVALAS** *(KOJAK)*

$\mathcal{A}$lthough most men finally capitulate to marriage, most do not find their fulfillment in marriage. Most women do. Now, does this mean that their standards are higher or lower, or their goals more realistic or humane than men's?
—**KURT COBAIN**

$\mathcal{I}$t was hard to tell whether our papas and mamas were happily married. The subject was not open for discussion, certainly not with their children. "Are you happy, Ma?" "I got nothing else to think about?" Nobody had ever told Mama that marriage was supposed to make her happy; certainly Papa hadn't. Nobody had promised him happiness either . . . only children talked of happiness.
—**SAM LEVENSON**

$\mathcal{T}$he first third of our lives we mostly deal with relatives. The second third with romance. The final third with ourselves—home at last.
—**JACK LEMMON**

$\mathcal{T}$ies of blood are blind, sometimes hollow. Ties of love bind, because voluntary, and because heartfelt.
—**WOODY GUTHRIE** (1912–1967)

Without meaning to, yet without being able to prevent what I chose to make inevitable, I have passed on the unhappiness of my childhood to my marriages and down to my children. —EUGENE O'NEILL

The darkness of too many families or marriages: bad behavior can be hidden within closed ranks, passed secretly from one generation to another. **—AUTHOR JOHN FOWLES** *(THE FRENCH LIEUTENANT'S WOMAN)*

Fairy tales and motion picture films have spoiled us for real life. The handsome boy and the pretty girl get married and then it's "happily ever after." That's a fiction depiction. Most people aren't that happy during. **—BOB HOPE SIDEKICK JERRY COLONNA**

The actual institution of marriage is a male-designed tool for regulating women. It's been sugar-coated by popular entertainment media and been modified in the last century or so, but that is still its main purpose. **—RALPH NADER, CONSUMER ADVOCATE AND POLITICIAN**

When the romance is said and done, marriage is basically so that a man can own a woman and claim her product, which is to say, her child—their child, really, but in name and status, his child.
**—ACTOR-COMPOSER IVOR NOVELLO**

In marriage, as in life, we often run from honesty. . . . Honesty has shattered more marriages than illicit sex. **—WRITER SAUL BELLOW**

The most beautiful things on earth are often useless, such as roses and peacocks. Not so, wives—the most useful things on earth, though to many men, still things.

—ASTRONOMER AND AUTHOR *(CONTACT)* DR. CARL SAGAN

The heart of the fool is in his mouth, but the mouth of the wise man is in his heart.   —BENJAMIN FRANKLIN

We're very private. We each got a career, we gotta be private. . . . When fans knock on the door of our bus, we tell them it's our home, so it's not appropriate.   —DARIO FRANCHITTI, PROFESSIONAL RACER AND HUSBAND OF ACTRESS ASHLEY JUDD; FOR TWENTY-TWO WEEKS A YEAR THEY SPEND THREE DAYS A WEEK ON THEIR BUS WHILE HE RACES

Beauty is very well at first sight; but who ever looks at it when it has been in the house three days?

—GEORGE BERNARD SHAW IN *MAN AND SUPERMAN*

Beauty will not buy beef.

—THOMAS FULLER IN *GNOMOLOGIA: ADAGIES AND PROVERBS*

Man is a fisherman. Woman's beauty is her bait. But the fish catches the fisherman.   —JULIO IGLESIAS

Love may be blind, but most men see with a single eye, further down. . . .   —MARILYN MANSON

Men in show business generally have money. So they go strictly for looks. Most other men have to be more practical, and their wallets figure somewhere in the equation of attraction and suitability— unless the man is well off or proud.

**—TALK SHOW HOST PIONEER STEVE ALLEN**

All heiresses are beautiful.

**—JOHN DRYDEN**

Beauty is a short-lived reign.

**—SOCRATES**

In tinseltown, most men are more concerned with the loss of their hair than the loss of a wife. Makes sense: hair is very difficult to replace.

**—TED BESSELL** *(THAT GIRL)*

A [male] friend married is a friend lost.

**—HENRIK IBSEN**

I've had women friends and I've had women lovers, and I'll tell you this: friends can wind up as lovers, but I have yet to see lovers turn into friends.

**—THEN-BACHELOR WARREN BEATTY**

Before I married, my fiancée and I had the best times. Life was fun and fancy-free. My married life is not fun—anything but. It's not that marriage ruined everything, it's that I didn't marry my fiancée.

Would you buy a car you knew you were supposed to keep for life, without ever test-driving it? "Cohabitation" may not be a beau-tiful word, but it's the most practical one ever invented. Would you buy a house, the only house you'll have in your whole life, without living in it at least one weekend? I ask you.

**—DUDLEY MOORE**

$\mathcal{I}$ caught the flu once, but I didn't have to keep it.
—MARTY FELDMAN, ON WHY HE FAVORED DIVORCE

$\mathcal{B}$y forty, women get the faces they deserve and men get the wives they deserve.   —TALK SHOW HOST TOM SNYDER

$\mathcal{A}$n ideal wife is any woman who has an ideal husband.
—BOOTH TARKINGTON

$\mathcal{H}$e tells you when you've got on too much lipstick,
And helps you with your girdle when your hips stick.
—OGDEN NASH IN *THE PERFECT HUSBAND*

$\mathcal{I}$mmature love says: "I love you because I need you."
Mature love says: "I need you because I love you."   —ERICH FROMM

$\mathcal{I}$'ve never heard it put in a song, but I once read it, and I tried to memorize it, and boy, is it true. Listen: Getting married with love is like going to heaven with your eyes shut, but getting married without love is like going to hell with your eyes open.
—SINGER WAYLON JENNINGS

$\mathcal{T}$he clog of all pleasures, the luggage of life,
Is the best that can be said for a very good wife.
—JOHN WILMOT, THE EARL OF ROCHESTER, IN *ON A WIFE*

$\mathcal{W}$ife: a former sweetheart.   —H. L. MENCKEN

The difference between a wife and a girlfriend is the difference between routine acquiescence and enthusiastic cooperation.

—ANONYMOUS

The kiss originated when the first male reptile licked the first female reptile, implying in a subtle, complimentary way that she was as succulent as the small reptile he had for dinner the night before.

—F. SCOTT FITZGERALD

Blondes have the hottest kisses. Redheads are fair to middling torrid, and brunettes are the frigidest of all. It's something to do with hormones, no doubt. —THEN-ACTOR RONALD REAGAN

The first kiss is stolen by the man; the last is begged by the woman.

—H. L. MENCKEN

After you're married long enough, you get to do everything alone—even suffer alone. —KEVIN COSTNER

Marriage doesn't really change a man, it changes his habits.

—YUL BRYNNER *(THE KING AND I)*

Marriage changes your life. And if your married life's going to last, you'd better change too. —JON BON JOVI

To have a good marriage, just be a good husband. End of speech.

—OSCAR-WINNER DR. HAING S. NGOR *(THE KILLING FIELDS)*

As my wise and darling wife Carol always says, when you speak of other people's marriages, you're really saying something about your own.                                                                    **—WALTER MATTHAU**

Marriage is the one fortress that cannot be destroyed from without. That can only happen from within.          **—RICARDO MONTALBAN**

They say that every success eventually is a failure, that you can't stay on top forever. Professionally, if you reach the top, it's a brief stay. Thank goodness that in marriage this isn't so. Anyone can reach the top, and in a good marriage can remain there.   **—PATRICK DUFFY** *(DALLAS)*

# Broken Marriages

They weren't really weddings, just long cocktail parties.
**—PEGGY LEE, ON HER VARIOUS ABBREVIATED MARRIAGES**

Some people talk a lot on their divorces. But there's not much to say or you'd want to say on this.    **—JANET JACKSON ON HER 1984 MARRIAGE TO SINGER JAMES DEBARGE, WHICH WAS ANNULLED**

Annull, rhymes with dull. Tell me about it. I had a few [marriages] that should have been annulled.    **—ERROL FLYNN, MORE NOTED FOR HIS ACTIVE LOVE LIFE THAN HIS MARRIAGES**

It's been reported that Kevin Costner might be getting married to his longtime girlfriend. Costner says he wants to plan the wedding, which means it will last three hours and lose $200 million.

**—CONAN O'BRIEN IN 2001**

Women should appreciate a great husband—the supply is so small. The house beautiful for the husband dutiful. But for the husband straying, the house decaying.    **—PHYLLIS DILLER**

A lot of men are Jekyll-and-Hydes. They're one thing before the conquest, and another thing afterward. Men are always looking around. They're looking at the young ones with the miniskirts. I'd rather be single than live like that. They all cheat.
　　　　　**—ETHEL MERMAN ON HER FINAL MARRIAGE, TO ACTOR ERNEST BORGNINE,**
　　　　　　　　　　　　　　　　　　**WHICH LASTED MANY WEEKS**

It's unfortunate of course, but sometimes one gets very angry with a wife.　　　**—SIX-TIMES-MARRIED NORMAN MAILER, WHO STABBED HIS SECOND**
　　**WIFE ADELE (WHOSE BOOK ABOUT THE MARRIAGE WAS TITLED *THE LAST PARTY*)**

It was a very wounding experience, but I got rid of it by writing about it.　　　　　　　　　　　　**—V. S. PRITCHETT, ON HIS FIRST MARRIAGE**

I believe that all those painters and writers who leave their wives have an idea at the back of their minds that their painting or writing will be the better for it, whereas they only go from bad to worse.
　　　　　**—AUSTRALIAN NOBEL PRIZE–WINNING AUTHOR PATRICK WHITE**

In some marriages, one and one equals less than two.
　　　　　　　　　　　　　　　　　**—CALISTA FLOCKHART**

Marry me—or you can't see your baby!　　**—DEBBIE ROWE, REPORTEDLY**
　　**IMPREGNATED BY OR VIA MICHAEL JACKSON (THE INEVITABLE FUTURE DIVORCE**
　　　　　　　　**HAD ALREADY BEEN DUBBED *ROWE V. WEIRD*)**

Jane Fonda—from Barbarella to Stepford Billionaire's Wife.
　　　　　**—BRITISH TALK HOST DAVID FROST, DURING FONDA'S TED TURNER PHASE**

$\mathcal{I}$ know a lot of people didn't expect our relationship to last. But we've just celebrated our two months' anniversary.
　　　　　　　　　　　　**—BRITT EKLAND, THEN-WIFE OF PETER SELLERS**

$\mathcal{T}$his should be my wedding day, not hers. I should be the famous one!　　**—PAULA CICCONE, UPON BURSTING INTO THE POWDER ROOM ON THE**
**DAY OF HER SISTER MADONNA'S WEDDING TO SEAN PENN**

$\mathcal{W}$e started as husband and wife, but it ended like brother and sister.
　　　　　　　　　　**—ELIZABETH TAYLOR, ON HER SECOND MARRIAGE,**
　　　　　　　　　　　　　**TO OLDER ACTOR MICHAEL WILDING**

$\mathcal{S}$he lets me be me. For the first time in a long time, I don't feel like I am walking on eggshells. She'd be the perfect wife.　　**—TED TURNER,**
**SIXTY-ONE, ON HIS FIFTY-YEAR-OLD FRENCH GIRLFRIEND (AFTER THE END OF HIS**
**MARRIAGE TO JANE FONDA AND BEFORE HE SWITCHED TO A GIRLFRIEND IN HER THIRTIES)**

$\mathcal{O}$nce you reach a certain age, you realize that men aren't as important as you once thought they were. It's awfully hard to make marriage work. I've tried twice, and I don't know how. To have to think of somebody else so much of the time . . . it's such a compromise.
　　　　　　　　　　　　　　　　**—FAYE DUNAWAY**

$\mathcal{N}$ever marry an actress. They never stop acting.　　**—REX HARRISON**

$\mathcal{N}$ever marry an actor. They perform in every room of the house except the kitchen and sometimes the bedroom—unless it has a mirror in it.　　　　　　　　　　　　**—BRIGITTE BARDOT**

*I* knew it was time to stop cheating when I was with my girlfriend and I found myself fantasizing about my wife. —MICK JAGGER

*L*et's not kid ourselves. There's all this thing about "Men just don't understand. . . ." But men don't give a shit! They want to get laid, a lot of them. The general consensus is that women are there for three purposes: to be in the bedroom and the kitchen, and to have a kid. Why do you think men, once they get married and have kids, don't want their wives—they want a stripper with huge silicone boobs? Because they don't really care about women anyway. They care about sex. —JACKIE COLLINS, AUTHOR OF *HOLLYWOOD WIVES*

*W*ell, my marriages just aren't, or weren't, really long enough to discuss at length. —TWO-TIME WIFE DREW BARRYMORE

*A*n ugly trend has emerged of late, with husbands and wives airing their dirty linen in public. Frequently in restaurants. It's the lack of self-control I object to . . . a general lack of maturity. . . . Jim Carrey and his [soon to be divorced] wife [Lauren Holly] got together for dinner . . . with the version I read saying it became a screaming match after she began to cry and got up to leave. Then he runs after her.

See, such episodes did not take place in times past, flawed though they were. Stars wouldn't behave that way in public. They cared enough not to. —GOLDEN-ERA STAR KIRK DOUGLAS

*I* married my first husband [barber Frank White] because he smelled so good. My second [gambler Nick Arnstein] because he looked so good. And my third [producer Billy Rose] because he thought so good—mostly about the shows he was starring me in.
—FANNY BRICE (PLAYED BY BARBRA STREISAND IN *FUNNY GIRL* AND *FUNNY LADY*)

We loved deeply and we quarreled soundly. . . . When Elizabeth was present, she had more presence than anyone else . . . and I have at times found since we went our separate ways that no one else's absence could be so absent.

**—RICHARD BURTON, AFTER HIS FIRST DIVORCE FROM ELIZABETH TAYLOR**

A broken marriage is so sad. Doesn't matter if it was long or short. Really, the only thing to do with it is to remember the good things, and to use the rest for a reminder when you try again.

**—BROOKE SHIELDS**

It wasn't as dramatic as the [breakup of her] first one. Perhaps I'm older and wiser. . . . All he wants to do is have dinner and go to boring Hollywood parties. You live and learn and I have no regrets.

**—DREW BARRYMORE ON HER SPLIT FROM SECOND HUSBAND TOM GREEN**

Don't say it, it's too easy.   **—NICOLAS CAGE TO A REPORTER WHO ASKED IF HE WERE LIVING IN "HEARTBREAK HOTEL" (CAGE WAS REPORTEDLY DEVASTATED WHEN LISA MARIE PRESLEY ENDED THEIR RELATIONSHIP IN 2002 AND RETURNED TO HER FORMER FIANCÉ; LATER IN THE YEAR, PRESLEY DID MARRY CAGE)**

We discovered we each needed a wife to take care of us. That role is not for me, and it is certainly not for Shirley [MacLaine]. She is a very strong woman. She is Warren Beatty's older brother, not his sister. . . . We just couldn't live together.

**—RUSSIAN DIRECTOR ANDREI KONCHALOVSKY**

$\mathcal{K}$en is so tired, his sperm are on crutches. —EMMA THOMPSON ON
THEN-HUSBAND KENNETH BRANAGH, BY WHOM SHE HAD NO CHILD
(SHE DID, NEXT TIME AROUND)

$\mathcal{B}$eauty and the beastie. Seems Brooke [Shields] is being influenced by
her recent hubby [Andre Agassi], as she's finally back in the news, but
for talking dirty at tennis matches. I thought by now she'd be old
enough to know better than to take up new bad habits, if not bad boys.
—ERIC IDLE OF MONTY PYTHON

$\mathcal{J}$ohn wanted a stay-at-home wife, and I liked being a mother. It's
nice when what a husband wants and what his wife wants coincides.
Because that isn't permanent. —THEN-RETIRED ACTRESS TATUM O'NEAL,
LOOKING BACK ON MARRIAGE TO TENNIS BAD BOY JOHN MCENROE

$\mathcal{D}$arling, she's old enough to take care of herself. And him too.
—MARITAL VETERAN ZSA ZSA GABOR ON ELIZABETH TAYLOR'S LATEST SPLIT,
FROM LARRY FORTENSKY

$\mathcal{I}$ guess I'd like to get back with Pamela [Anderson], but there's a lot
of baggage there, like children and a new boyfriend. —SWEDISH MODEL
MARCUS SCHENKENBERG IN 2001, AFTER BEING DUMPED IN FAVOR
OF RAPPER KID ROCK

He pressured me to play the role of trophy girlfriend twenty-four hours a day. I'm not going to be a trophy. That's it. If you expect me to be in the kitchen cooking breakfast in high heels and a sable coat, it's not going to happen. I may be alone but I'm not lonely. I feel very content since Flavio is out of my life. I feel great. **—MODEL NAOMI CAMPBELL IN 2002, ON ENDING HER TWO-YEAR RELATIONSHIP WITH BENETTON FORMULA 1'S FLAVIO BRIATORE, OLD ENOUGH TO BE HER FATHER**

My ex-husband, he was so jealous. Of other guys, like just costars, even. But also [of] my career. When you're moving up, you don't want someone who tries to hold you down. **—JENNIFER LOPEZ**

I quit with one of my wives because she couldn't get enthusiastic about my work. **—ERNEST HEMINGWAY, WHO HAD FOUR WIVES**

Few husbands are as absorbing as one's work, especially for a writer. Tradition dictates that wives be absorbed by their spouses . . . it's husbands who, for the most part, are nonabsorbent, leaky sponges. **—WRITER MARY MCCARTHY *(THE GROUP)*, WHO HAD FOUR HUSBANDS**

"I'm very famous, you know. I'm world famous." And that's not like me at all. But it didn't help. He didn't understand what I was saying. After we were married, when the first photograph appeared, he just couldn't handle it. **—MYRNA LOY, ON WHAT SHE TOLD HER FOURTH HUSBAND BEFORE WEDDING HIM**

$\mathcal{T}$he biggest drawback to fame is that, in the States particularly, it doesn't allow you much privacy or any secrets. Every move, every flirtation or infidelity, the press is there. The only time they turn a blind eye is if the VIP in question is a homosexual.     —REX HARRISON

$\mathcal{R}$ex never could understand why I wouldn't leave my new husband to come back to him. He thought I behaved very badly.
—ACTRESS LILLI PALMER, WHO'D AGREED TO DIVORCE REX HARRISON SO HE COULD MARRY HIS MISTRESS (ACTRESS KAY KENDALL), WHO WAS FATALLY ILL; AFTER SHE DIED, REX RETURNED TO LILLI WHO, HOWEVER, MEANWHILE FELL IN LOVE AND MARRIED ANOTHER ACTOR

$\mathcal{W}$ell, there were three of us in this marriage, so it was a bit crowded.
—PRINCESS DIANA ON TELEVISION, ABOUT HER HUSBAND AND HIS MISTRESS

$\mathcal{I}$f you were my husband, I'd put poison in your coffee.
—LADY ASTOR, TO SIR WINSTON CHURCHILL (HIS REPLY: "IF I WERE YOUR HUSBAND, I'D DRINK IT!")

$\mathcal{I}$ used to think if I had a daughter I'd want her to marry a royal. Not anymore. First, they are the most spoiled rotten people on the planet. Second, it's an outrageously archaic system—they can't marry Catholics, never mind Jews; the gay ones have to marry regardless; the female inherits nothing unless there's no male, . . . plus being a royal simply means that your ancestors killed more people than a "common" person's ancestors.     —*OLIVER!* COMPOSER LIONEL BART

*I* was married to a French aristocrat. Titles may impress, but I'd seen those manners before—among the working people, ones who actually earned their keep.   **—GLORIA SWANSON** *(SUNSET BOULEVARD)*

[*T*here's] nothing to it. I was out of town making a movie, and Barbra is cheap. She hates to buy her own meals. Sharif was just somebody to pick up the tabs.   **—ELLIOTT GOULD, ON OMAR SHARIF'S DINING WITH HIS *FUNNY GIRL* COSTAR AND GOULD'S SOON-TO-BE-EX-WIFE STREISAND (MOST OF THE DINNERS WERE CONSUMED IN SHARIF'S SUITE IN THE BEVERLY WILSHIRE HOTEL)**

*T*here was an upside to playing a nymphomaniac on TV. I'm not married anymore.   **—TÉA LEONI**

*I* can believe Charlie Sheen's a sex maniac . . . also very rude and loves to shock for the sake of it. He has problems.   **—ERIC STOLTZ, AFTER SHEEN PUBLICLY SAID HE'D LIKE TO HAVE SEX WITH STOLTZ'S THEN-GIRLFRIEND BRIDGET FONDA**

[*B*urt Reynolds] was a very macho man, and I got the show business break first. The more I did well, the more invalidated he felt as a man, and consequently the more destructive he became. It started with pushes and slaps. As things got worse, it was very painful. I was terrified of him.   **—JUDY CARNE, THEN-WIFE OF THE ASPIRING STAR**

*I* left Sean Connery after he bashed my face in with his fists.   **—ACTRESS DIANE CILENTO**

Like so many women, I thought by not fighting [during the relationship] everything would work out. . . . "Daddy" would take care of it all. But I learned "Daddy" would only take care of "Daddy."
    —SONDRA LOCKE, REFERRING TO FORMER LONGTIME COMPANION CLINT EASTWOOD

You're boring, stupid, and I don't have any fun with you. Goodbye.
    —NICOLLETTE SHERIDAN'S FAREWELL NOTE TO HARRY HAMLIN

The Antichrist
    —ACTOR HART BOCHNER'S NICKNAME FOR EX-GIRLFRIEND SHARON STONE

She knew more days on which gifts could be given than appear on any holiday calendar.    —CONRAD HILTON ON EX-WIFE ZSA ZSA GABOR

She's like that old joke about Philadelphia. First prize, four years with Joan. Second prize, eight. —FRANCHOT TONE ON EX-WIFE JOAN CRAWFORD

During the five years I was married to Zsa Zsa Gabor, I lived in her sumptuous Bel Air mansion as a sort of paying guest. . . . I was allotted a small room in which I was permitted to keep my personal effects until such time as more space was needed to store her ever-mounting stacks of press clippings and photographs.

I was accustomed to austerity and it was no great sacrifice for me to dispose from time to time of some of my belongings so as to empty drawers in my room and make them available for the more vital function of housing Zsa Zsa's memorabilia. All of the tables, walls, cupboards, and closets of various kinds were pressed into similar service.    —GEORGE SANDERS, WHOSE AUTOBIOGRAPHY WAS
    TITLED *MEMOIRS OF A PROFESSIONAL CAD*

This girl and I . . . we were going steady and I thought it could become a long thing, you know. But she always kept bringing over her friends. Never just her and me. She had to fill my place with her friends. Which at first I resented it, no privacy. Then I thought, hey, does she need all those people "cause I'm not enough?   **—CHRIS FARLEY**

Years back, I worked with an actor who married a girl who moved practically her whole family into his mansion. They were all there by the time the happy couple returned from the honeymoon. He wasn't happy for long. He stood it as long as he could, but nothing kills intimacy as quickly as a bunch of relatives.

**—IRENE RYAN (GRANNY ON *THE BEVERLY HILLBILLIES*)**

Tom Arnold was a third-rate comedian. Then he married Roseanne. Great example of a guy who made something of himself, by the sweat of his frau. Or is it the sweat of his sow?   **—PINKY LEE (WHEN PEE-WEE HERMAN WAS COMING UP, HE WAS DESCRIBED AS "THE NEW PINKY LEE")**

Not unless I have to. We have absolutely nothing in common. I think he's a bit of a sad character.

**—CHER ON SPEAKING WITH HER EX-HUSBAND SONNY BONO, BEFORE HIS DEATH**

The critics fell all over him. I read how Marlon [Brando] was such a wonderfully complex actor. But they didn't have to try and live with this man and his many complexes.   **—EX-WIFE ANNA KASHFI**

A friend asked me when Michael Jackson married the Presley girl, "What are you giving the happy couple?" I said, "About two months."

**—COMEDIAN RODNEY DANGERFIELD**

Sometimes you can tell which actors are gay because they're so terrified of being disclosed or discloseted that they keep on marrying, right up to their death. Especially when it's an old dude like Cary Grant or Fred Astaire and the wife is decades younger. It's not a marriage of winter passion; it's a marriage of eternal image.

Cary Grant I know for a fact was gay. Astaire, I don't know; I question whether he was anything. But it was desperately, pathetically important to both men that they continue to be thought of as heterosexual. So those final marriages lasted till the very end.

**—DESIGNER HALSTON**

One of my wives admitted her insecurity over all the marriage and other proposals I received regularly in the mail. Scads of them were not from girls. . . . **—BLOND SEX ICON TROY DONAHUE**

How's this for a rumor? You can't confirm anything; [director] Stanley Kubrick's keeping a completely closed set [on *Eyes Wide Shut*]. But it's been reported that Kubrick has hired a sex therapist to counsel Tom Cruise and Nicole Kidman on enacting the relationship between their characters, who are married.

**—HOLLYWOOD REPORTER AND ARCHIVIST JIM KEPNER**

An inveterate liar who lived in a fantasy world.

**—EX-MODEL KELLY LEBROCK ON EX-HUSBAND STEVEN SEAGAL**

*I*'m glad I'm no better-looking than I am. It can do things to your head, man. Some time back, I costarred with this actor known for his looks. I knew he was deceiving his wife right and left . . . when she caught him out, he even bragged about how many girls there'd been. She was beside herself, but his excuse was he didn't go looking for them, they came after him, and he was just doing them a favor—letting his fans in for a treat. **—CHUCK CONNORS**

*W*hat can I do? I'm hot.
**—JACK NICHOLSON, WHEN LONGTIME COMPANION ANGELICA HUSTON DISCOVERED HE'D BEEN HAVING AFFAIRS WITH YOUNGER WOMEN**

*S*ome women do look for father figures or father substitutes. But I just don't think very many men out there are looking for mother figures—in either sense of the phrase. **—MADELINE KAHN**

*I* knew a gal, almost made the mistake of marrying her. Great girl, very nice, great legs, and so on. But the longer we were together, the more she kept going into motherly mode. I suppose familiarity breeds motherhood. **—GEORGE PEPPARD**

*W*e all enjoyed our tremendous success at first, and Bjorn and I continued enjoying it. . . . I think the end began for us because my wife felt guilty about being away from her offspring. We would tour or have to make an appearance, a promotion, be away three days, for instance, and she missed being mama. I didn't feel it was terrible, being away and doing what we had to do, but she did, and it affected the four of us, and the two of us. **—BENNY ANDERSSON OF ABBA, WHICH INITIALLY COMPRISED TWO MARRIED COUPLES**

My first marriage was [to author] Thomas McGuane—I was cast in a movie he directed in 1975 . . . he broke up with his wife [who later wed Peter Fonda] and his girlfriend [actress Elizabeth Ashley] to marry me, and we had a daughter. It lasted about three years . . . I married an actor [John Heard] for a few weeks, and the third time was to a director [Philippe de Broca] for about nine months. But none of this is so unusual, not these days or in this business.

—MARGOT KIDDER (*SUPERMAN'S* LOIS LANE)

I counted eight. —BONNY LEE BAKLEY, MURDERED WIFE OF ACTOR ROBERT BLAKE, ON THE NUMBER OF HER MARRIAGES PRE-BLAKE; WHEN A REPORTER TOLD HER AT LEAST ONE MORE MARRIAGE WAS DOCUMENTED IN THE COUNTY RECORDER'S OFFICE IN BAKLEY'S HOMETOWN OF MEMPHIS, TENNESSEE, SHE ADDED, "OH, NINE THEN"

I think he was called Poison [Sean] Penn before Madonna married him. She knew what she was getting into, though a lot of people want to feel sorry for her. But after he allegedly tied her to the chair and did all those things to her, and then the police report, it was over. She'd finally had enough of him.

—EX-MADONNA-PAL SANDRA BERNHARD

George C. Scott. Fine actor. Big drinker. Wife beater. What else do you want to know? —ACTRESS COLLEEN DEWHURST ON HER EX-HUSBAND

Originally, it was very satisfying—the attention, the romance, it made me feel like an American star too. But she never became my wife, I was always the husband of Ginger Rogers. Not even an equality. I would never be a bigger star than her, or as big. Not even in my own country. —FRENCH ACTOR JACQUES BERGERAC

*I*'m frequently asked what I saw in Mickey Rooney. In retrospect, I think one reason that I married him was what he saw in me. . . . Don't forget, he was one of the biggest movie stars at the time, and I was fresh from the cotton and tobacco fields of North Carolina.

**—AVA GARDNER, WHO EVENTUALLY BECAME THE BIGGER STAR**

*I*n France I have not always been respected as an artist, but as a commercial director, yes. Brigitte Bardot became, she was like a mushrooming cloud, more than a star. She was an international phenomenon. The most famous and desired woman in the world. And I was just the husband or the director of that beautiful blonde.

**—ROGER VADIM, WHO LATER WED JANE FONDA**

*I* hate hearing that I was in love with Brad Pitt! That's so embarrassing. **—ACTRESS JULIETTE LEWIS, FORMER GIRLFRIEND OF THE BEAUTIFUL BLOND**

*I* was losing myself more and more in the marriage to a handsome actor playing the suave, glamorous James Bond. At the same time, he was losing himself in the usual intimate places and persons husbands eventually do. **—LUISA MATTIOLI, EX OF ROGER MOORE**

*W*hen Fernando [Lamas] proposed to me, he said, "Let me take you away from all this." And I said, "Away from all what? I'm a movie star!" **—ESTHER WILLIAMS**

*I*sn't it terrible? What memory is . . . I can remember so many quarrels, what the husband said or what I said to him. But for the life of me, I can never remember what it was we were quarreling about.

**—JUDY GARLAND**

*I* recall too many arguments over the years. Marriage has too many spats and flare-ups. Which you don't have when you date. . . . I don't recall the sex acts, beyond the fact that they took place, of course. Which you could say, if you were in a Proustian mood, there are, alas, no sexual madeleines. **—OLIVER REED**

*I*'ve had a happy marriage, knock wood—don't knock each other—but I remember this cute story. When somebody asked a psychiatrist how to forgive a spouse who has been unfaithful. The shrink said it reminded him of the old prayer that went, "Oh, Lord, let me forgive those who sin differently than I do." **—FILM CRITIC GENE SISKEL**

*D*oes adultery destroy, or break, a marriage? It sure as shooting doesn't strengthen it! But whether [the marriage] goes on, that has to be up to the cheated-upon party. He or she makes that decision, and then the transgression should be forgotten or at least never ever mentioned again. **—COWBOY STAR TEX RITTER (FATHER OF JOHN)**

*I* think Jane Fonda secretly turned to religion because Ted Turner had turned to another woman, or women. Jane has kept quiet so far about that, although she's busy writing a book. But Turner went public with his irritation over his wife's interest in organized religion. **—COLUMNIST DELPHINE ROSAY**

*R*ex [Harrison] was nicer to his leading ladies than his wives. They got the pleasant public face. The wives get the cold reality. If we hadn't been shackled together, he'd have flirted with me on the set, just for appearances, for his credentials—those get more important as a man gets older. Rex was always afraid of being past it. **—EX-WIFE AND EX-COSTAR RACHEL ROBERTS**

*I* met an ex-beau of mine by accident in a restaurant, and I couldn't get over how nice he was to me. I asked myself if I'd done the right thing in breaking off with him. When I got home and the effect of the wine had worn off, it dawned on me that he's an actor and everyone is on display at the Russian Tea Room.

—ACTRESS SUSAN STRASBERG

*Y*ears later, [producer] Robert Evans informed me he'd had a big crush on me but hadn't done anything about it because he couldn't get involved with a woman whose voice was lower than his!

—SUZANNE PLESHETTE

*Y*ou gotta check a woman like you check a horse, see? The teeth, the behind, . . . you got to know what you're gettin'. I knew this one chick, a smile like the sun, a voice like honey. . . . She was lookin' to tie the knot, only she didn't get to tie it over on me. She was like a bee all right—she had honey in her mouth and poison in her tail.

—BOXER MUHAMMAD ALI

*W*hy do rock stars like Bruce Springsteen and Rod Stewart always wed blondes and models? Why don't they ever marry someone like Janis Joplin or Bette Midler? You want to know why? Those guys know they aren't that talented. They couldn't stand the comparisons.

—JILL IRELAND (SHE MIGHT HAVE ADDED "WED AND SHED . . .")

*Y*ou see an awful lot of smart guys with dumb women, but you hardly ever see a smart woman with a dumb guy. —WRITER ERICA JONG

$\mathcal{V}$incente Minnelli, my second [husband], was too busy for me. . . . [He] snored louder and longer than any man in the world. After two years of this I was going crazy. We only had one bedroom, so . . . one night I sat up in bed and hit him as hard as I could with my fist—the one on which I wore my heavy wedding and engagement rings. I broke the poor man's nose. I quickly took some of the blood and smeared it on his night table and convinced him he had thrown himself against it during a nightmare.

It didn't cure Vincente's snoring, but he did build another wing on the house so I could sleep in peace.     **—JUDY GARLAND IN THE AUGUST 1967** *LADIES' HOME JOURNAL* **(HER MARRIAGE TO MINNELLI WAS FOSTERED BY THEIR STUDIO, MGM)**

$\mathcal{T}$he men I married, I chose because they were intellectuals—Charlie Chaplin, Burgess Meredith, and Erich Maria Remarque. They were my second, third, and fourth. I don't count my first husband—it wasn't memorable, and he was not an intellectual.     **—PAULETTE GODDARD**

$\mathcal{Y}$ou never see a man walking down the street with a woman who has a little pot belly and a bald spot.     **—COMEDIAN ELAYNE BOOSLER**

$\mathcal{Y}$eah, sure. Why not come clean? I'd dump my woman if she got fat or bald. If she got both, I'd sue her too!     **—COMEDIAN SAM KINISON, WHO WAS BOTH FAT AND BALDING**

$\mathcal{D}$id John F. Kennedy propose to me? I think you're aware of the answer [yes]. . . . The fact is, had he married me, he couldn't have had the political career that he did. In those days, it was that simple.     **—MOVIE STAR GENE TIERNEY, A DIVORCÉE**

This [Dodi] al-Fayed guy, he's dated more than his share of models and actresses, and from what I've heard he's been bad news for most of the girls he went with. This latest one, the [model] represented by [attorney] Gloria Allred, he allegedly promised to marry her, then dumped her for Princess Di. . . . Like I say, he's far from Prince Charming himself, but how tragic that for Diana he was fatal.

**—LITERARY AGENT CONNIE CLAUSEN**

Some men collect women . . . trophies. Onassis got the world's most famous opera singer [Maria Callas], then had her give up her career. Then cast her off for John F. Kennedy's widow. . . . Dodi Fayed went through umpteen celebrity blondes, working his way up to Diana. If she had lived to marry him—and I pray she wouldn't have sunk that low—it would have been interesting to see how he'd have topped himself after Diana.

**—COLUMNIST DELPHINE ROSAY**

I lived with Jane Fonda, and I wanted to marry her. But she'd been very sheltered as a child, growing up inside Henry Fonda's mansion and in his giant, usually absent shadow. So Jane tended to come to things late—[including] she married late. . . .

**—ACTOR JAMES FRANCISCUS (WHO PLAYED JFK IN *THE GREEK TYCOON*)**

I was just really young. I don't know what his excuse is, but that's mine.

**—WINONA RYDER ON HER BREAKUP WITH JOHNNY DEPP**

Richard Gere and Cindy Crawford. Such a pair, and what a concept—his body's by Nautilus and her mind's by Mattel.

**—SAM KINISON**

$\mathcal{D}$on't marry an ambitious bisexual female, girls.
—**MELISSA ETHERIDGE'S ADVICE TO LESBIANS (SHE AND HER FEMALE PARTNER BROKE UP SOON AFTER ANNE HECHE LEFT ELLEN DEGENERES)**

$\mathcal{M}$y marriage to Angela Lansbury lasted several months. It's always in my résumé, never in hers. She chooses to forget that I was her first. Husband, that is.
—**ACTOR RICHARD CROMWELL, WHOM LANSBURY HAS SINCE ADMITTED WAS GAY**

$\mathcal{G}$ilbert Roland was a wonderful husband. In one room of the house. . . .
—**CONSTANCE BENNETT, ONCE THE MOVIES' HIGHEST-PAID ACTRESS**

$\mathcal{O}$f course I married Artie Shaw. Everybody married Artie Shaw!
—**AVA GARDNER (AMONG THE MUSICIAN'S OTHER WIVES WERE ACTRESSES LANA TURNER AND EVELYN KEYES)**

$\mathcal{I}$ was married to the brother of St. Nick. You know that picture, *Miracle on 44th [34th] Street*. The one who played Santa Claus—I forget his name [Edmund Gwenn]. Anyway, his brother—that's who I was married to. I forget his name as well.
—**ACTRESS ESTELLE WINWOOD, WHO LIVED TO 101 AND HAD SEVERAL HUSBANDS**

$\mathcal{I}$ married a designer [Oleg Cassini]. The thing is, I wasn't the only person he had designs on.
—**GENE TIERNEY**

$\mathcal{A}$rtie [Shaw] used to tell a joke that Ava [Gardner] hated. "What do you call it when a man hates the woman he loves? . . . His wife."
—**LANA TURNER**

With my first husband, I liked him too much to stay married to him. Crazy but true.
—GILDA RADNER

What's it like being married to [Olympic ice skater] Dorothy Hamill? Sometimes it's like skating on thin ice.
—DEAN PAUL MARTIN (DEAN MARTIN'S SON, WHO DIED IN A PLANE CRASH)

It didn't help our marriage when I became known as Barbra Streisand's husband. When we met, I was the leading man; she was the newcomer.
—ELLIOTT GOULD

People think it's melodramatic when the husband in *A Star Is Born* walks into the ocean and kills himself. Those people have never lived among the show biz set.
—ROBERT BLAKE, WHO ONCE AUDITIONED FOR A MOVIE STARRING BARBRA STREISAND, WHO LATER PRODUCED A REMAKE OF *A STAR IS BORN*, ABOUT A FEMALE PERFORMER WHO EVENTUALLY BECOMES A BIGGER STAR THAN HER HUSBAND

Most of my liaisons with men ended because of money. My brief relationships were with rich men, my longer ones, I had more money. And for a man, to convince himself he is the boss, he wants to be my manager, handle my money. Which as I grow older, I'm not stupid enough to let him.
—JOSEPHINE BAKER

As good an actor as Richard Burton was, he was rather threatened by my father being [acting coach] Lee Strasberg. I hate to say it, but so often, there in bed, the shadow of my father was lying right beside us. . . . Richard liked it that I wasn't a very famous actress. Just a very pretty one at the time.
—SUSAN STRASBERG

𝓘t's just always something in marriage. Until maybe you get too old to care. But first we argued over our relatives. A few years later, once we'd broken away from them, we argued over money—spending habits. Then it was jealousy or imagined jealousy. Then—aw, what the hell—by then we'd gone our separate ways.

—GEORGE REEVES, TV'S SUPERMAN

𝖂ith one wife, it was big fights over the money we didn't have. With another wife, it was fighting over the money we did have. . . . I think marriage lost a lot of its stability when they let the broads get involved with the husbands' money. —JACKIE GLEASON

𝓐mong polite company, it used to be you avoided talking about religion or politics. Between married people, it's talking about sex or money that's the most sensitive areas. Have sex, don't discuss it. And put the one with the math smarts in charge of the dough.

—SYLVESTER STALLONE

𝓘 don't know if opposites really always attract, unless you choose to mean women and men. But I know that if you pair a saver and a spender, it may not last too long. And if it's a miser and a spendthrift, forget it. —MODEL KATE MOSS

𝓜oney talks, and in marriage sometimes it dictates.

—ECONOMIST JOHN KENNETH GALBRAITH

$\mathcal{S}$uccess and money happen to you if you're lucky, and what happens is they give you plenty of choices you didn't have before. And the more choices you have, the less willing you are to settle only for what you've already got.

—DEAN MARTIN, REFERRING TO THE END OF HIS MARRIAGE

$\mathcal{A}$fter the work sort of diminished and became less important, family became more important to Dean again. . . . He spent more time with his family, and we became better friends than we had been while we were married.
—JEANNE MARTIN

$\mathcal{M}$en are like kids with toys. Like, he's had a toy, say, a teddy bear, a long time. He's loved it. He'll continue loving it or liking it, but he wants all the newest, latest toys—several at once or, if he's more mature, one at a time. But you can count on it: wait long enough, he'll want a new toy to replace the old one.

—JACKIE STALLONE, SLY'S MOTHER

$\mathcal{Y}$ou had enduring, for-better-or-worse marriages among famous people in the old days. It's all changed. When the national average is one out of two broken marriages, it means in Hollywood the chances are that every marriage since around 1970 will maybe sooner, maybe later legally dissolve.     —DIRECTOR CARL REINER

$\mathcal{I}$n show business, the majority of marriages fall victim to ego or libido.
—JULIA ROBERTS

With actors and actresses getting hitched, it's just as much about two careers as it is two people. It has to be coordinated . . . like a merger. Except that with companies, after they've merged, they stay merged.

—HUGH GRANT

Everyone's heard the old saw about how a lot of men owe their success to their first wife but they owe their second wife to their success. It's old but it's true.

—ESTELLE GETTY

A man and woman build a life, a family, and his career together, then he hits it big. Not just show biz, any biz. He drops the wife because he's getting older but it's her getting older that reminds him he's no kid anymore. So he wants a chick to make him think he's a young rooster. . . . The ex-wife gets alimony, as well she should, and he gets a new lease on life and everyone's congratulations.

—BEA ARTHUR

If it's true that women age faster, then it could be that some men shed a wife once she's primarily a mommy—and not just her kids" mommy. . . .

—ROSEMARY CLOONEY, SINGER (AND GEORGE'S AUNT)

Certain men don't want to be reminded of where and what they came from . . . the long, hard road up to the peak. A wife who began that journey with him is certainly a constant reminder.

—SONDRA LOCKE, CLINT EASTWOOD'S FORMER PARAMOUR

$\mathcal{I}$t's peculiar . . . marital relationships so often wind down on account of he's tired of being a husband, tied down to one wife, or else she's tired of being just a mom and housekeeper, tied down to one life. . . . Men seldom get tired of being a dad, 'cause for them it's a part-time job. Women seldom tire of being a wife, 'cause that's what most women want to be—preferably without too much house-work or sex involved.   **—COUNTRY-STYLE COMEDIAN MINNIE PEARL**

$\mathcal{T}$he myth is that marriages end because the couple's sex life is over. They are much more apt to end because the couple no longer share affection and intimacy—kissing or cuddling, caressing, hugging, or simply, literally sleeping together in the same bed. Expressive affec-tion is crucial to lasting relationships.   **—DR. RUTH WESTHEIMER**

$\mathcal{E}$veryone believes the worst of men in the industry. That they're all unfaithful, kinky, and anticommitment. It's the nature of the business, really. You put a man in a situation where he's surrounded by young, ambitious beauties, where kissing scenes are part of the mix, and almost anything goes, and it'll be the same if he's from Tampa, Cleveland, or Hollywood.   **—TALK SHOW HOST JERRY SPRINGER**

$\mathcal{O}$ne thing's improved. Whenever a man strayed, it was said he wouldn't have to if the wife was more accommodating. Now we know it's not Mrs. Doormat's fault, it's the nature of the beast—he's a two-faced, insatiable whoremonger, that's all.   **—KIM CATTRALL**

$\mathcal{T}$he impulse to marry and remain married is one toward together-ness and commitment. It starts weakening the more a spouse feels like a prisoner, rationally or irrationally.   **—JACK LEMMON**

$\mathcal{I}$ think it would be smarter for girls to look for nice widowers than well-heeled divorced men. A widower misses his wife to one degree or another, probably appreciates her and feels some guilt. . . . Divorced men are often just goats, looking for the next rutting partner. A widower's almost guaranteed to be more sensitive. Thing is, where do you go to meet nice, preferably well-heeled widowers? They should form a club—but that might be morbid.   **—GILDA RADNER**

$\mathfrak{M}$any widows don't want to get back into the market, and why should they? At that age—unless he died prematurely or was significantly older—who wants a new boss? But some women always want a man around, and unlike a divorcée, a widow didn't have to get her freedom and her financial reward the tough, bitter way.

**—AUTHOR EUDORA WELTY**

$\mathfrak{W}$ives are a materialistic breed, speaking as a rule. Young single girls are happier and more easily entertained. They're more grateful, not always playing the angles. . . . Women's eyes age the fastest: that what's-in-it-for-me look.   **—RICHARD PRYOR**

$\mathcal{I}$t's the breaks, man. Female bodies age faster. They can do all those tricks with their hair and on the face with makeup, but the rest of it. . . . Listen, if women had to get erections to perform, they'd go out hunting for younger bodies too.   **—VANILLA ICE**

$\mathcal{I}$ cheated. With younger women. This was after I'd been a husband for some time. I didn't mind the perhaps understandable lessening of sex in marriage so much. It was the routineness. The reluctance with which a wife will grant sex. . . . I found girls who were eager for sex, eager to share their bodies.

It may be—medically, scientifically, whichever—that women do reach a sexual peak later than men, but you couldn't prove it by me. I think the longer a woman's married, the less pro-sex she becomes.

—GEORGE C. SCOTT

$\mathcal{Y}$ou know a marriage has hit the skids and needs a tune-up when you go to a restaurant together and spend less time talking while waiting for your food than you did in the car coming over—mostly commenting on or arguing about the traffic.

—DREW CAREY

$\mathcal{M}$y wife and I keep the romance in our marriage by going out to dinner twice a week to a beautiful, romantic restaurant with fine wines and exquisite food. She goes Fridays, I go Saturdays.

—MILTON BERLE

$\mathcal{W}$e found ourselves stuck, stale . . . it wasn't fresh anymore. We were enacting intimacy. Out of habit and from fear of admitting it, it was gone from our life together.

—UK PLAYWRIGHT JOHN OSBORNE

$\mathcal{I}$ don't know what happened, or how. But I would have conversations with perfect strangers, and I had more in common with them, could relate better to them, than to my own wife.

—JOHN LENNON, ON HIS FIRST MARRIAGE

We write books because our children aren't interested in us. We address ourselves to an anonymous world because our wives plug their ears when we speak to them.
—**AUTHOR MILAN KUNDERA** *(THE INCREDIBLE LIGHTNESS OF BEING)*

When he's your boyfriend or your partner, he has to listen to you. He may not like it, but he'll listen. Husbands don't listen. They don't have to. They've got a long-term lease. —**DEBORAH HARRY OF BLONDIE**

It's not good for a relationship when your husband is your manager. The romance goes out the window when you feel you're married to your father. —**DORIS DAY, WHOSE HUSBAND-MANAGER AND HIS ASSOCIATE LOST HER OVER $20 MILLION, AS SHE FOUND OUT AFTER BECOMING A WIDOW**

My mother, who'd wanted to be an actress, let her mother ruin her hopes, professionally. Then she let my father ruin her life, personally. I was her only hope. —**BETTE DAVIS**

Any woman who lets a man walk over her is a dumb idiot and deserves no better. —**CHANTEUSE EDITH PIAF**

My father, an old-fashioned Greek, divorced my mother without informing her. She read about it later in the paper. Of course, like many marriages of that era, it had really been over for many years.
—**MARIA CALLAS**

$\mathcal{V}$ivian was ashamed of divorce . . . she didn't admit to all her marriages and divorces, publicly. . . . I tried to tell her that the fact that she divorced—once, twice, or three times—proved that she thought enough of herself to not continue in a negative situation. If I'd been her psychiatrist, she'd have agreed.

**—LUCILLE BALL, ON *I LOVE LUCY*'S VIVIAN VANCE**

$\mathcal{I}$ know a man who used to compare his wife to younger women. In public. So she went and had a face-lift. She looked marvelous. Better than her dapper but aging producer husband. But he left her because he was afraid to have a face-lift.      **—SANDRA BULLOCK**

$\mathcal{I}$t's always painful when a man leaves his wife for another woman. Typically a younger one. There's worse, though. I have a friend whose husband left her for an older woman.      **—LUCY LIU (*ALLY MCBEAL*)**

$\mathcal{I}$ don't take marriage very lightly, it's not my nature. But some men . . . one of my husbands was in the habit of telling me how much he needed me. He was quite a needy type, and when he left me, he took with him quite a bundle. He needed me, all right—he kneaded me for my dough.      **—GINGER ROGERS**

$\mathcal{S}$ometimes you both leave because you want to salvage your friendship. We were together about two years, it was serious, but we were both on the road, and he tired of being alone so much. . . . I'm young, and at this point I have to put my career first.

**—BRITNEY SPEARS IN 2002, ON FORMER BEAU JUSTIN TIMBERLAKE**

*I*t's funny—Lucy and I get along better now than we did when we were married. —DESI ARNAZ IN 1970

*I*f a woman 'spects to stay married with me, she's got to be understandin'. We're like bees, you know, and a man goes from flower to flower. If a woman can't forgive and forget, all the Latin guys would be bachelors! —DESI ARNAZ, WHOM LUCILLE BALL SAID WAS "ADDICTED TO WINE, WOMEN, AND GAMBLING, NOT NECESSARILY IN THAT ORDER"

*W*hen you let go, you have to let go of the jealousy, and that's the one relief. The rest can be painful, sad, but not having to care who he's sleeping or cheating with, that's the best part of good-bye. And in some cases good riddance. —SHELLEY WINTERS

*L*iving together really gets you involved with somebody else, like it or not. It's not easy. I think the perfect lover is someone who turns into a pizza at two in the morning. —JON STEWART *(THE DAILY SHOW)*

*W*oman would be more charming if one could fall into her arms without falling into her hands. —WRITER AMBROSE BIERCE

*I* think you have to be honest. A lot of women have low libidos. I would say that is true for the majority of married women. —WRITER MARABEL MORGAN ON WHY MANY MARRIAGES BREAK UP

More marriages break up when the people go down the aisle too young. They don't know what they want. Well, we know what men always want. But a woman should wait, should develop her own sense of self, her own style, her own goals. She should be more vogue than vague.          —FILM CRITIC PAULINE KAEL

Marriages usually end because men have a very short . . . not a short attention span, but a short sexual or affectional or commitment span. They're restless. They're born restless. Look at little girls; they can sit and play, solo or together, in one place for an hour. Little boys are like jumping beans; a few minutes after starting one thing, they're ready for the next.

Honestly, sometimes I wish I were a lesbian. Lesbians don't have to deal with men on a daily, or an hourly, basis.

          —CASSANDRA *ELVIRA, MISTRESS OF THE DARK* PETERSON

Are women books? says Hodge, then would mine were An Almanac, to change her every year.          —BENJAMIN FRANKLIN

A lot of grown men are still afraid of women. They'd rather have visiting rights than connubial responsibilities.

          —COMEDIAN ELAYNE BOOSLER

A woman is the only thing I am afraid of that I know will not hurt me.          —ABRAHAM LINCOLN

Those were B-movies. If [Ronald Reagan] had been in *Casablanca,* he wouldn't have become governor and president. . . . If he'd been married to his current wife [instead of] a successful actress [Jane Wyman], his ego could have handled not being a top-flight actor.
—A-LIST DIRECTOR GEORGE CUKOR (REAGAN HALF-JOKINGLY NAMED *JOHNNY BELINDA,* THE FILM THAT WON WYMAN HER OSCAR, AS CORESPONDENT IN HIS DIVORCE)

I remember after I was first on television and I became famous overnight and my pictures were on every magazine cover. George [Sanders] and I, we walked on the street one night in Hollywood, and some teenagers came up to us and said, "Zsa Zsa, Zsa Zsa, can we have your autograph?" And one young girl said to George, "You are so familiar. What is your name?" When I saw his face, I knew that was the end of my marriage.
—ZSA ZSA GABOR *(QUEEN OF OUTER SPACE* AND *MOULIN ROUGE)*

I had the pretty wedding. I made the pretty house. I had the pretty baby. I had the handsome husband. I had the career, he had the career, with me at the gate, waving. And the reality is: I'm flawed and he's flawed.  —MELISSA RIVERS, JOAN'S DAUGHTER, SEPARATED AS OF 2002, PARTLY DUE TO THE STRAINS OF A TWO-CAREER MARRIAGE

To mothers it's natural. But a lot of men are shocked when it happens—even though they'd expect the same from their own mothers. But when a baby enters the marriage, suddenly it has to come first, not the husband. It takes a mature man as well as a loving father to really accept that.  —ACTRESS GLENN CLOSE

The majority of girls who marry will be predominantly a wife or predominantly a mother. Unless you want to head up a clan or be a petty paterfamilias, choose a wifely woman. How you do that, I don't know—blind luck, I suppose—but if you can do that, the romance and pleasure of a marriage meant for two have a chance to flourish and endure. **—GENE RAYBURN, HOST OF *THE MATCH GAME***

Leaving behind books is even more beautiful—there are far too many children. **—PRIZE-WINNING NOVELIST MARGUERITE YOURCENAR**
**(*THE MEMOIRS OF HADRIAN*)**

A man cannot know what reserves of patience he has until he has dealt long-term with a wife or with children, or both.
**—JAMES STEWART**

Most women grow up with a father and at least one brother, but the depth of her [sic] patience is ultimately tested and sometimes destroyed by living with a man—a mate, more so one to whom one is contractually obligated. **—SINGER ROSEMARY CLOONEY**

It's clear that after a woman's had her children, the husband becomes rather redundant. Unless he's necessary for paying the bills. Which outside of show business, usually he is, and therefore fewer divorces outside of show biz. **—AUDREY MEADOWS *(THE HONEYMOONERS)***

$\mathcal{I}$f you're not a children type of guy, they'll get on your nerves or you'll end up feeling like the eldest one of your wife's kids. And to be frank, a lot of guys don't mind that. In marriage, most guys just want to be looked after. **—TV PRODUCER JAMES KOMACK**
**(THE COURTSHIP OF EDDIE'S FATHER)**

$\mathcal{I}$t destroys one's nerves to be amiable every day to the same human being. **—BENJAMIN DISRAELI**

$\mathcal{M}$y wife asked me what more I wanted in our marriage, a few years on. I said space. She took offense. I thought she wanted me to be honest. A little more freedom might have saved that marriage.
**—JOHN HUSTON**

$\mathcal{D}$epending, but too much honesty in marriage can be as dangerous as infidelity. **—DR. RUTH WESTHEIMER**

$\mathcal{T}$he worst thing a spouse can tell you is whatever follows "I'm only telling you this for your own good . . ." or "I'm only saying this because I love you. . . ." **—*PLAYBOY* FOUNDER HUGH HEFNER**

$\mathcal{I}$f you ask your husband or wife a question that begins with "Now, be honest, honey," then be prepared for the answer. After all, you asked for it. **—ACTION STAR JACKIE CHAN**

$\mathcal{W}$hen it's about an indiscretion, and I don't mean a long affair with some matrimonially minded single gal, I feel that what your wife doesn't know won't hurt your marriage. **—CHUCK CONNORS *(THE RIFLEMAN)***

Eighty percent of married men cheat in America. The rest cheat in Europe.                                     **—COMEDIAN JACKIE MASON**

Call me a philanderer. If you can pronounce it. But . . . I believe in the institution of marriage and I intend to keep trying until I get it right.                                     **—RICHARD PRYOR** *(SILVER STREAK)*

It has to be said. Cheating is like drugs. If you give in and do it once, chances are you'll do it again. . . . After my marriage survived my first affair, I reasoned it would survive a second one, and later a third, and so on. It's a trap, and do I admire any man who's honestly and quietly faithful. He's either got terrific self-discipline or very high morals. And possibly a low sex urge, besides.
                    **—JASON ROBARDS** *(PHILADELPHIA, ALL THE PRESIDENT'S MEN)*

Infidelity's funny. Or our personal excuses are. After I'd been married a while, I convinced myself cheating was a way to keep the spice in my marriage. I rationalized that for a man it was a virtual necessity. After my wife found out, she saw divorce as a necessity, and by that point I couldn't really blame her, even though she didn't know the half of it all.        **—GEORGE PEPPARD** *(BREAKFAST AT TIFFANY'S)*

For me, having extramarital flings was just . . . exciting. Like getting away with something. It was, in a way, leading a secret life, it was stealing extra thrills and experiences. I even compared it to shop-lifting, but without any true possibility of getting arrested. Man, it was great. But even that finally got boring.        **—GEORGE C. SCOTT** *(PATTON)*

$\mathfrak{M}$en are marrying later than ever. It's a good trend. Sow your wild oats first. . . . Lots of guys cheat because they're afraid they'll miss out. If all you've ever had is your wife, well, you are missing out. That one and only special girl for life, that's out of fairy tales. But guys, after you do marry, try and stay the course.

**—FORMER NBC HEAD BRANDON TARTIKOFF**

$\mathfrak{I}$t's just tough trying to juggle the two, but Julia and I are in love.

**—JULIA ROBERTS'S 2002 BOYFRIEND, DANNY MODER, WHOM THE SUPERSTAR FOUND OUT SPENT A NIGHT WITH HIS ESTRANGED WIFE VERA (ROBERTS MARRIED HIM ANYWAY)**

$\mathfrak{O}$ne woman's stud muffin is another woman's cheating s.o.b.

**—COMEDIAN JUDY TENUTA**

$\mathfrak{I}$f a man doesn't think I'm thin, that's it. I need the validation, and I'm not proud of it, but if a husband can't do it, who, besides your mother, will? I'm not exactly heavy now, but I still go through life thinking of myself as a chubby little redhead.

**—ANNE ROBINSON, HOST OF *THE WEAKEST LINK***

$\mathfrak{T}$act is something too few married people practice within the home. We all need boosting, not only before our friends and family, but on that one-to-one, intimate basis. Tact and diplomacy begin at home, or should. **—HILARY SWANK (*BOYS DON'T CRY* OSCAR-WINNER)**

Men think tact and diplomacy are for fighting off war or keeping trade relations. They don't see them as tools for fighting off hurt feelings or keeping a relationship happy and healthy. . . . Tact lets you describe your loved ones as they see themselves.   **—CATHERINE DENEUVE**

In my opinion, she has little to crow about. The guy should just shut up and act.   **—COLUMNIST DELPHINE ROSAY ON DANIELLE SPENCER, ON-AND-OFF GIRLFRIEND OF ACTOR RUSSELL CROWE, FAMED FOR HIS ROVING EYE**

I may or may not be lucky enough to find that person. If you're going to commit to marriage, it shouldn't be, "Well, I'll see how this goes."   **—RUSSELL CROWE IN 2002, WHILE LIVING WITH DANIELLE SPENCER, HIS OFF-ON GIRLFRIEND FOR FOURTEEN YEARS, WHOM HE TOOK BACK AFTER BREAKING UP WITH ACTRESS MEG RYAN**

How do you know love is gone? If you said that you would be there at seven and you get there by nine, and he or she has not called the police yet—it's gone.   **—MARLENE DIETRICH**

Some men kiss and don't tell. Some kiss and tell. Cary Grant told but didn't kiss.   **—BARBARA HUTTON ON HER GAY OR BISEXUAL FORMER HUSBAND**

My mother and father and I now lived in the intimacy of estrangement that exists between married couples who have nothing left in common but their incompatibility.   **—SOUTH AFRICAN NOVELIST NADINE GORDIMER IN *THE LYING DAYS* (1953)**

Marriage doesn't get in the way of love. . . . I was married at the time, mid-1940s, in love with a married woman, but beginning a romantic friendship that lasted about thirty-five years. With a third woman, Pauline. . . . In 1950 I married Enrica [mother of Anjelica Huston], and that was my longest marriage [until her death in a car accident in 1969]. But of all the ladies in my life, the one I still miss most is Pauline, who was a friend.

—JOHN HUSTON, WHO, BY THE WAY, HAD FIVE WIVES

Men aren't that easy to stay married to, they're so self-involved. Actors—the most. If he's a male lead, do you know how much time he'll spend—in front of the mirror, in front of the TV, and in front of you—preparing for those close-ups by tweezing his nostrils?

—MARY JANE CROFT *(I LOVE LUCY, THE LUCY SHOW)*, MARRIED TO A PRODUCER

I was on the cover of the *National Enquirer* for six months because of [his seven-month marriage in 1980]. It was a mistake. The Joyce stuff was all her lawyer's doing. Her lawyer wanted the publicity.

—ERIK ESTRADA *(CHIPS)* ON SOCIALITE JOYCE MILLER, HIS EX-WIFE

Miller alleges that Estrada threatened to shoot her, indulged in black magic rituals and kinky sex acts, and worst of all, picked at his toes at the dining room table.    —HOLLYWOOD COLUMNIST JOYCE HABER

I wouldn't have a Hollywood wife. I'd throw her out on her ear. British girls are more down to earth—where they belong. A typical movie star wife doesn't scrub floors. Right-o. But before long she won't do sex either—not without protest. Or profit.

—UK STAR OLIVER REED *(TOMMY)*

At least with the American wife, there is a big opportunity to be friends after it is *finis* [finished]. You end up not with an enemy. You don't have someone you must avoid no matter what. You have, instead, a very friendly acquaintance. I don't know how good wives Americans make, but they seem to be excellent ex-wives.

—**FRENCH DIPLOMAT AND NOVELIST ROMAIN GARY, EX-HUSBAND OF U.S.**
**ACTRESS JEAN SEBERG** *(BREATHLESS, PAINT YOUR WAGON)*

I had four husbands. Sometimes I think if I could have had them all at once, I could have picked and chosen the best qualities of each— since not one of them was a bona fide prize. I could also have saved myself so much time, heartache, and agonizing over what I imagined to be wrong with me. And had a ball, besides!    —**BETTE DAVIS**

To love is to deny oneself.    —**LATIN PROVERB**

Giving of yourself for love feels good. But too much sacrifice, and you feel cheated, the more so if sacrifice is not mutually equal, which it rarely is. There would be more marital splits if women weren't taught to believe they must shoulder most of the sacrificing.

—**VIVIEN LEIGH** *(A STREETCAR NAMED DESIRE)*

The sentence "You're my wife" can be a wonderful or an awful one, depending entirely on the man saying it and how he says it.

—**ACTOR-WRITER RUTH GORDON** *(ROSEMARY'S BABY)*

In my marriage I had so much to say and no one to really listen. I was so willing to listen, but he had so little to say.

—**ACTRESS-DIRECTOR IDA LUPINO**

Loneliness is never more cruel than when it is felt in close propinquity with someone who has ceased to communicate.

—GERMAINE GREER

I think so many things were pulling at us that somewhere along the way we forgot to ask each other, "How was your day?"

—MELISSA RIVERS, EXPLAINING HER BREAKUP AFTER THREE YEARS
OF A TWO-CAREER MARRIAGE

A relationship is something that bridges the space between two people's distances. We're like one soul in billions of separate bodies, caged or separated, constantly comparing ourselves to each other and constantly craving communication—to share, to express, to experience each other. In a good and growing relationship of any kind, we move toward oneness.

Marriages that don't last are especially tragic because you had two people moving closer and closer together, then pulling apart in disappointment or embarrassment after the happiness of mutual pairing and growth.　　　—THE PHILOSOPHY OF BUDDHIST ACTOR PETER FINCH

Communication is the bloodstream of matrimony. When and if it dries up, the relationship withers into mere coexistence.

—TALK SHOW HOST STEVE ALLEN

If you must part, move on. Don't regret. You can't build a future on regret, you can only wallow in it.　　　—BARBARA WALTERS

In our culture, men are supposed to be ambitious. When you're getting to know them, they say so many things they don't mean. They have so many plans for themselves, for you and your relationship. It takes quite a few years and sometimes quite a few men to realize that you should ignore most of their talk and instead judge by their actions.   **—ACTOR TURNED DIRECTOR PENNY MARSHALL**

They shouldn't just give sex ed classes, they should give you a dose of reality. . . . I used to think once I had a husband, matrimony would just carry my life along, like perfume on a breeze. I guess I thought the marriage certificate was like a magic wand. But being married changed so very little. I was still me, the old problems remained, now there were new ones. . . . I naively thought when you're a married lady, it all gets done for you . . . things, wonderfully, just . . . happen.   **—TINA TURNER**

Some women marry because they don't want to work. Are they ever in for a surprise! Even if a woman marries rich, she earns what she gets. Men see to that . . . [and] usually, in due time, the wife rebels. Reforms are made, or if not, the lawyer is paid.   **—PEGGY LEE**

It occurred to me when I was thirteen and wearing white gloves and Mary Janes and going to dancing school, that no one should have to dance backward all their lives.   **—U.S. GOVERNMENT OFFICIAL JILL RUCKELSHAUS IN 1973**

What a girl of sixteen puts up with in terms of behavior and self-limitations, only a foolish woman of thirty-two would put up with.   **—DAME DIANA RIGG *(THE AVENGERS)***

People call me a feminist whenever I express sentiments that differentiate me from a doormat or a prostitute.
—NOVELIST DAME REBECCA WEST IN 1913

The more men talk about chivalry, watch out! Too often, it's a substitute for the real, equitable things in life. . . . My ex would always open a door for me, but he wouldn't open a checking account for me.
—JAYNE MANSFIELD

The happiest moment . . . takes place after the loved one has learned to accommodate the lover and before the maddening personality of either party has emerged like a jagged rock from the receding tides of lust and curiosity.
—QUENTIN CRISP

Gable's first two wives were older women and decidedly not beauties. But rich. . . . He may have been, initially, a gigolo at heart. That may be why his persona was treating women badly, which was not unacceptable then. Clark used his first wives to work his way up. . . . He may have been a divine sex symbol, but he wasn't a prize husband.
—MOVIE SUPPORTING ACTRESS EVE ARDEN

In a faltering marriage, thoughtlessness is the male's failing and vindictiveness the female's.
—JOHN LENNON, PRE–YOKO ONO

My marriage to Sheila began to end when she wouldn't accommodate my drinking and began concentrating on her own career. I think the wife I should have had would be a stay-at-home alcoholic. Someone like Dixie Lee, who was married to Bing Crosby. I'd have been kinder to her than Crosby was, and she'd have been more sympathetic to me. **—SINGER-ACTOR GORDON MACRAE** *(OKLAHOMA!, CAROUSEL)*

I think being a woman is like being Irish . . . everyone says you're important and nice but you take second place all the same.

**—IRIS MURDOCH**

You could say I got a younger model . . . he's male, certainly, but not a male model. **—MODEL SOPHIE DAHL, WHO LEFT MICK JAGGER FOR YOUNG ACTOR CHARLIE HUNNAM** *(QUEER AS FOLK)*

I want another child. . . . [George Clooney] is gorgeous and younger than my last boyfriend. I would be happy if someone would introduce me. A mini-Mick and a mini-George, now that would be quite a team. **—BRAZILIAN MODEL LUCIANA MORAD, WHO RECEIVES $10,000 A MONTH FOR HAVING HAD A SON BY MICK JAGGER**

I don't have the right wife. **—MICK JAGGER, THEN MARRIED TO JERRY HALL, ON WHY HE WASN'T GOING INTO POLITICS**

Adultery may or may not be sinful, but it is never cheap.

**—WRITER RAYMOND POSTGATE**

No adultery is bloodless. **—WRITER NATALIE GUINZBERG**

They call it adultery, but it seems to me it's a very unadultlike thing to do. Not to mention unladylike, of course.

—COUNTRY COMIC MINNIE PEARL

After my husband stopped having eyes for me, I found a man friend who wasn't blind to my charms. We enjoyed romantic lunches, long walks in the park, sparkling conversation—a rarity in marriage—and as to whether our romantic friendship progressed any further, that remains a secret between a gentleman and a lady.

—HERMIONE GINGOLD, WHO HAD TWO HUSBANDS

One man's mate is another man's passion.     —WRITER EUGENE HEALY

Finding a boyfriend or even a lover is, for some reason, like finding a job. It's easier if you already have one.     —MARILYN MONROE

The most hazardous of all occupations known to man: drying a widow's tears. . . .     —COLUMNIST JAMES BACON, REFERRING TO '50S CROONER EDDIE FISHER, FRIEND OF PRODUCER MIKE TODD, WHO CONSOLED TODD'S WIDOW, ELIZABETH TAYLOR, AND THEN LEFT HIS WIFE DEBBIE REYNOLDS AND THEIR TWO CHILDREN FOR HER

No man can be friends with a woman he finds attractive. He always wants to have sex with her. Sex is always out there. Friendship is ultimately doomed and that's the end of the story.

—WRITER-DIRECTOR NORA EPHRON *(WHEN HARRY MET SALLY)*

We pardon to the extent that we love.

—FRANÇOIS, DUC DE LA ROCHEFOUCAULD

Once a woman has forgiven her man, she must not reheat his sins for breakfast. —**MARLENE DIETRICH IN *MARLENE DIETRICH'S ABCS***

Happiness is having your girlfriend's lipstick the same color as your wife's. —**PHIL HARTMAN *(NEWSRADIO)***

Every man should love his wife.
But a promise can't make you love.
It only makes you lie. —**J. L. WILLIAMS IN *WHY MARRY?***

Vows can't change nature. —**ROBERT BROWNING**

In this era of X-rated home videos, phone sex, escort services, easy pick-ups, and do-it-yourself mail-order machines, a man only really needs a free housekeeper, not a whole wife. —**BILLY CRYSTAL**

I knew this girl, she married an old geezer for his money. I asked her how their sex life was, she said, "He's holding his own." I said, "No, I meant your sex life together." —**DREW CAREY**

. . . wives are a dying need. —**UNA STANNARAD IN *MRS. MAN***

The terrible question which confronts all brides is whether to pin up their curls and cream their faces before going to bed. —**VIRGINIA GRAHAM IN *EVERYTHING'S TOO SOMETHING***

The big question is whether to go to bed together to go to sleep or not? —**SARAH JESSICA PARKER**

Widows have all the advantages of marriage and almost none of the minuses. The "almost" depends on how often you need "it."
—**EIGHT-TIMES-WED LANA TURNER**

Rich widows are only secondhand goods that sell for first-class prices. —**BENJAMIN FRANKLIN**

Is it chauvinistic to say that women, wives especially, have a price, and that they know their price exactly? Women know the market-place thoroughly, and I talk too much and too honestly. No wonder my wives sometimes tell me to shut up and sing. —**SAMMY DAVIS JR.**

He who hesitates is bossed. . . . On my shows, in my marriages, there is one boss. I try to be a benevolent one. —**JACKIE GLEASON**

Don't worry about the fighting. There will be fighting. Worry about how often you fight, is it always about the same thing, and what comes after the fighting—resentment or making up and starting over? Consider the quality of your fights. . . . —**DUDLEY MOORE**

The way to fight a woman is with your hat. Grab it and run.
—**JOHN BARRYMORE**

When women decline to argue, it means their husbands no longer hold their interest. To differ, to resist, to fight back, one must be interested. —**JENNIFER LOPEZ**

Never argue with a woman when she is tired—or rested.
—H. C. DIEFENBACH IN NOVEMBER 1960 *READER'S DIGEST*

Women are natural guerrillas. Scheming, we nestle in the enemy's bed, avoiding open warfare, watching the options, playing the odds.
—SALLY KEMPTON IN JULY 1970 *ESQUIRE*

The kind of spouse you get has little to do with your talents of discernment, more to do with luck. The length of your marriage, that does have to do with you, with how much you can take, and how much you're willing to give.   —MARTY FELDMAN *(YOUNG FRANKENSTEIN)*

Matrimony or matriphony? Half the marriages in Hollywood, well, they're like tennis—where love means nothing.
—JERRY COLONNA, BOB HOPE'S SIDEKICK

To be strictly veracious, I'd have to question 80 percent of the marriages I report about.   —GOSSIP COLUMNIST LIZ SMITH

Their careers are real, their marriage isn't. It's matriphony.
—COLUMNIST LANCE BROWNE OF THE HOLLYWOOD KIDS, ABOUT
A BRIEF CONTRACTUAL MARRIAGE BETWEEN A BISEXUAL MOVIE STAR
AND A BISEXUAL SUPERMODEL

Love has no gender, and its value isn't increased by a contract.
—RUPERT EVERETT *(MY BEST FRIEND'S WEDDING)*

How real is love? Not necessarily as real as you think it; it's as real and true as the kind and selfless way you treat your partner.
— **RELATIONSHIPS EXPERT LEO BUSCAGLIA**

No, I don't believe Katharine Hepburn ever said that [that she divorced Ludlow Ogden Smith so she wouldn't be known as Kate Smith]. That marriage lasted only a few weeks. There were other, extremely personal reasons. . . . Two of her close friends have said she prefers friendships with men to marriage with them. — **FRANCES DEE, HEPBURN'S *LITTLE WOMEN* COSTAR (KATE SMITH WAS A HUGELY SUCCESSFUL, HUGELY OVERWEIGHT RADIO SINGING STAR)**

Love is moral even without legal marriage, but marriage is immoral without love. — **ELLEN KEY IN THE *MORALITY OF WOMEN* (1911)**

Love, the strongest and deepest element in all life, the harbinger of hope, of joy, of ecstasy; love, the defier of all laws, of all conventions; the freest, the most powerful molder of human destiny; how can such an all-compelling force be synonymous with that poor little State- and Church-begotten weed, marriage?
— **AUTHOR-ACTIVIST EMMA GOLDMAN IN 1910**

All these reverend gentlemen who insist on the word "obey" in the marriage service should be removed for a clear violation of the Thirteenth Amendment to the Federal Constitution, which says there shall be neither slavery nor involuntary servitude within the United States. — **WOMEN'S RIGHTS PIONEER ELIZABETH CADY STANTON IN 1898**

$\mathscr{I}$ have not laughed since I married.
—MRS. INCHBALD IN *EVERY ONE HAS HIS FAULT* (1793)

$\mathscr{O}$ne who no longer wishes to laugh had best marry. . . . They will soon find that it is no laughing matter.    —CHARLOTTE-ELISABETH, DUCHESSE D'ORLÉANS IN 1699 (MARRIAGE WAS MORE SERIOUS THEN—IN EVERY WAY)

$\mathscr{W}$ell, I'd been Eddie Fisher's wife for many, many months, and to be perfectly candid, I thought it was finally someone else's turn.
—ELIZABETH TAYLOR IN 1999, AFTER PUBLICATION OF FISHER'S VERY UNFLATTERING (TO HIS EX-WIVES) MEMOIRS

$\mathscr{T}$here was this nursery rhyme I heard as a child: "Needles and pins, needles and pins, when a man marries, his trouble begins." It meant nothing to me at the time; now I marvel at the realistic philosophy embedded into that short little kiddies' rhyme.    —MICK JAGGER

$\mathscr{T}$he trials of life in fact begin with marriage.    —QUEEN VICTORIA IN A LETTER WRITTEN UPON THE ENGAGEMENT OF GRANDSON ALBERT VICTOR, WHOM SHE NAMED AFTER HER HUSBAND AND HERSELF

$\mathscr{W}$e remain very married. . . .    —RICHARD GERE IN A 1994 NEWSPAPER AD, VAINLY TRYING TO DISPEL RUMORS ABOUT HIS MARRIAGE TO CINDY CRAWFORD; MONTHS LATER, THEY DIVORCED

$\mathscr{M}$y ex-husband said someday he'd go far; I said I hope you stay there.    —DREW BARRYMORE

My ex said he hadn't been wrong once during our marriage. Except for the time he thought he made a mistake. I conceded. I said I had been wrong once—back when I said "I do."

—ACTRESS EVELYN KEYES

In France we have a saying about marriage: All beginnings are lovely. Make of it what you will. Make of marriage what you will.

—BRIGITTE BARDOT

What a holler would ensue if people had to pay the minister as much to marry them as they have to pay a lawyer to get them a divorce.

—OSCAR-WINNING ACTRESS CLAIRE TREVOR *(KEY LARGO)*

I don't think marriages break up because of what you do to each other. They break up because of what you must become in order to stay in them.

—CAROL MATTHAU [WALTER'S WIFE] IN *AMONG THE PORCUPINES*

Telling lies is a fault in a boy, an art in a lover, an accomplishment in a bachelor, and second nature in a married man.

—HUMORIST HELEN ROWLAND

Any good marriage involves a certain amount of play-acting.

—MARGARET MILLAR IN *A STRANGER IN MY GRAVE* (1960)

There is not one in a hundred of either sex, who is not taken in when they marry. . . . It is, of all transactions, the one in which people expect most from others, and are least honest themselves.

—JANE AUSTEN IN *MANSFIELD PARK* (1814)

Before marriage, a man will go home and lie awake all night thinking about something you said; after marriage, he'll go to sleep before you finish saying it. —HELEN ROWLAND IN *A GUIDE TO MEN*

My ex-husband would often get lost in thought—it was unfamiliar territory. —CHER (SHE DIDN'T SPECIFY WHICH EX)

The honeymoon is not actually over until we cease to stifle our sighs and begin to stifle our yawns. —HELEN ROWLAND

The honeymoon is not over until either one of you thinks that it is. So, synchronize your thinking, please. —ACTOR DR. HAING S. NGOR

Last time I tried to make love to my wife nothing was happening, so I said to her, "What's the matter, you can't think of anybody either?" —RODNEY DANGERFIELD (WHO LATER WED A YOUNGER BLONDE)

When turkeys mate they think of swans. —JOHNNY CARSON

My former husband did not change, though God knows I tried. He did change physically—used to be handsome, svelte. But I always knew that under his cool exterior, be it lean or flabby, beat a heart of ice. —ESTELLE WINWOOD (THE MISFITS)

Marriage is not a reform school. —COLUMNIST ANN LANDERS

$\mathcal{I}$ built a friendship and a fantasy, then a marriage, around a gorgeous smile. . . . He had a winning smile—everything else, a loser.
 **—ACTRESS ANN SHERIDAN ON HER TWO-YEAR MARRIAGE TO ACTOR GEORGE BRENT**

$\mathcal{M}$arriage is the tomb of friendship.       **—RICHARD BURTON**

$\mathcal{I}$f you can no longer be friends with hubby, at least you can have him as a friend to your kids.     **—TATUM O'NEAL, THEN-WIFE OF JOHN MCENROE**

$\mathcal{G}$ood marriage or bad marriage, the best a man can do for his children is to love their mother.       **—JACK LEMMON**

$\mathcal{O}$ne thing I'll say for Hollywood. Most of the relatively few pregnancies there are planned. Those people want their children. Most anywhere else, the attitude is more like sow your wild oats on Saturday night, then pray for a crop failure on Sunday morning.
      **—RITA HAYWORTH**

$\mathcal{I}$t doesn't get noted very often—it's more than a little shameful— but several marriages sour when the husband stops being the apple of his wife's eye in favor of their offspring. That is an immature man, and that is the most senseless form of jealousy.
      **—MAE QUESTEL, THE VOICE OF BETTY BOOP AND OLIVE OYL**

$\mathcal{A}$ lewd bachelor makes a jealous husband.
      **—H. G. BOHN IN *HANDBOOK OF PROVERBS***

$\mathcal{I}$n a way, we got married because of jealousy . . . we started out being friends. . . . On our second date we played a game at the beach: who could get the most phone numbers from the opposite sex. . . . Of course I won. But [producer Robert Smith] was definitely on my tail, and I started to get jealous of the women he was approaching. And I'm like, "Why am I getting jealous? This is just Bert, this is nothing, why am I getting jealous?" And that day I knew that it was something special.                    **—SINGER-ACTOR BRANDY** *(MOESHA)*

$\mathcal{M}$an is jealous because of his [self-pride]; woman is jealous because of her lack of it.                    **—AUTHOR GERMAINE GREER**

$\mathcal{W}$omen can be jealous of other women, sometimes of men. But men can also be jealous of things. I don't know if it's chemical, or what. My husband was very jealous of my career, specifically, my success. I don't know if he'd have minded my career as much if I'd been a flop or been poorly paid. But in many women's cases, achievement is part of your personality, and if my work came between him and me, so be it.                    **—AUDREY MEADOWS** *(THE HONEYMOONERS)*

$\mathcal{F}$rank had his work; I had my nothing.
                    **—ALIX KATES SHULMAN IN** *MEMOIRS OF AN EX-PROM QUEEN*

$\mathcal{A}$ man loves a woman so much, he asks her to marry—to change her name, quit her job, have and raise his babies, be home when he gets there, move where his job is. You can hardly imagine what he might ask if he didn't love her.
                    **—GABRIELLE BURTON IN** *THE NEW YORK TIMES* **IN 1981**

*I* have yet to hear a man ask for advice on how to combine marriage and a career. **—GLORIA STEINEM IN A SPEECH IN 1975**

*P*eople think marriage is my life's work, but I married for love several times. Except the first time—that was to show my mother that I could. **—ZSA ZSA GABOR**

*I*t is ridiculous to think you can spend your entire life with just one person. Three is about the right number. Yes, I imagine three husbands would do it. **—PLAYWRIGHT CLARE BOOTHE LUCE, WIFE OF TIME-LIFE FOUNDER HENRY LUCE**

*I* don't think it's natural for two people to swear to be together for the rest of their lives.
**—JANE FONDA IN 1961; SHE'S SINCE HAD THREE HUSBANDS AND THREE DIVORCES**

*W*ho knew? I married a hypochondriac. Then I read the best cure for that is to forget about your own body and get interested in someone else's. Which advice she was already taking—with a handsome young bodybuilder. **—COMEDIAN JACK E. LEONARD**

*S*he was a regular Martha Stewart of matrimony. She worked so hard to make a go of her marriage, that he went.
**—CESAR ROMERO, ON PAL JOAN CRAWFORD'S MARRIAGE TO ACTOR FRANCHOT TONE**

*H*e married to beget children and get rid of small talk.
**—DIANE CILENTO ON EX-HUSBAND SEAN CONNERY**

$\mathcal{A}$ recent survey of young children in the United States found that, forced to choose, most would pick their television set over their father. One wonders what most husbands would choose: the telly or the wife? Perhaps it's better not to ask.

—**EMMA THOMPSON** *(SENSE AND SENSIBILITY)*

$\mathcal{A}$ couple is strolling along a New York City sidewalk. A mugger comes along, holds them up with a gun, and tells the man, "Your money or your wife." The man doesn't say anything. Finally the mugger repeats the question, and the man says, "I'm thinking, I'm thinking!"

—**MILTON BERLE**

$\mathcal{M}$ arriage can end up like a mugging. Not as much via your spouse, but the government, the divorce lawyers, and the longtime friends who suddenly choose up sides.  —**ANGELA LANSBURY**

$\mathcal{I}$ thought marriage was for sharing a life. Or at least trying to dovetail two lives. But my first husband was always telling me how to live my live . . . every detail, down to how and where to shop. And meanwhile his life was set apart and immune to any suggestions on my part, not to mention criticism.  —**RITA HAYWORTH**

$\mathcal{W}$ e finally got to fighting over whether to put rice in the salt shaker. I said it was practical, he didn't like the look of it. One day something clicked in my head, and I thought, I don't like the sound of this marriage. It's over, and farewell.  —**ACTRESS VIVECA LINDFORS**
*(THE WAY WE WERE)*, **EX-WIFE OF** *DIRTY HARRY* **DIRECTOR DON SIEGEL**

Quarreling—and making up—aren't for interview or publication, in my book. It's too personal. **—JULIA ROBERTS**

The best part of married life is the fights. . . . I pity the woman whose husband slams the door and walks out of the house at the beginning of an argument. . . . When I felt tired I'd start a good bloodwarming fight and it'd take ten years off my age.

**—FROM THORNTON WILDER'S PLAY *THE MATCHMAKER***
**(THE PREMUSICAL BASIS OF *HELLO, DOLLY!*)**

Don't you believe it. Most of the time, aggression only yields more aggression, and letting it out just leads to letting more out. Generally, fighting is not a good thing, in or out of marriage. **—DIANE SAWYER**

As far as I am concerned I would rather spend the rest of my life in prison than marry again. **—AUTHORESS GEORGE SAND IN 1837**

In an impossible marriage, either your relationship breaks—and you move toward divorce—or else your spirit does. **—PAMELA ANDERSON**

If you feel like getting a divorce, you are no exception to the general rule. **—WRITER ELIZABETH HAWES**

There is one thing I can't get in my head—
Why do people marry the people they wed?

**—POET-PLAYWRIGHT CAROLYN WELLS**

If you made a list of the reasons why any couple got married, and another list of the reasons for their divorce, you'd have a hell of a lot of overlapping.   **—HUMORIST MIGNON MCLAUGHLIN**

Marriage is an extraordinary thing, and I doubt if any outsider—even a child of the marriage—has the right to judge.

**—AGATHA CHRISTIE**

We can judge the relative quality of a relationship—one compares, after all, it being human nature. But often we may not fathom the reasons that people remain in a bad marriage or why a good one turns bad or irretrievably bland.

**—DIRECTOR GUY RITCHIE, MADONNA'S SECOND HUSBAND**

You take each other for better or for worse, but you shouldn't take each other for granted.   **—LUCILLE BALL**

# Divorce

Divorces are made in heaven.

—OSCAR WILDE

Divorce can mean heartache or it can mean relief or freedom or joy. Or all the above.

—JENNIFER LOPEZ

I don't think divorce would result in so much anger and bitter feelings if money wasn't involved.

—SEAN CONNERY

I say that alimony is the biggest killer of romance there is.

—ZSA ZSA GABOR

Alimony . . . it's the high cost of loving.

—JOHNNY CARSON

Alimony is the screwing you get for the screwing you got.

—DREW BARRYMORE

Alimony is proof that you pay for past mistakes. And pay. . . .

—PETER O'TOOLE

Alimony is like buying oats for a dead horse.
—EDDIE CANTOR IN THE FILM *KID MILLIONS* (1934)

Since our breakup I have been required to live in an environment in which Elizabeth would never reside.
—EX–TRUCK DRIVER AND FORMER MR. ELIZABETH TAYLOR LARRY FORTENSKY

Why the courts don't tell a husband who has been living off his wife to go out and get a job is beyond my comprehension.
—JOAN LUNDEN

You never realize how short a month is until you pay alimony.
—JOHN BARRYMORE (DREW'S FAMOUS GRANDFATHER)

Instead of getting married again, I'm going to find a woman I don't like and give her a house.
—LEWIS GRIZZARD

If he needed the money so badly, I'd have given him alimony.
—JANE FONDA, AFTER READING EX-HUSBAND (AND DIRECTOR)
ROGER VADIM'S TELL-ALL MEMOIRS

Why do Hollywood divorces cost so much? Because they're worth it.
—JOHNNY CARSON

Darling, I'm a marvelous housekeeper: every time I divorce a man, I keep the house!
—ZSA ZSA GABOR

A woman never used to have to worry about paying alimony. Today, the liability is two-sided, and a man can make a fortune out of marrying the wrong woman—or, temporarily, the right woman!

—LANA TURNER, WHOSE BRIEFEST MARRIAGE [SIX WEEKS] COST HER $35,000 [DECADES LATER, WHEN JOAN COLLINS DIVORCED RECORD EXECUTIVE RON KASS SHE PAID HIM A REPORTED $1 MILLION, AND STILL LATER, JANE FONDA SETTLED SOME $10 MILLION ON POLITICIAN TOM HAYDEN)

A divorce is a public admission that either or both of you made a mistake. It hurts or embarrasses. It's even worse to conceal the mistake and continue living together in a private hell.    —BURT REYNOLDS

Furniture-hurling has never been my style. And we were beyond the point where that kind of anger could have done any good.

—LONI ANDERSON IN HER MEMOIRS, ABOUT BREAKING UP WITH BURT REYNOLDS

Meg Ryan and Dennis Quaid may not want to stay married but they both want custody of their guru, Gurumay. Instead of fighting over their eight-year-old son, Jack, they are arguing over who is going to get custody of their yoga teacher. They have both been disciples of yoga for years. Meg carries a picture of her guru and now she wants her all to herself.

—COLUMNIST ARLENE WALSH IN AUGUST 2000, IN *BEVERLY HILLS (213)*

A man's real face comes out during divorce. A woman has to protect her kids and her investments . . . he's often more interested in protecting his pride.                              —CHER

You never really know a man until you have divorced him.

—ZSA ZSA GABOR

While married to Nicole Kidman, Tom Cruise named his Gulf Stream jet *Sweet Nic*. However, Tom apparently wants to erase as much of Kidman from his current life as possible because he recently filed paperwork to change the name of the plane. Its new moniker: *Sweet Belle,* after adopted daughter Isabella.

—2001 ITEM IN CATHY GRIFFIN'S *BEVERLY HILLS (213)* COLUMN

Hollywood is the only place in the world where an amicable divorce means each one getting 50 percent of the publicity.

—LAUREN BACALL, WHOSE FIRST MARRIAGE, TO HUMPHREY BOGART, LASTED
UNTIL HIS DEATH (UNLIKE THE ONE TO ACTOR JASON ROBARDS)

Jane [Fonda] and I were together for ten years, and eight and a half of them were the happiest time of my life. —TED TURNER IN 2000

I was married for eight years. I think that's pretty damn good, being in this industry. And I think a great deal of that was from not having people in your business. —JANET JACKSON, WHO IN 1991 SECRETLY WED
HER SONGWRITER PARTNER RENE ELIZONDO JR., WHOM SHE CONTINUED TO CALL
HER "BOYFRIEND"; WHEN THEY SPLIT IN 1999, ELIZONDO SUED JACKSON FOR
$10 MILLION AND REPORTEDLY DECLARED THAT SHE WAS GAY OR BISEXUAL

The only way I'd ever marry again was if the man was very rich, very old, and had a terminal disease. —BETTE DAVIS

They went to bed with Gilda but woke up with me.   **—SEX GODDESS RITA HAYWORTH *(GILDA)*, ON HER HUSBANDS' DISAPPOINTMENT WITH REALITY**

Tell a woman anything she wants. What does it cost you? But never put it in writing.   **—ORSON WELLES (ONE OF RITA HAYWORTH'S HUSBANDS)**

It's interesting. The men who make the most noise about alimony often seem to be the ones who can best afford it.   **—UMA THURMAN**

Never loan an ex-husband any money . . . he will only use it on other women. And what can hurt more than knowing that your ex-husband is off in Rome with a girl who looks like Sophia Loren's daughter—on your money?   **—ZSA ZSA GABOR**

Janet Leigh was years ago! Nowadays I wouldn't be caught dead married to a woman old enough to be my wife!   **—TONY CURTIS**

I thought it was very humanitarian of Sean Penn and Madonna to marry each other. That way, they make only two people miserable instead of four.   **—LIFELONG BACHELOR CESAR ROMERO**

My ex-husband was so dumb, when we were in divorce court and the judge yelled, "Order in the court!" he said, "Two cheeseburgers and a fries."   **—MOMS MABLEY**

I wanted [daughter Chastity] to grow up, get married, have a child, get divorced, and live happily ever after.   **—CHER, NOW A MEMBER OF P-FLAG (PARENTS AND FRIENDS OF LESBIANS AND GAYS)**

Gay people have the same right to lose half their stuff as everyone else. **—HETEROSEXUAL COMIC RICHARD JENI, ON SAME-SEX MARRIAGE**

One thing about it: whenever a woman goes from married to divorced, she raises the intelligence quotient of both categories. **—ANGELA BOWIE, EX-WIFE OF DAVID**

Dark and light, yin and yang. Divorce is necessary, if only for contrast. Without hell, what would paradise be? **—JACKIE GLEASON**

A wife lasts only for the length of the marriage, but an ex-wife is there for the rest of your life. **—STAND-UP COMIC JIM SAMUELS**

Without being unduly vulgar, but my ex-husband was so far up his own ass, he could polish his own ulcers. **—HERMIONE GINGOLD**

I'll admit my ex-wife was no beauty. I'm being very kind here. But I don't care what anyone says, she was no hypocrite. If she were two-faced, would she be wearing that one? **—JOE E. LEWIS**

Mike's recently published book, *You're Only as Good as Your Next One,* never mentions their nearly ten years of marriage. Patricia Duff helped Mike reach the status of mover and shaker, but it seems to have escaped his memory. **—2002 ITEM IN ARLENE WALSH'S COLUMN, ABOUT FORMER STUDIO CHIEF MIKE MEDAVOY**

[Editor] Michael Korda has revealed that in [Ronald] Reagan's memoir he originally made no mention at all of his first, more successful wife [actress Jane Wyman]. Korda had to persuade him to finally include any reference to that whole chunk of his life. . . . The question is, did Reagan omit her because she was a bigger star than he or because Nancy didn't want her acknowledged? You know, Eva Peron tried to pretend she was [Juan] Peron's first wife. . . .

—HAROLD ROBBINS

Experience is what happens to a man during marriage. Hope is what he still has if he remarries.   —BOB HOPE

It was the triumph of hope over experience.   —DR. SAMUEL JOHNSON
IN 1770, WHEN INFORMED THAT A GENTLEMAN WHO'D BEEN
UNHAPPILY MARRIED HAD QUICKLY REMARRIED AFTER HIS WIFE DIED

[Samuel] Johnson had a very positive view of marriage, though it is sometimes forgotten that he was himself married for a while.

—ANONYMOUS BIOGRAPHICAL PAMPHLET

I know we didn't work together. I wasn't sure if we'd been married.

—LEX "TARZAN" BARKER, ON EX-WIFE ARLENE DAHL

My ex-husband Fang—you remember him, don't you?—sorry—he had a memory like an Etch-a-Sketch. He'd shake his head and forget everything.   —PHYLLIS DILLER

There was one divorce . . . what I remember about it is the very next day I got married. I did it to help erase the memory. I guess it worked. —JOHN HUSTON

Darling, wherever my ex-husbands are, they should only stay there. —EVA GABOR

Custody of the children is pretty easy to figure out. You keep all the young children, and let their father have all those that are over eighteen or twenty. This is because of three reasons: First, the older ones are never home anyway. Second, the older ones are a big headache to take care of. Third, they give away your age. —ZSA ZSA GABOR

Divorce is the one human tragedy that reduces everything to cash. —WRITER RITA MAE BROWN

A divorce is like an amputation; you survive, but there's less of you. —MARGARET ATWOOD

However often marriage is dissolved, it remains indissoluble. Real divorce, the divorce of heart and nerve and fiber, does not exist, since there is no divorce from memory. —WRITER VIRGILIA PETERSON

What divorce? The guy's still there in my dreams—or nightmares. And they say sleep is one third of your life. . . . —MARTHA RAYE

One of the comedienne's marriages was doomed from the start. She kept a gun under her pillow, in case her new husband got fresh in bed.   **—HOLLYWOOD HISTORIAN MARTIN GREIF ON MARTHA RAYE**

A husband who shall remain nameless, if not blameless. . . . I couldn't trust him with other women or with my money. I once challenged him when I heard he'd stolen some item at a store for which I couldn't find a receipt. He said he hadn't shoplifted, he'd just been so confused that he'd forgotten to pay. I couldn't help thinking that he'd never been so confused that he forgot and paid twice.

**—LANA TURNER, EIGHT TIMES MARRIED**

It has been my experience that one cannot, in any shape or form, depend on human relations for lasting reward. It is only work that truly satisfies.   **—BETTE DAVIS IN *THE LONELY LIFE* (1962)**

My marriages didn't usually last . . . my father was always looking over my shoulder. He was overprotective, an old-fashioned Italian-American head of the family. . . . Most of the men he introduced me to, trying to set me up, were either gay or about to become priests.

**—SINGER CONNIE FRANCIS**

My divorces have been painful things which I prefer not to speak about.   **—RAYMOND BURR *(PERRY MASON)*, WHO WAS SECRETLY GAY, HAD ONE DIVORCE, AND ONE MALE PARTNER FOR OVER THIRTY YEARS BUT FABRICATED SOME EXTRA DIVORCES AND A SON WHO "DIED"**

Rock Hudson let his gay agent marry him off to his secretary because he didn't want people to get the right idea.

—GAY ACTOR TONY PERKINS

One of my marriages was so short I was afraid if we didn't wait, we'd have to give the wedding presents back. —TROY DONAHUE

Yes, we were married, but it only lasted a few months, so it's not really worth answering in detail.

—TROY DONAHUE ON HIS 1964 MARRIAGE TO SUZANNE PLESHETTE

Two of the more trivial topics I never discuss are my marriage [of three weeks] to Wallace Beery and those frozen dinners which have become famous with my name on them.

—GLORIA SWANSON *(SUNSET BOULEVARD)*

I don't know. I was married to him a few weeks, a few months, whatever. It was very unmemorable and hurtful. —ETHEL MERMAN ON
HER FINAL MARRIAGE, TO ACTOR ERNEST BORGNINE (IN HER MEMOIRS,
SHE DESCRIBED IT WITH A BLANK PAGE)

My marriages was [sic] so short because each man gave me all he had to give and it was sweet while it lasted, but it never lasted long till they wanted me to support them, and I don't work for no man!
—HATTIE MCDANIEL *(GONE WITH THE WIND)* ON HER FOUR MATRIMONIAL EXCURSIONS

Heaven help him if he comes near me again! . . . It was strictly a green card situation. —DREW BARRYMORE ON HER FIRST MARRIAGE,
WHICH LASTED TWENTY-NINE DAYS UNTIL SHE FILED FOR DIVORCE

Tom Green's funny as a comedian [but] it wasn't funny or a very fun marriage.   **—DREW BARRYMORE ON HER SECOND, WHICH LASTED THREE MONTHS**

Joan Collins is a commodity who would sell her own bowel movement.                 **—EX-HUSBAND ANTHONY NEWLEY**

Yes, Vanessa Redgrave is controversial. Her enemies hate her, and her friends dislike her.                **—EX-HUSBAND TONY RICHARDSON**

Desi [Arnaz] is a loser. A gambler, an alcoholic, a skirt-chaser . . . a financially smart man but self-destructive. He's just a loser.
                                            **—EX-WIFE LUCILLE BALL**

Lucy isn't a redhead for no reason. She has a big comic talent, but she also has a big, not very funny temper. . . . Her tongue is a lethal weapon. She can be very cruel when she wants to be.
                                            **—EX-HUSBAND DESI ARNAZ**

Of course I hit him! But only after he hit me. . . . Actors love to act out . . . or as they now say, to let it all hang out.
          **—BETTE DAVIS ON FINAL HUSBAND GARY MERRILL, HER ONLY ACTOR SPOUSE**

I'm not upset about my divorce. I'm only upset I'm not a widow.
                                            **—ROSEANNE ON TOM ARNOLD**

Tom Arnold's penis is three inches long. Okay, I'll say four, 'cause we're trying to settle.                          **—ROSEANNE**

Even a 747 looks small when it lands in the Grand Canyon.
—TOM ARNOLD

Oh. They consider him a star? —ROSEANNE, ON BEING INFORMED THAT
EX-HUSBAND TOM ARNOLD HAD BEEN VOTED THE MOST BORING FILM STAR

I did used to be a [nightclub] bouncer. So what? Roseanne, my ex-wife, *bounces.* Not her checks, of course. Her. —TOM ARNOLD

When I call my ex-husband anal, people think I'm being intellectu-al or Freudian. But I'm merely using a polite word for what he really is, deep down. —LANA TURNER ON LEX "TARZAN" BARKER

[Women] live longer for several reasons. . . . We can cry whenever we wish . . . we don't have to be soldiers or play dangerous games [sports] or worry about things like paternity and impotence and alimony. . . . I also think women are generally more sensible.
—BRITISH ACTRESS ATHENE SEYLER (1889–1990)

I'll be eighty this month. Age, if nothing else, entitles me to set the record straight before I dissolve. I've given my memoirs far more thought than any of my marriages. You can't divorce a book.
—GLORIA SWANSON

$\mathcal{I}$ went from closet to closet, emptying his personal things and throwing them from the house, where his limo driver scooped them up and stacked them in the car. I sang, "Happy birthday to me, happy birthday to me." I thought, This is my birthday present to myself. I'm getting rid of my cheating husband once and for all!

—GRACE WILLIAMS, WHO SPLIT WITH MONTEL AFTER FINDING OUT
HE HAD A BLONDE GIRLFRIEND (WHOM SHE TELEPHONED)

$\mathcal{I}$f I ever get married again, and I won't, I should have my head examined. As far as I'm concerned, only gay people should get married. It doesn't seem to work for heterosexuals.

—ELIZABETH TAYLOR IN 2000

$\mathcal{I}$ have no comment. But nothing surprises me anymore.

—ELLEN DEGENERES, AFTER BISEXUAL ACTRESS ANNE HECHE ENDED
THEIR RELATIONSHIP TO MARRY A MAN

$\mathcal{M}$ost of America will never know the truth. We're talking big business, big bucks, big closets. [But] it seems X, who was interested in his bisexual wife's male costar, caught her having an affair with him. . . . There was no explanation for the divorce, and he instantly acquired, via his own publicity firm, a new "girlfriend."

—COLUMNIST DELPHINE ROSAY IN 2001

$\mathcal{A}$ gentleman doesn't tell.

—ELTON JOHN, WHEN ASKED IF HIS EX-WIFE WAS, LIKE HIM, GAY

Let's say I am still recovering from the aftereffects of divorce. I have nothing more whatsoever to say on the subject. —BARBARA STANWYCK, LESBIAN OR BISEXUAL STAR, FORMERLY MARRIED TO GAY OR BISEXUAL STAR ROBERT TAYLOR

Divorce is a bitch. And so's half the people who do it. —SAM KINISON

I suppose so. Hope springs infernal.
—GROUCHO MARX, ASKED IF HE WOULD CONSIDER MARRYING AGAIN

I suppose alcoholism, on the part of a husband, could be regarded more or less as a violent third party inside of a marriage.
—WILLIAM HOLDEN

Hollywood's Unhappiest Couple? —FAN MAGAZINE CAPTION OF A PHOTO OF WILLIAM HOLDEN AND BRENDA MARSHALL, WHO GAVE UP HER ACTING CAREER TO BE HOLDEN'S WIFE FROM 1941 TO 1971

You'd think the longer you're together, the more logical it is you should be friends after you divorce. Doesn't work out that way.
—JOHNNY CARSON

How can I feel amiable or well disposed toward a woman I'm stuck paying for when I don't have any say-so on how she spends her money? —ERROL FLYNN, AFTER HIS FIRST DIVORCE

$\mathcal{I}$'m ready to turn matchmaker and find my ex-wife a suitable new husband so I can stop paying her alimony. But Ivan the Terrible is dead, isn't he?                                    **—PETER O'TOOLE**

$\mathcal{L}$isten, to stop the alimony, I'd remarry the broad myself—if I didn't have to live with her.                        **—GEORGE C. SCOTT**

$\mathcal{D}$arling, all my husbands get along beautifully. They even get a 25 percent discount at the Hilton Hotel restaurants and each one will tell you his favorite movie is *The Moon and Sixpence.*    **—ZSA ZSA GABOR, WHOSE MARITAL MENAGERIE INCLUDED CONRAD HILTON AND ACTOR GEORGE SANDERS *(THE MOON AND SIXPENCE)***

$\mathcal{I}$ didn't stay married to Donna McKechnie for long [three months], but we became the best of friends . . . that can last for decades. I don't get the expression "just friends." What's "just" about friends who last a lifetime?                  **—CLOSETED DIRECTOR-CHOREOGRAPHER MICHAEL BENNETT, WHO WED HIS A *CHORUS LINE* STAR FOR COVER**

$\mathcal{I}$ tried being friends with my ex-wife, but it's kind of like pretending your mom is your sister. It's spooky!    **—PETER LAWFORD OF THE RAT PACK**

$\mathcal{T}$he sad thing about divorce when it does turn into a friendship— yeah, that's nice—is that sex becomes almost an impossibility. But that might be just as well. Sex probably had something to do with starting a lot of the problems. . . . For a man, sex is probably better with people you don't have to talk to afterward.    **—DEAN PAUL MARTIN**

$I$ knew my marriage was in trouble when we went to a Hollywood party and I overheard a starlet ask my husband if he was married and he said, "Occasionally." **—PRODUCER JULIA PHILLIPS** *(THE STING)*

$D$ivorce means never having to say you're sorry again.
**—RYAN O'NEAL** *(LOVE STORY)*

$T$he great thing about our not being married on paper is we'll never have to go through a legal divorce. **—FARRAH FAWCETT,**
**LONGTIME COMPANION OF RYAN O'NEAL AND PREVIOUSLY**
**CONTRACTUALLY MARRIED TO LEE MAJORS**

$N$ow I can wear high heels! **—NICOLE KIDMAN AFTER HER**
**DIVORCE FROM SHORTER ACTOR TOM CRUISE**

[$T$om] Cruise left [Nicole Kidman] three days before their tenth anniversary, which meant he escaped having to support her for the rest of her life by seventy-two hours. **—COLUMNIST JACK MARTIN IN 2001**
**(KIDMAN GOT TO KEEP THREE HOUSES AND JOINT CUSTODY OF**
**THEIR ADOPTED CHILDREN)**

$T$he real her is as different from her image as night and day.
**—CLAIM BY RESTAURATEUR BARRY COMDEN, DORIS DAY'S LAST HUSBAND,**
**WHO TRIED UNSUCCESSFULLY TO SELL A BOOK ABOUT HIS LIFE WITH THE**
**FORMER NO. 1 MOVIE SUPERSTAR**

$H$e wasn't prepared to be a husband. **—JOAN COLLINS, UPON DIVORCING**
**FOURTH HUSBAND PETER HOLM, A YOUNGER BLOND**

$\mathcal{I}$ like girls, not women. Wives are women. They're not much fun.
—DEAN MARTIN

$\mathcal{Y}$eah, I got an old battle axe. Somewhere. . . . I never got divorced 'cause I'm never gonna get married again. You can bet your life on it!
—WILLIAM FRAWLEY, A.K.A. FRED MERTZ ON *I LOVE LUCY*

$\mathcal{I}$f divorce has increased by 1,000 percent, don't blame the women's movement. Blame the obsolete sex roles on which our marriages were based. —ACTIVIST-AUTHOR BETTY FRIEDAN IN 1974

$\mathcal{I}$t's all in the family, darling, which I love it. Now I am the sister-in-law to my former husband. It's very civilized, not like when they could burn a woman at the stake for marrying her late husband's brother! —ZSA ZSA GABOR, ON GEORGE SANDERS WEDDING HER
SISTER MAGDA (IT LASTED SEVERAL WEEKS)

$\mathcal{I}$t's like, "Is [sic] there any more at home like you?" People acted like it was some strange thing that Dorothy had a sister I might be interested in, but I don't know why. It was her sister. It's sort of normal, I think, not such a stretch. —DIRECTOR PETER BOGDANOVICH, SIXTY-TWO,
AFTER HIS THIRTY-FOUR-YEAR-OLD WIFE LOUISE HOOGSTRATEN ENDED THEIR
TWELVE-YEAR MARRIAGE (LOUISE IS THE HALF-SISTER OF BOGDANOVICH'S
LOVER DOROTHY STRATTEN, THE ACTRESS AND FORMER *PLAYBOY* MODEL
MURDERED BY HER ESTRANGED HUSBAND)

$\mathcal{P}$eter Bogdanovich left Polly Platt, his wife of eight years, for up-and-coming Cybill Shepherd, whom he directed in *The Last Picture Show.* Hollywood, or the public, ended their relationship when every movie he thereafter directed Shepherd in lost money. In show biz, money is the bottom line of most everything.

**—AUTHOR PAUL ROSENFIELD *(THE CLUB RULES)***

$\mathcal{O}$h, yes, definitely. But only to a man who has never seen even one of my movies. I'm really bored and tired of competing with the "original" Hedy Lamarr. **—FORMER SCREEN SIREN HEDY LAMARR, ASKED IF SHE WOULD EVER MARRY AGAIN (SHE DIDN'T)**

$\mathcal{W}$hen you're younger, men might really marry you for love. When you're older—and less beautiful for them—they marry you for ambition, and the tragedy is you marry so not to be lonely but still knowing that it's only a matter of time until divorce happens.

**—RITA HAYWORTH**

$\mathcal{Y}$ou fall in love with a man, you marry. Then you have children and they become the loves of your lives. Maybe the husband is not so wonderful anymore. And perhaps you two get divorced—it's not life's biggest tragedy. Losing your child or losing your looks—those are real tragedies. So is, I imagine, losing a husband if you had to depend on him for all your money.

**—ACTRESS ROMY SCHNEIDER *(WHAT'S NEW, PUSSYCAT?)***

$\mathcal{I}$ married to have children and I divorced to not have a husband. *¿Comprende?* **—FORMER SCREEN SIREN VERONICA LAKE, TO A HISPANIC REPORTER**

When I can no longer bear to think of the victims of broken homes, I begin to think of the victims of intact ones.

**—WRITER PETER DEVRIES**

The reason grandparents and grandchildren get along so well is that they have a common enemy.   **—SAM LEVENSON**

During those periods, all too frequent in a young and tender life, when my parents were—to put it mildly—not getting along, I fervently wished they would divorce. When I realized such a radical step would not be undertaken, I wished I could divorce them and go away and live with my beloved grandmother.   **—TENNESSEE WILLIAMS**

It was so long ago . . . I slapped my wife [actress Katherine DeMille, Cecil's daughter] on our wedding night [because] she wasn't a virgin. I was so disappointed. But it was a very long time ago.

**—ANTHONY QUINN ON HIS FIRST WIFE**

I admit it. I left [longtime wife Yolanda] because a younger wife makes fewer demands and she can give me more children. I am an actor and a father first.   **—ANTHONY QUINN, TWO-TIME OSCAR-WINNER**

No matter how much housewives want to believe in them, novels are fiction. . . . Robert Waller became a multimillionaire from *The Bridges of Madison County*, about a middle-aged marriage that outlasts passion and temptation. He wrote it so convincingly, he moved so many housewives . . . [but] now he's divorced from his wife of thirty-five years and is living with a woman who's twenty-three years younger than his ex-wife.

**—ACTRESS TURNED LITERARY AGENT CONNIE CLAUSEN**

𝔇ivorce is a disturbing business: to the clergy, to statisticians, to those who engage in it, and to their offspring, but the men and women who lead the lives of quiet desperation rather than resort to it, no matter how grim their condition, contribute little to the general welfare. **—ILKA CHASE**

ℋelen Hayes had the extreme bad taste to mention one of my two ex-husbands, both of them experiences too dreadful to discuss. She had no provocation for mentioning him. So now she's on my enemies list. **—DAME JUDITH ANDERSON *(SANTA BARBARA)***

𝔅eing married to Arlene Dahl was very nice, at nighttime. But in the daytime, it was like being married to Elizabeth Arden. That is where she spent most of her time. If you asked her which was more important to her, her home life or her career, she would have to tell you the truth: her face! **—FERNANDO LAMAS, WHOSE SON VIA DAHL IS TV ACTOR LORENZO LAMAS**

ℒiving with Jane [Fonda] was difficult in the beginning. . . . She had so many—how do you say?—bachelor habits. Too much organization. Time is her enemy. She cannot relax. Always there is something to do—the work, the appointment, the telephone call. She cannot say, "Oh, well, I'll do it tomorrow." This is her weakness. **—FRENCH DIRECTOR ROGER "MAÑANA" VADIM**

𝔄li MacGraw is a good wife for me. We're both actors, but neither of us is a great, big, fat talent, and she's not all wild-eyed about her career, which suits me fine. **—STEVE MCQUEEN, WHO POST-ALI WED A MODEL**

*I* always knew he'd end up in bed with a boy!
**—AVA GARDNER, AFTER EX-HUSBAND FRANK SINATRA WED SKINNY MIA FARROW**

*J*oan Crawford's first marriage was very shrewd on her part. She married for social position in Hollywood. It didn't matter a bit that it was Douglas Fairbanks Jr. Joan had set her sight on Mary Pickford as an in-law; she married into Pickfair. It just happened that Junior was the son of Douglas Fairbanks Sr. and the stepson of Mary Pickford. That put Joan on the map, and she more than took it from there!
**—CHARLES "BUDDY" ROGERS, PICKFORD'S LAST HUSBAND**

*J*oan [Crawford], who had one of the biggest, longest Hollywood careers, was ambitious from day one. Billy [Haines, silent movie star] befriended her, and so she proposed to him, to boost herself and to give him a "beard." He declined, saying it usually worked better with a lesbian actress and a gay actor—whether or not they divorced a few years later. . . . So, to my knowledge, all Joan's husbands were straight.   **—JIMMY SHIELDS, LIFETIME PARTNER OF WILLIAM HAINES**

*T*wo of my wives resented me because they thought I was better-looking than they were. That came out during one of our fights. Another one resented that I looked younger than her. I can't help any of that. I thought I married pretty girls. . . .
**—MATINEE IDOL JEFFREY HUNTER (1925–1969)**

*I* begged Richard [Dawson] not to go to the States. You know what happens to most British actors who go there—they finish by playing butlers or opening fish-and-chips stands. With Dickie, it was worse: He became host of something called *Family Feud*.
**—SEX SYMBOL DIANA DORS**

ℛex Harrison is so pompous, he expects a lady to open the door for him! **—WELSH ACTRESS RACHEL ROBERTS ON HER ENGLISH EX-HUSBAND**

ℐ was married to Glenn Ford. But now I feel as if I'm married to God, and in the nicest, purest sense. **—DANCER-ACTRESS ELEANOR POWELL, WHO BECAME AN ORDAINED MINISTER**

𝒟ivorce scares me. When I was a kid, I was told if you got married and then got divorced, you went to hell. Your chances for heaven were shot—except here on earth, while the sex was good. **—TED KNIGHT *(THE MARY TYLER MOORE SHOW)***

𝒲hy do people think blame must be attached, if a marriage ends? If a car conks out after twenty years, is the driver to blame? It can be what's to blame, like boredom or adultery, although boredom only requires one and the other takes three. . . . Anyhow, I feel: Work on your own bloody marriage and let other people's divorces be. **—JOHN CLEESE**

𝒜 union definitely not made in heaven. I continued after I married her to live by myself. **—ANDY GRIFFITH ON HIS 1975–1979 MARRIAGE TO GREEK ACTRESS SOLICIA CASSUTO**

$\mathcal{A}$ comedian's wife has a hard job. It's a constant state of giving. A continual satisfying of the other's needs, because a comic is like a child. Everything must revolve around him. . . . He frequently lives in a world so completely surrounded by himself that often he doesn't even hear me.

A person who deals in himself and in his emotions is bound to be more sensitive than a butcher. So we try to soft-pedal when Andy has had many tensions building. Otherwise, you can never tell when it's that last trivial thing which will be the straw that broke the camel's back.    **—BARBARA GRIFFITH, ANDY'S FIRST WIFE,**
**FOR TWENTY-THREE YEARS (UNTIL 1972)**

$\mathcal{O}$ lder wives were reared to think the husband is more important than the wife. But the wife of a successful, famous actor is made to feel like nothing. He's one hundred times as "important" as you. He gets all the adulation, every bit of the attention. In public together, you're treated as if you're invisible and you even get jealous resentment from many of the fans. It's not a lifestyle most wives can endure for long, despite the outer trappings.    **—ANONYMOUS EX-WIFE OF**
**A BRITISH STAR, QUOTED IN THE *SOUTH CHINA MORNING POST***

$\mathcal{Y}$ ou cannot believe how many letters the studio received over the years, urging that it pressure Greer Garson and myself into marriage! Some even urged that we divorce our respective spouses in order to be free to marry each other. . . . That's when I learned that "fan" is short for "fanatic."    **—WALTER PIDGEON, GARSON'S FREQUENT COSTAR**
**(*MRS. MINIVER, MADAME CURIE,* AND SO ON)**

Being married to Dyan Cannon was no picnic, but we had a child together, my only child. It seems that each new marriage is more difficult to survive than the last one. I'm rather a fool for punishment— I keep going back for more, don't ask me why.

—CARY GRANT (BORN ARCHIBALD LEACH)

I know they nicknamed us "Cash and Cary," but I never asked [Woolworth heiress] Barbara Hutton for a penny. I never married a woman for money, that's the God's truth. I may not have married for very sound reasons, but money was the least of them. —CARY GRANT

Rudolph Valentino was no Italian stallion, at least where the ladies were concerned. He had two wives [both reportedly lesbian], but neither marriage took off. Apparently Rudy thought "consummate" meant to make soup. —SINGER-ACTOR RUDY VALLEE

The scuttlebutt was that Virginia Valli was more butch than Charles Farrell, ditto Mary Livingstone vis-à-vis Jack Benny. More than a few of your celebrated actor-actress marriages aren't entirely what they seem. . . . —ACTOR-AUTHOR DAVID NIVEN

I will always feel married to Mr. Olivier, in one way or another.

—VIVIEN LEIGH ON HER EX, LAURENCE OLIVIER

The irony is that Larry's first wife [actress Jill Esmond] was a reputed lesbian, and they did have offspring. Larry and Vivien, who was . . . heterosexual, did not. Then he married one more actress, and they have offspring, yet I understand she is heterosexual. . . . Is Larry heterosexual? I'm the wrong chap to ask. —PETER FINCH

$\mathcal{A}$ctress Leigh Taylor-Young, former wife of Ryan O'Neal, once had been married to studio head Guy McElwaine, being told she was his third wife. "Then at a fitness class, I mentioned I was a newlywed, married to Guy, and another girl in the class said she knew his fifth wife. I finally found out I was wife number seven."

—HOLLYWOOD COLUMNIST JAMES BACON

$\mathcal{I}$ might wear red this year. . . .  —NICOLE KIDMAN, OSCAR NOMINEE, ON THE ACADEMY AWARD CEREMONIES IN 2002; EX-HUSBAND TOM CRUISE NEVER LIKED HER IN RED (SHE COMPROMISED AND WORE PINK)

$\mathcal{H}$e said he hoped to pay his alimony bill with a smile, but I told him I wanted cash.  —DEBBIE REYNOLDS ON EDDIE FISHER, WHO LEFT HER FOR ELIZABETH TAYLOR

$\mathcal{N}$icolas Cage and Patricia Arquette were married for six years but hadn't seen each other since their divorce. Patricia [went to a 2002 Oscar party] with her girlfriend Gina Gershon and didn't know her ex had been invited. Cage spotted her across the room and after a brief conversation, Patricia and Gina left knowing that the dreaded moment was finally over with.  —ARLENE WALSH

$\mathcal{O}$n our final anniversary, as a present, I cooked him a homemade meal. He said, as a present, he'd eat it.  —NELL CARTER *(GIMME A BREAK)*

$\mathcal{S}$ome stuff does bother me about being married . . . like having a husband.  —ROSEANNE BARR, AS SHE THEN WAS

𝒥'm too busy to think of marriage. . . . Sometimes I think life is too short . . . and how could I marry a man and then ignore him? It would be so unkind, Besides, I could never consent to a divorce.
— THE DEEPLY CLOSETED LILLIAN GISH, WHO NEVER WED A MAN AND BECAME A STAR IN 1915 IN *BIRTH OF A NATION* (SHE LIVED TO NINETY-NINE)

𝒟ivorce becomes part of your record. Like being fired from a job, only worse. — CONFIRMED BACHELOR SHERMAN HELMSLEY *(THE JEFFERSONS)*

𝒱ery few people realize how much Larry King has done for the youth of America—he married seven of them! — PHYLLIS DILLER

𝒴ou buy a bad car, it breaks down, what are you going to do?
— CHARLIE SHEEN ON WHY HE WAS LEAVING HIS WIFE OF FIVE MONTHS

𝔐y sister was wailing and moping round after her first divorce. I finally says to her, "Honey, husbands ain't copyrighted. There's plenty more where he came from." — MAE WEST

𝒥f you adopt a child, what happens when the marriage goes sour? When Burt Reynolds and Loni Anderson fought, they could always leave Quinton [sic] with Dom DeLuise. But what about the kids who aren't that lucky? — BILL MAHER

𝓑eauty and the horsey. — BRITISH ACTOR IAN CHARLESON ("GANDHI") ON PRINCESS DIANA AND PRINCE CHARLES

$\mathfrak{M}$y sex-mad husband was driving me to distraction. I wanted to know where he spent his nights. Then one night I went home and there he was.                              **—COMEDIAN TOTIE FIELDS**

$\mathcal{I}$ can truthfully say that the first years of my marriage were happy. Compared to what came later.

**—DAN ROWAN** *(ROWAN AND MARTIN'S LAUGH-IN)*

$\mathfrak{M}$y favorite divorce lies that will never die are: We'll still be good friends; I'm not bitter; and I'm glad he's found someone who makes him happy.                **—SEVEN-TIMES-MARRIED ARTIE SHAW**

$\mathfrak{T}$he truth is, we [women] live like bats or owls, labor like beasts, and die like worms.   **—MARGARET CAVENDISH, DUCHESS OF NEWCASTLE, IN 1662**

$\mathcal{I}$ think a lot of people first entertain thoughts of divorce when at some point they realize that their marriage is turning into their parents' marriage.   **—ANETA CORSAUT (HELEN CRUMP ON *THE ANDY GRIFFITH SHOW*)**

$\mathfrak{O}$kay, I take it back, but . . . yeah.           **—KIRSTIE ALLEY, WHO'D SAID OF EX-HUSBAND PARKER STEVENSON, "HE HAD SO MANY FAULTS, HIS NICKNAME WAS SAN ANDREAS"**

$\mathfrak{F}$ar be it from me to criticize any of his highly rated works, few of them perfect, however. I did once start to offer a dissenting view of his latest work, and my sweet, unspoilt husband stopped me. He said, "Excuse me. You obviously have me confused with someone who values your opinion."

**—JILL BENNETT *(THE NANNY)* ON EX-HUSBAND JOHN OSBORNE**

$\mathcal{I}$'m not about to listen to criticism of my divorces. I alone know what I went through, and for how long, before I decided not to keep going through it.  **—CHER**

$\mathcal{H}$ollywood husbands work hard. At being bastards. Hollywood wives work hard too. On their tans. . . . In Tinseltown they're all drama queens. I think most of them enjoy their divorces more than their weddings, for two reasons. Divorces last longer to take effect, and they get more sympathy.  **—NOVELIST HAROLD ROBBINS**

$\mathcal{I}$ had a career before we married. He was so rich, I figured why work? Take a five-year vacation or something. . . . One friend gave me for a wedding present a "matrimonial memory book." To write down all the things and events in my new married life. After six months, I hadn't filled three pages. And most of it pertained to him. Like the time he wrote the president of Purina and asked why he didn't make mouse-flavored cat food?

He finally said what I'd only thought: outside of sex, we weren't communicating. Of course, he's a communications expert . . . a man who screens all his calls on answering machines but has call-waiting so he won't miss any calls from anyone he didn't want to talk with in the first place. . . . In the end, we divorced, he trading me in for a heart attack and me trading him in for something better than most VIP husbands: my work and a big promotion.  **—ANONYMOUS HOLLYWOOD EXEC, "MS. X," QUOTED IN THE *SYDNEY MORNING HERALD***

$\mathcal{A}$ couple all wrapped up in themselves make a very small package. Some people do retreat into marriage, as behind a fortress. Which is not to say that they won't finally divorce or, *au contraire,* remain as one over the long, selfish haul.  **—TALK SHOW HOST JERRY SPRINGER**

When a woman marries again it is because she detested her first husband. When a man marries again, it is because he adored his first wife. Women try their luck; men risk theirs.    **—OSCAR WILDE**

Eddie Fisher's successes grew with his marriages to famous women like Elizabeth Taylor, Debbie Reynolds, and Connie Stevens. They all divorced him, his career plummeted, and he married a Chinese woman. So everyone felt sorry for him, being out of the limelight, no longer a success. . . . The woman was worth $100 million, and under California's community property laws, Eddie has inherited $50 million from her estate. Who's having the last laugh?

**—COLUMNIST JAMES BACON IN 2002**

My friend Rachel [Roberts] was a talented actress who married a major, Hollywood-style star [Rex Harrison]. Thereafter her talent and career took second place. She loved the new lifestyle, and when divorce took it away, she kept hoping they'd someday remarry or at least get back together. No way—Rex wanted younger meat. When this finally sank in, Rachel planned to get back at Rex as best she could, short of murder.

She timed her suicide to coincide with the Los Angeles opening of Rex's *My Fair Lady* stage tour. For maximum embarrassment, because decades before, actress Carole Landis had committed suicide over Rex, whose mistress she was; he was married. Rachel planned her suicide meticulously, but it backfired. The Latin American gardener didn't show up to find her body on the day he should have, and so it didn't affect Rex's triumphant return. And they have so many murders in American cities that the L.A. coroner at first believed it was murder, not suicide. Certainly not suicide as revenge.

**—UK DIRECTOR LINDSAY ANDERSON (*THIS SPORTING LIFE*)**

$\mathcal{I}$ had a friend who married a model. She came very close to being anorexic . . . and they divorced. He said that it takes strength to care about another person, and the thinner she got, the less strength or interest she had; her relationship had become that between her and food, that was No. 1.  **—MALE MODEL JOE MACDONALD**

$\mathcal{H}$ow come these so-called psychics finished up divorcing, like anyone else? Couldn't they foresee it would be a bad marriage?
**—COMEDIAN CAROLINE RHEA**

$\mathcal{M}$y bitter half, as I call him, took an IQ test—the results were negative.  **—VIVIAN VANCE ON ACTOR PHIL OBER, WHO BECAME A DIPLOMAT IN MEXICO**

$\mathcal{S}$ean [Penn] tried to be a good husband. He just tried too hard. . . .
**—MADONNA**

$\mathcal{I}$ should have married Rita Hayworth instead of Bette Davis. With Bette, it should have remained a love affair. When an affair burns itself out, it's best to make a clean break. But when the affair within a marriage—the sex—burns out, you're still stuck with each other, and things can turn very messy.  **—GARY MERRILL *(ALL ABOUT EVE)***

Shirley Jones should have become a bigger star than she did. She can do more than play a goody-goody, but she had the bad luck to be a good-looking blonde who is not a sex symbol. I admit that her stardom, when she was in *Oklahoma!,* was very attractive to me. I wanted to be a movie star, myself. I married Shirley, and with time I found out that in this life you almost never get what you want, or you end up not wanting what you got.    **—JACK CASSIDY, FATHER OF DAVID AND EX-HUSBAND OF SHIRLEY, BOTH STARS ON TV'S *THE PARTRIDGE FAMILY***

The more they want us to get divorced, the more married we stay.
**—WHITNEY HOUSTON ON MEDIA REPORTAGE OF HER TURBULENT MARRIAGE TO "BAD BOY" BOBBY BROWN**

Change is inevitable. Except from a vending machine or in a stale marriage.    **—LARRY KING**

Being a motivational speaker, sometimes I inadvertently bring my work home with me. So far, my wife has not asked for a divorce. Like the time I hugged her and said, "I hope you sincerely know that you are unique, just like everyone else."    **—LEO BUSCAGLIA**

A bore is a person not interested in you. I'm sorry to say I once married a bore . . . although less sorry than if I'd remained married to him.    **—GLYNIS JOHNS (BROADWAY'S *A LITTLE NIGHT MUSIC*)**

$\mathcal{A}$ child absolutely belongs to you, for a long time. A husband, perhaps, never belongs to you. I think that's why most everyone that I know is either divorced or has never bothered with the getting married to begin with.　—MODEL TURNED ACTOR-PRODUCER ELIZABETH HURLEY, WHO BECAME A MOTHER IN 2002 (NOT BY FORMER LONGTIME PAL HUGH GRANT)

$\mathcal{I}$ married and divorced several beautiful, sexy, much younger girls. For pleasure and for my career, which was always my biggest pleasure. Oddly, I was often asked why I married these women, not why we divorced.　—BAND LEADER XAVIER CUGAT, WHOSE WIVES INCLUDED ABBE LANE AND CHARO

$\mathcal{T}$he sole consolation I found in my previous husband's presence was his ultimate absence.　—HERMIONE GINGOLD

$\mathcal{I}$ leave before being left. *I* decide.　—BRIGITTE BARDOT

$\mathcal{V}$ariety is the only actual and foolproof aphrodisiac. If your spouse is open-minded and flexible, sometimes literally, you're lucky. If not, and if the variety takes you outside the marital nest, then you're lucky if you don't get caught or you have a very understanding mate. And if you do get or you don't have, then you must choose between an ongoing wonderful sex life, which means divorce, or sticking it out together for the approval of relatives and strangers, who are really the same people except for your growing up with the former bunch.　—WALLY COX *(MR. PEEPERS)*

$\mathcal{T}$he happiest time of anyone's life is just after the first divorce.　—ECONOMIST JOHN KENNETH GALBRAITH

The difference between divorce and legal separation is that legal separation gives a husband time to hide his money. **—JOHNNY CARSON**

Judges, as a class, display, in the matter of arranging alimony, that reckless generosity that is found only in men who are giving away somebody else's cash. **—AUTHOR P. G. WODEHOUSE**

It's interesting how most females seem to get energized when they hear that a woman has left her husband. **—DREW BARRYMORE**

In our family we don't divorce our men—we bury them. **—RUTH GORDON (HAROLD AND MAUDE)**

He thought that she'd come to reconcile. But she came to serve him papers and told him, "Get your tongue out of my mouth, I'm kissing you goodbye." **—BILL MAHER**

The thing with rock stars is that women keep chasing after them—they're not like normal guys. With normal guys it's bad enough, but things calm down. My girlfriends are always saying, "I could never do it. I don't know how you stand it." Because after all these years, all these girls are still chasing after him.

**—JERRY HALL ON MICK JAGGER; SHE FINALLY HAD ENOUGH IN 1999,**
**AFTER HIS LATEST INDISCRETION AND BABY BY A YOUNGER MODEL**

It depends how much the guy goes for groupies. If he's gonna tie the knot, he'd better cut it way, way—I mean way—down. Like to zero. If he values his health. **—CHER, WHOSE ROCKER HUSBAND**
**GREGG ALLMAN INSISTED SHE CALL HIM "MR. ALLMAN"**

$\mathcal{D}$avid and I had so much in common . . . at times maybe too much.
**—ANGELA BOWIE (DAVID TOLD *PLAYBOY* MAGAZINE, "WHEN WE MET,
WE WERE BOTH LAYING THE SAME BLOKE," A MALE RECORD EXECUTIVE)**

$\mathcal{D}$omesticity is death.  **—MICK JAGGER**

$\mathcal{M}$arriage is worse than dying. Why stay with one person for fifty
years?  **—JOEY RAMONE**

$\mathcal{I}$ know people theorize that Mick thought it would be amusing to
marry his twin. But actually he wanted to achieve the ultimate by
making love to himself.
**—BIANCA MACÍAS ON HER LOOKALIKE EX-HUSBAND, MICK JAGGER**

$\mathcal{C}$an you handle the fact that I don't love you?
**—DAVID BOWIE'S ANTIROMANCE MARRIAGE PROPOSAL TO ANGELA,
FUTURE MOTHER OF THEIR SON ZOWIE**

$\mathcal{M}$y wife was a model. Not a model wife.
**—ROD STEWART ON EX-WIFE RACHEL HUNTER**

$\mathcal{B}$esides the obvious age difference, he was obsessed with sports.
Almost the only thing that excited him—besides his music.
**—RACHEL HUNTER ON HER EX, NOT-SO-HOT ROD**

$\mathcal{H}$i, I'm Tommy—nice to touch you.  **—TOMMY LEE'S INTRODUCTORY
LINE TO FUTURE WIFE AND EX-WIFE HEATHER LOCKLEAR**

In some ways, rock stars are as childish as little boys and as chauvinistic as old men, even if they are kind of lovably irresistible.
—**PAMELA ANDERSON, FORMER WIFE OF TOMMY LEE**

I've never bought that open marriage thing. I've never seen it work. But that doesn't mean I believe in monogamy. Sleeping with someone else doesn't necessarily constitute an infidelity.
—**CARLY SIMON, FORMERLY MARRIED TO JAMES TAYLOR**

Divorced individuals, like brand-new lovers, are often embarrassed to be alone in the same room.    —**ELVIS PRESLEY**

Many great hatreds spring from great loves. . . .   —**"MAMA" CASS ELLIOT**

What we controlled or influenced but do so no more, we develop contempt for. What resists us, we begin to hate.    —**DUSTY SPRINGFIELD**

The cruelest lies are often told in silence.    —**ROBERT LOUIS STEVENSON**

Parting is not sweet sorrow but a dry panic.    —**JOHN STEINBECK**

In this society, it's like we expect men to be rough, aggressive, even violent. It's encouraged, it is tolerated. I thought my husband was not that unusual . . . then one day he held a gun to my head for what seemed eternity. Something like half an hour. After I survived that, I decided, I don't care what men are like or what wives are supposed to be like, I'm getting out of here.
—**NOW OPENLY GAY SINGER-COMPOSER JANIS IAN ("AT SEVENTEEN")**

The trouble with my ex-wife is she was a whore in the kitchen and a chef in bed.                                    —GROUCHO MARX

The average ex-wife, in the morning first thing, would terrify Hansel and Gretel.                                    —TOM ARNOLD

Men often judge women in the harshest terms and themselves not at all.          —LYNN REDGRAVE, WHO DIVORCED AFTER DISCOVERING THAT HER LONGTIME HUSBAND AND MANAGER HAD IMPREGNATED THEIR SON'S GIRLFRIEND

Weak women are drawn to difficult men; they may have a masochistic need for disaster or degradation. . . . At least one of Marlon's lady friends tried to kill herself after their breakup, and another one tried and succeeded. . . . His dark side is the whole other side of the moon, but as a man and actor he has been so respected that in the press there is no criticism of him.          —DIVORCÉE ANNA KASHFI BRANDO

My boyfriends don't talk about it while we're an item, and I don't discuss my breakups or my divorce. My personal life is private, but once in a while a happy tidbit sneaks out because when I'm in love I tend to be more expressive.          —JULIA ROBERTS

The d-words. I hate to talk about those. Dieting, divorce, and death. Anything else, I can handle. Including fat and even including the occasional, and wrong, bad review.          —SHELLEY WINTERS

They'd like me to write a book, and I'm like, What about? What could I write a book about? Books aren't my scene. But after I thought about it, I decided there's two subjects I'd someday like to write a book about. One's reincarnation, another's divorce—both deep and heavy subjects. But I'd have to die to write the one, and get divorced to write the other, and if I divorced her, Courtney [Love] would kill me.  **—KURT COBAIN OF NIRVANA**

I think they have a good idea in the Muslim world. All a man has to do to divorce is spin his wife around or walk around her, I'm not sure, and say three times, "I divorce thee." And it's over with. No muss, no fuss. Of course in Europe the bureaucrats wouldn't like it— no red tape involved. The feminists wouldn't either—women can't divorce their husbands.  **—PETER SELLERS**

The religious fundamentalists are so scary. They want America to scrap its laws and use the Bible instead, like they use the Koran in Arab countries. That means adultery on the part of a wife is instant grounds for divorce, and can be punished by stoning—to death. But adultery on the part of the husband is never grounds for divorce. In fact, nothing is. It just amazes me that there are female fundamentalists.

**—ELAYNE BOOSLER**

One of the drawbacks of divorce is the end of a reassuring daily household routine. Another is that one's wife acts as a sort of watch-dog against feminine intruders. You can't begin to imagine the number of ambitious actresses and other females who are drawn like magnets to a successful motion picture director no matter what his age or weight. Alma protects me against all that.   **—ALFRED HITCHCOCK**

ℛita [Hayworth] doesn't think I was a terrible husband . . . but you divorce a gorgeous, popular actress like Rita, and the media and the public think you must be an ogre. No matter the reality, you become an overnight brute or, at the least, a cad. "How could you leave such a beautiful woman?" I was scolded, reprimanded, accused, insulted . . . never mind who left who or why. And if I hadn't lived this long and had rather a colorful existence, if I had died after divorcing Rita or within five or ten years of doing so, I would be remembered solely as the man who made *Citizen Kane* and the man who divorced Rita Hayworth.                                                  —ACTOR-DIRECTOR ORSON WELLES

𝒟ivorcing Mary Pickford will make me the most hated and reviled man in America.                          —DOUGLAS FAIRBANKS SR. IN A LETTER TO HIS SON
(DFS WAS THE SECOND BUT MOST FAMOUS HUSBAND OF
"AMERICA'S SWEETHEART," WHO HAD THREE)

𝒜fter they divorced, I don't believe [playwright] Arthur Miller got alimony from Marilyn [Monroe]. But he managed to squeeze every penny from that matrimonial experience by writing a not very good play about it called *After the Fall*. If I ever get divorced, I would want to put it behind me, not put it before an audience, paying or otherwise.
                                    —BILLY WILDER, WHO DIRECTED MONROE TWICE

ℬeing in business with your husband isn't easy. . . . Our company was named after me, but I was his employee, I couldn't take a vacation without his permission, do anything outside the house without his permission. When we divorced, he sued me, and not just one lawsuit; it wasn't just a marriage ending, it was busting up a corporation, and money hurts men where they live.
                                    —CHER, FORMERLY OF SONNY AND CHER

Divorce can be a very hurtful, stupid, macho thing that a man does to a woman when he's tired of her or thinks that he's done with her.
—JOHN LENNON, ON HIS ONLY DIVORCE

One of my husbands and I, we weren't musically compatible. That may not sound serious if you're not in the music business. . . .
—PEGGY LEE

I had one fool husband was a hypochondriac. That's not a guy who likes needles or the bad stuff, that's a man what's always worrying if an ambulance'll take longer to reach your house than a pizza. One day he called for both of 'em, just to time them. That was one sorry hypochrondriac: The pizza got there first. And they got the order wrong—with anchovies. But the story has a happy ending: My ex ate the anchovies anyway, got sick, and took the ambulance to the hospital.
—MOMS MABLEY

It's lonely at the top, but you eat better. Especially if you're divorced and can eat whatever and whenever you want to, courtesy of your own professional cook.
—DAVID LETTERMAN

Our wedding vows, well, one thing we said was to "honor and respect each other's goals and ambitions." That was important. But one of my goals was more of a family life at home, and one of his was staying a party animal.
—CHRISTIE BRINKLEY ON THE LIFESTYLE CLASH WITH HER EX, BILLY JOEL

*I*f [Rod Stewart] wants to go out with a series of mindless, moronic young models rather than being with me and the children, I don't think I'm losing anything.  **—ALANA HAMILTON STEWART, WHOSE OTHER FAMOUS EX WAS ACTOR GEORGE HAMILTON**

*I*f you have a long-lasting and genuinely happy marriage, congratulations. But I think too many people's emotional lives or marriages are like deserts punctuated by very few and far-between palm trees. These are symbolic of beauty, growth, and nourishment. The less you seek happiness, the more you allow fear or convention to trap you, and the fewer palm trees you'll have.  **—KIM BASINGER**

*D*ivorce: a safety valve. One is vaguely pleased that it's there, in the background, but one hopes sincerely never to have to use it.
**—LAURENCE OLIVIER, WHO DIVORCED TWICE**

*D*ivorce has gotten a really bad rap, mainly thanks to overly organized religion. Yet it boils down to one undeniable fact: divorce means hope. For something better, more livable.  **—WOODY ALLEN**

*D*on't think many of the people that bad-mouth divorce aren't jealous. The moralists, of course, and also people who just haven't got the guts. Divorce is a bit scary—sometimes a lot. But if things are bad enough, have the self-respect to try and change the situation. Let's be thankful [that] after so many centuries, divorce is available to people without personal access to the pope.  **—CYNDI LAUPER**

After they circumcised David, they tossed out the wrong bit.
—IRENE MAYER SELZNICK (DAUGHTER OF MGM'S LOUIS B. MAYER)
ON EX-HUSBAND DAVID O. SELZNICK (PRODUCER OF *GONE WITH THE WIND*),
WHO LEFT HER FOR ACTRESS JENNIFER JONES

Relationships which do not end peacefully do not end in our lifetime.
—HINDU PHILOSOPHER RABINDRANATH TAGORE

# Lasting Marriage

❧

Keep your eyes wide open before marriage, half shut afterward.
—**BENJAMIN FRANKLIN**

Never go to bed mad. Stay up and fight. —**PHYLLIS DILLER**

Three ingredients to a successful marriage, in no particular order:
two people earning, yearning, and learning. —**SARAH JESSICA PARKER**

Most marriages last as long as they need to. . . . —**SHIRLEY MACLAINE**

Marriage is not just spiritual communion, it is also remembering to
take out the trash. —**DR. JOYCE BROTHERS**

Communication in marriage is all. Honest, frequent communication.
And choosing your arguments carefully. —**LUCILLE BALL**

Marriage is one long conversation, chequered by disputes.
—**ROBERT LOUIS STEVENSON**

The husband who wants a happy marriage should learn to keep his mouth shut and his checkbook open.  —GROUCHO MARX

Marriage isn't meant to make you happy. It's meant to make you married.  —MEL BROOKS

There is nothing more admirable than two people who see eye to eye keeping house as husband and wife, confounding their enemies, and delighting their friends.  —HOMER

One reason my marriage has lasted so long is I wanted to spite my wife's mother, who didn't give us a wedding present, she gave us three months. . . . Did you know, I just got back from a pleasure trip? I drove my mother-in-law to the airport.  —HENNY YOUNGMAN

Chains don't hold a marriage together. It's threads, hundreds of tiny threads which sew people together through the years. That's what makes a marriage last—more than passion or even sex.
—SIMONE SIGNORET, MARRIED TO YVES MONTAND UNTIL HER DEATH

Why fool around with hamburger when you have steak at home?
—PAUL NEWMAN, LONGTIME HUSBAND OF JOANNE WOODWARD
(HE DID ADD, "THAT DOESN'T MEAN IT'S ALWAYS TENDER")

Okay, so Brad [Pitt] is better-looking than me. He's better-looking than most people. But he dresses down. So I can dress up. That helps even things out.  —JENNIFER ANISTON *(FRIENDS)*

"Happily ever after" isn't an ending, it's a beginning. The beginning of all the work that goes into maintaining a marriage.
—ANGELINA JOLIE, WHOSE WEEKLY MARITAL MAINTENANCE WITH
BILLY BOB THORNTON INCLUDED HIS-AND-HERS MANICURES

The best way to start being a good wife is to impersonate one. Your mother or someone in the movies, a fictional heroine, whatever. Often, you find that you become what you're modeling yourself on.
—RUTH GORDON *(ROSEMARY'S BABY)*

A model husband is one who doesn't compare his wife to any other. Whether she's your first wife or your fourth, let her be the first wife that ever was—and praise her frequently for pioneering such a difficult role.   —ROBERT YOUNG *(FATHER KNOWS BEST)*

Don't be afraid to seek out a marriage counselor. One can really help. Going to one is not an admission of failure. Rather, it's proof that you care enough about your marriage to try and improve it.
—NATALIE WOOD, WHO MARRIED ROBERT WAGNER TWICE

I had suggested going to this marriage therapist, and then my husband found out the gentleman had never been married. I had to remind Robert—a Frenchman, yet—of Flaubert's dictum that the less you feel a thing, the more objective and fit you are to discuss and analyze it.   —NATALIE CANTOR, DAUGHTER OF EDDIE AND WIFE OF ROBERT
*(HOGAN'S HEROES)* CLARY, TO WHOM SHE WAS MARRIED UNTIL HER DEATH

All this talk about working on your marriage . . . how much work is enough if it doesn't work on its own, and how much is too much? It's supposed to be pleasant, for gosh sakes, not a graduate course.

—JERRY SEINFELD

Don't work on your marriage. Don't work on your husband. Work on yourself.

—YOKO ONO

It's okay to try and be a better wife if he's trying to be a better husband.

—MADONNA

A man must not be afraid to tell his wife if she's turning into his mother. You don't treat a man like a child. That cannot last.

—BRITISH PLAYWRIGHT JOHN OSBORNE *(LOOK BACK IN ANGER),* WHO HAD FIVE WIVES

If I were a sexist, I'd say what a lot of men think: A wife should be obscene and not heard. But I'm not a sexist man, so I'll just think it. Especially during hard times.

—AUTHOR HENRY MILLER, WHO ALSO HAD FIVE WIVES

For a man, sex is fundamental. Lots of marriages dissolve because he still wants it and she doesn't. Maybe she just used it as a lure. . . . I'm sorry, moralists, but the only way to find out if you and she are sexually compatible is to have plenty of sex before marriage. Isn't it worth it, if it makes it longer?

—JERRY SPRINGER

The only thing I like more than my wife is my money. And I'm not about to lose that to her and her lawyers, that's for damn sure. And you can quote me on that.

—ROCKER-ACTOR JON BON JOVI

$\mathcal{I}$ love being a man. I like shaving and I like [soccer]. But if I was saying who's superior, I'd say women. They look better. They last longer. And they're more compassionate. My wife [filmmaker Trudie Styler] agrees. —STING

$\mathcal{W}$ho wears the pants in this house? I do, and I also wash and iron them. —DENIS THATCHER, HUSBAND OF THEN-PRIME MINISTER MARGARET THATCHER

$\mathcal{T}$here is so little difference between husbands, you might as well keep the first. —WRITER ADELA ROGERS ST. JOHNS

$\mathcal{A}$ successful wife needs a sense of humor. She who laughs, lasts. —MARY TYLER MOORE

$\mathcal{D}$o you know why [new husband Michael Douglas] doesn't do weights any more? Because he has sacrificed his home gym for my closet. We have a Stair Master and stuff in there, but the rest had to go, and the closet still isn't big enough. —CATHERINE ZETA-JONES IN 2000

$\mathcal{J}$ust because I'm on *Sex and the City,* people think I'm this wild thing. But it's not like that. I met Matthew [Broderick] in 1991. We moved in together in 1992, then in 1997 we got married in a synagogue, 'cause we're each half Jewish. And we have a Border Collie named Sally. We're all very happy together. —SARAH JESSICA PARKER

$\mathcal{I}$'ve been married twenty-eight years, so I must be doing something right. . . . One important thing, besides love and romance, is accepting yourselves, individually, and accepting each other. As you are. No big makeovers, please. —SOAP ACTRESS PATRIKA DARBO

𝒥 married a man who is for me a wonderful companion, a fellow thinker and artist, and a good husband. Like most men, he has a wandering eye. He also, I am happy to say, has a very strong sense of guilt. **—SIMONE SIGNORET ON YVES MONTAND**

𝒥f someone is very special to you, is it really that important if every now and then he takes off and has a liaison with someone else? I mean, is it really catastrophic? **—SUSAN SARANDON, LONGTIME COMPANION OF YOUNGER ACTOR-DIRECTOR TIM ROBBINS**

𝓕idelity is possible. Anything is possible if you're stubborn and strong. But it's not that important. Traditional marriage is very outdated. I don't think people should live together the rest of their lives suppressing frustrations. **—MICHELLE PFEIFFER**

𝒥f you want to improve a friendship, use courtesy. If you want to improve a marriage, use love. **—BEATRIX POTTER, CHILDREN'S AUTHOR**

𝒪ne of my Academy Awards is from *The Diary of Anne Frank,* and Anne Frank said, or wrote, a wonderful thing. "How wonderful it is that nobody need wait a single moment before starting to improve the world." And that goes for all of us, in all situations, even marriage. **—SHELLEY WINTERS**

𝒯he secret to a successful and enduring marriage is loyalty. Loyalty can improve any relationship; certainly it is a requirement of friendship. **—SESSUE HAYAKAWA *(THE BRIDGE ON THE RIVER KWAI)***

We value loyalty in our pets. I think women value it in a husband. The sad thing is, a lot of husbands eventually find it annoying or intimidating in a wife. Even so, men, unlike women, demand loyalty.
—SONGWRITER LAURA NYRO

The key to a wonderful relationship isn't sex. It's friendship. And between two loving partners, it's more than friendship. It's being in love.
—ACTOR RAUL JULIA

Let's remember, a lasting marriage is one that lasts, not necessarily one that's happy. On the other hand, some people and a huge percentage of women, don't mind, or even like, being directed . . . being dominated. Independence can be frightening if you don't think you can cut it. —GEORGE TOBIAS (MR. KRAVITZ ON *BEWITCHED*), WHO NEVER MARRIED

Malcolm Lowry would rise early and go for a swim. His wife was only allowed to stir in the house when she heard the animal-like noises that he would make once he had entered his trancelike state of creation. —AUTHOR TERENCE BLACKER ON THE AUTHOR OF *UNDER THE VOLCANO*

John Galsworthy installed his wife in the room next door to his study and required her to play the piano quietly.
—TERENCE BLACKER ON THE BRITISH WRITER'S CREATIVITY RITUAL

For the last three years they've told her that I am not welcome in their homes. They are forcing Shirley to choose between her husband and her children. And that's not fair to her. —MARTY INGELS TO
*TV GUIDE* IN 2000; NONETHELESS HE AND SHIRLEY JONES, WHOSE THREE
SONS INCLUDE PATRICK AND SHAUN CASSIDY AND WHOSE STEPSON IS DAVID
CASSIDY, HAVE CONTINUED THEIR LONG-RUNNING MARRIAGE OF OPPOSITES

*I* never really felt at home in England. When I first set foot on American soil as a very young man, it came to me like a flash: This is what I like. Here I'd like to stay. And when I married an American, I hoped we would live in America. But as fate would have it, my wife hates America and only wants to live in France. That's the way it goes. —**THE DUKE OF WINDSOR, FORMER KING OF ENGLAND**

*I* married him for better or worse, but not for lunch.
—**THE DUCHESS OF WINDSOR [FORMERLY WALLIS SIMPSON], WHOSE BUSY SOCIAL LIFE WAS INVIOLABLE**

*I*t turns out that back in 1980, Hillary Clinton invested in sugar, hogs, and cattle. She got the idea from watching her husband eat breakfast. —**CONAN O'BRIEN**

*S*teve [Parker] lived in Japan and I was mostly in Hollywood or on location. I had several affairs, he had his relationships. We knew and understood that. Our marriage lasted a long time and was right for us. If we'd been intolerant of each other's emotional and physical needs, the marriage would have ended that much sooner.
—**SHIRLEY MACLAINE ON HER ONE AND ONLY HUSBAND**

*S*ex, in or out of marriage, breeds so many insecurities. . . . When all's said and done, sex is no way to hold on to somebody. Except figuratively speaking. —**BLONDE BOMBSHELL JAYNE MANSFIELD**

Once sex peters down to a realistic level that pleases both partners, or even if it peters out altogether—so long as the two don't feel guilty about it—that's when marriage becomes more comfortable and—something young people cannot yet believe—more happy and content. Once sex isn't at the forefront, that's when you can know whether or not your marriage is for the rest of your lives.
—GARY MORTON, LUCILLE BALL'S SECOND AND LONGER-LASTING
(UNTIL HER DEATH) HUSBAND

Actors make lousy husbands . . . no, I should say they make more temporary husbands. I mean, they're forever surrounded by girls who are beautiful and have no scruples. So they're always ready to trade in for a new model. Or actress. Or bimbo. Or whatever.
—ACTRESS COLLEEN DEWHURST, FORMER WIFE OF GEORGE C. SCOTT

My late wife Maggy and I had a lovely life together. . . . We had no children . . . my costumes are my children. The best thing is a marital friendship. . . . They say Hollywood is full of temptation, but I never felt it. Besides, really, there is temptation everywhere, if you look for it.
—HOLLYWOOD DESIGNER JEAN LOUIS, WHO AFTER MAGGY'S DEATH ENTERED
INTO A PLATONIC MARRIAGE WITH HER BEST FRIEND, LORETTA YOUNG

Love and tennis keep us going. We're a team.  —ANDRE AGASSI ON WIFE
AND TENNIS CHAMP STEFFI GRAF (PREVIOUSLY, AGASSI WAS MARRIED TO
NONATHLETE BROOKE SHIELDS)

Times have changed, and ladies who have careers tend to seem more interesting to men. I find Elizabeth more fascinating, magnetic, and delightfully frustrating than ever I would a little housewife waiting for me at the end of each day. Housewives expect you to keep regular, accountable hours.

—RICHARD BURTON, WHO MARRIED ELIZABETH TAYLOR TWICE

A husband in the same business makes for better compatibility, I think. At the least, he should be in some business. —ELIZABETH TAYLOR
ON FIRST HUSBAND NICKY HILTON, AN ALCOHOLIC, WIFE-BEATING PLAYBOY
WHO LIVED OFF HIS HOTELIER FATHER CONRAD HILTON

The danger in being in the same profession, let alone working together, is that after hours you don't always want to talk shop. And if a project you do together fails expectations, it can cast a pall over his reaction to you. —SONDRA LOCKE, SEVERAL OF WHOSE FILMS COSTARRED
AND WERE DIRECTED BY LONGTIME LOVER CLINT EASTWOOD

What counts in making a happy marriage is not so much how compatible you are, but how you deal with incompatibility.

—LEO TOLSTOY, IN PREDIVORCE DAYS

I'm rich and my wife comes from a classy background and has a healthy respect for money and its responsibilities. That's a marital bond that goes a long way. —*TIME* MAGAZINE COFOUNDER HENRY LUCE,
MARRIED TO PLAYWRIGHT CLARE BOOTH LUCE *(THE WOMEN)*

$\mathcal{P}$eople in England tend to marry within their own class. But actresses pick up and wed their hairdressers or bodyguards or a lorry [truck] driver. Such pretend-unions can't last.  **—UK WRITER ANTHONY BURGESS, ALLUDING TO BARBRA STREISAND (WHO DIDN'T ACTUALLY WED JON PETERS), ROSEANNE, AND ELIZABETH TAYLOR**

$\mathcal{O}$nly two things are necessary to keep one's wife happy. One is to let her think she is having her own way, and the other is to let her have it.  **—PRESIDENT LYNDON B. JOHNSON, WHO WED THE WEALTHY LADY BIRD**

$\mathcal{T}$o keep your marriage brimming
With love in the loving cup,
Whenever you're wrong, admit it,
Whenever you're right, shut up.
  **—POET OGDEN NASH, IN "A WORD TO HUSBANDS" (1957)**

$\mathcal{E}$very politician should have been born an orphan and remain a bachelor.  **—LADY BIRD JOHNSON, WIDOW OF THE THIRTY-SIXTH U.S. PRESIDENT**

$\mathcal{B}$ehind every successful man is a surprised woman.
  **—MARYON PEARSON, WIFE OF A FORMER CANADIAN PRIME MINISTER**

$\mathcal{S}$ome of my friends said, "But he's older. He's a director . . . he's French, how will you get along?" But I didn't marry a nationality, I married an individual. . . . What further cemented our marriage was, of course, our daughter.  **—CANDICE BERGEN, WIDOW OF LOUIS MALLE**

My wife is fiercely beautiful, French, and largely in charge. She's very straight with me. Sometimes it hurts, but it's usually what I need. **—EWAN MCGREGOR *(MOULIN ROUGE, TRAINSPOTTING)***

Nancy was determined to give me a son. . . . It took a while, but I never doubted she would. Nancy usually gets what she wants.

**—RONALD REAGAN**

Marriage is marriage is marriage, as Gertrude Stein might have said. . . . Writing is something I do to feel. But I'd feel hollow and dead if I couldn't have children.

**—POET SYLVIA PLATH, A PARENT AND EVENTUAL SUICIDE**

Marriage without children is like ice cream without a cone. It's still tasty, but it's a different setting and mood, and there's no contrast. And with the cone, you can pretend it's in itself a small meal.

**—ESTELLE GETTY *(THE GOLDEN GIRLS)***

As far as I'm concerned, the only reason to get married today is to have kids. I know women aren't supposed to say they don't want children, but I'm being honest. When I was a kid, I sometimes thought I disliked everybody. When I grew up, I realized I only disliked kids. **—SHIRLEY HEMPHILL *(WHAT'S HAPPENIN')***

Generally speaking, women who marry give up their individual identity and their limited freedom in exchange for security and protection. Men marry, giving up some or much of their freedom and a sex life of choice for conformity and in order to beget heirs.

**—GEORGE PEPPARD *(THE A-TEAM)***

Romance isn't as easy once there are children in the picture. To my mind, there are fewer regrets and resentments later if a couple long and thoroughly enjoy their life together before children are conceived.

—MICK JAGGER

I blindfolded my wife—it's not what you think—and I led her into the bathroom. I'd already filled up the tub, sprinkled in rose petals, and lit 300 candles in there. Who says romance isn't fun? Or hard work?

—ACTOR HUGH JACKMAN

You want a cheerful, long marriage? Separate bathrooms. And don't ever let your loved one squeeze your toothpaste.

—GEORGE BURNS

Try not to ever see your wife in the bathroom. Or coming out of one. There is no greater romance-killer than shared bathrooms or bathroom details. In my house, we have lots of bathrooms. One toaster, but all the bathrooms you'd ever want.

—BOB HOPE

If you can help it, don't always eat together. A little separation helps . . . it's not exactly a pleasure or a romantic thrill to watch your husband making his way through three meals a day in front of you.

—PIONEERING FEMALE COMIC TOTIE FIELDS

You're my best friend, my soul mate, and the one I'll spend eternity with. I don't know what I did to deserve you, but I thank God you came into my life.     —WHAT BRAD PITT SAID AT AN EARLY-2002 PARTY HE THREW
FOR WIFE JENNIFER ANISTON; AFTER TOASTING HER, HE GAVE HER A PLATINUM
BRACELET AND LOCKET WITH A PHOTO OF THEM ON ONE OF THEIR EARLY DATES

No big deal. It's just a thing of blood. It's a romantic gesture. Really, truly, we're just the sometimes odd couple next door. Just normal people, not freaks. —BILLY BOB THORNTON, EXPLAINING THE LOCKETS HE AND WIFE ANGELINA JOLIE WORE AROUND THEIR NECKS THAT CONTAIN SOME OF EACH OTHER'S BLOOD

You cannot judge a marriage from the outside. Some brief ones are quite happy. Some lengthy ones are filled with forbearance and pain. A long one is often anything but monogamous. . . . Sometimes when we help celebrate a silver or golden wedding anniversary, we're merely paying lip service, putting quantity above quality. So why judge at all? —LEONARD BERNSTEIN

It really was a marriage . . . decades, but for me it was a lifetime of devotion. We had everything between us. Everything but a contract. . . . I never minded she was about thirty years older than me, 'cause we hit it off right away, we always had a barrel of laughs. Even in the last years, when I had to nurse her, it was fun mixed with heartache.

Why did we last? Because she was always Miss West to me, and I was there to help her whenever I could. Her career was bigger than her, and her image was bigger than the two of us. —FORMER MUSCLEMAN PAUL NOVAK, WHOM MAE WEST PUBLICLY PRESENTED AS A FAVORED ESCORT RATHER THAN HER PRIVATE MAINSTAY

He doesn't compete with me, and I don't compete with him, and we don't pay no mind to any of the gossip about us. —DOLLY PARTON ON HER MOSTLY LONG-DISTANCE BUT LONGTIME MARRIAGE TO CARL DEAN

We live apart half the year, so there's not enough time together for him to get in my hair or me to get into his—what's left of it.
—ESTELLE GETTY DURING THE 1980S TV HIT *THE GOLDEN GIRLS*

My wife has a sense of humor. She tolerates me while making it seem like she's lucky to have me. —LARRY HAGMAN

She knows when to baby me and when to let me be. She's a great mood reader, and as an actor, do I have moods! —MICHAEL J. FOX

Chains and children—both start with a ch. Ball and chain . . . I think kids give a man balls and a wife gives him chains, and all that keeps you bundled up together. Unless it's too, too terrible. —SAM KINISON

I'm not much of a celebrity to my wife. She knows me too well. . . . It's my children's hands that bring me down to earth.
—ACTOR DAVID DUKES

My publicity and the public raise me sky high. My wife helps keep my feet planted firmly on the ground. —TOM *(HAPPY DAYS)* BOSLEY

We live on foreign soil, although we love France and America. But we are both Italian and do not live in Italy. It makes us more close.
—SOPHIA LOREN, MARRIED TO FORMER FILM PRODUCER CARLO PONTI

Gloria and I remember how it was. We often remember how it was for us. I married late, but now I'm so damn old, we have a lot of past together. We do live in the present, but we enjoy and share our rather felicitous past. —JAMES STEWART

𝔐arlo [Thomas] and I share the same sociopolitical outlook. We're involved in the present . . . we look beyond ourselves. I guess we find each other exciting, just as we find life exciting. —PHIL DONAHUE

𝔉irst marriages tend to be for duty. Second marriages tend to be for pleasure. . . . You tell me. . . . —PHIL DONAHUE, WHOSE FIVE CHILDREN WERE VIA HIS PRE-MARLO WIFE

𝔚hen you lived to forty and had a twenty-year marriage, that was that. In this era, you live to be eighty, so what in hell's wrong with two or three twenty-year marriages? —SEAN PENN

ℐ know from endless conversations that a vast amount of people find comfort in the merging of identities that is a typical marriage. They become part of a unit, and several ladies have admitted to me they like losing themselves in either a man's identity or in the larger identity of a couple. As an actor, I can relate to that; I like losing myself in different roles. . . . Most actors, particularly rich and famous ones, don't want to merge their identities with anyone or anything else's. But who says actors are happier than average people? Some of the unhappiest people are big stars. —SOAP ACTOR JOEL CROTHERS
(*DARK SHADOWS, ANOTHER WORLD,* AND *EDGE OF NIGHT,* AMONG OTHERS)

[John F.] Kennedy's only complaint about Jackie in all the years I ever knew him was that she spent too much money. . . . "That Jackie," he'd yell. "She's unbelievable. She absolutely does not appreciate the value of money. Thinks she can keep on spending it forever. God, she's driving me crazy—absolutely crazy. I tell you . . . George, she's run through all the government funds and is drawing on my personal account. If the taxpayers ever found out what she's spending, they'd drive me out of office."   **—FORMER U.S. SENATOR GEORGE SMATHERS**

Her husband says that Jackie Onassis suffers from chronic affluenza.
**—COLUMNIST JOYCE HABER ON GREEK TYCOON ARISTOTLE ONASSIS, WHO NONETHELESS TOOK PRIDE IN THE AMOUNTS OF MONEY HIS WIFE SPENT**

I earn, she spends. Lucre will keep us together.
**—DONALD TRUMP ON THEN-WIFE IVANA**

Victoria Principal married a plastic surgeon. Isn't that convenient . . . and free.   **—JOAN RIVERS (THE EX *DALLAS* STAR NOW HAS HER OWN LINE OF BEAUTY PRODUCTS AND IS STILL AESTHETICALLY MARRIED)**

[Carole Lombard] was married to [Clark] Gable . . . I did a whole series of shows with her, and I said, "How are you and Gable getting along?" and she said, "He's the lousiest lay I ever had." **—GROUCHO MARX (LOMBARD ENJOYED HER OUTDOORS LIFESTYLE WITH HOLLYWOOD'S "KING")**

Bud [Abbott] loves his wife and he's got three dogs. I don't love mine and I've got two children. You figure it out.   **—LOU COSTELLO**

We share a lot of secrets, Charles and I. **—ELSA LANCHESTER, A.K.A. "THE BRIDE OF FRANKENSTEIN," NOT REFERRING TO HER LONGTIME HUSBAND'S CLOSETED HOMOSEXUALITY**

[Prince] Charles is finally with someone as shallow and pretentious as he is. Legal or not, this relationship will endure—they began when they were very young. . . . Diana was just too honest for him.
**—BRITISH COLUMNIST RICHARD GULLY ON THE CROWN PRINCE AND HIS MISTRESS CAMILLA PARKER-BOWLES**

I think I'm in so many of his pictures because no other actress would work with him. **—BRITISH ACTRESS JILL IRELAND, MARRIED TO COSTAR CHARLES BRONSON UNTIL HER DEATH FROM CANCER**

There really are a lot of marriages that survive because the wife has somehow decided she will hang on to the man or the position come hell or high water. **—BETTE DAVIS**

Sadly, the words "marriage" and "humiliation" are not strangers to each other. Particularly from the distaff side of things.
**—ESTHER ROLLE *(GOOD TIMES)***

Just ignore what I'm placing between you. She's very beautiful. Very stupid. She's just arrived from England, so Jack will want to have first crack at it. **—GORE VIDAL, CLAIMING TO QUOTE JACKIE KENNEDY AS SHE SEATED HIM NEAR JFK AT A WHITE HOUSE DINNER**

Kathie Lee Gifford just discovered what the whole country knows—that there is no Tuesday night football.
**—COMEDIAN NORM CROSBY**

She gushes endlessly . . . and her fetish about her husband, . . . It's like the gal who says how much her husband loves her, [until] you have to remind her that a real Frenchman loves his bidet too.

—GEORGE PEPPARD ON KATHIE LEE

If my wife Henny stepped out [cheated] on me, would I take the dear old thing back? Of course I would! What's sex got to do with our happily married life together?

—JIM BACKUS (THURSTON HOWELL III OF *GILLIGAN'S ISLAND*)

Thank God I've had a few wives who tolerated my infidelity, occasional though it has been. . . . The ladies are a more forgiving breed. When I found out my first wife [actress Margaret Sullavan] was seeing another man, it broke my heart. It effectively ended our marriage too.

—HENRY FONDA

My husband has done what a great number of husbands eventually do. Of course it hurts. It would hurt more to end what we still do have together . . . because so much of life is choosing the better of two alternatives.

—GERALDINE PAGE, MARRIED TO ACTOR RIP TORN (THEIR MAILBOX READ TORN PAGE)

Not all men cheat. Let's not generalize so wildly. If a man does, then for decency's sake, for her sake, he'd better keep it a secret. But if the wife finds out about it, then it's her turn, and she may as well go out and have an affair of her own.

—BETTE MIDLER

$\mathcal{I}$ found out the guy I was with, my steady, regular guy, was two-timing me. As fate would have it, soon after that I bumped into a guy I'd dated years back—such a big crush. What'd I do? I dated him again—I won't say more than that. But it made me feel a whole lot better, 'stead of moping and feeling sorry for myself.

—**SINGER MINNIE RIPPERTON ("LOVING YOU")**

$\mathcal{I}$ could barely handle it if my husband had a woman on the side. But if he had another man? How could I hope to compete with that?

—**ACTRESS MAUREEN O'SULLIVAN, MARRIED TO DIRECTOR JOHN FARROW (PARENTS OF ACTRESSES MIA AND TISA)**

$\mathcal{I}$ discovered that my first wife was a lesbian. That sort of thing has a very discouraging effect on a young man. . . . I was more careful the second time out. I think so many first marriages are predicated on a passing fancy—or a passing fanny. —**ALAN NAPIER, WHO PLAYED ALFRED THE BUTLER ON TV'S *BATMAN* SERIES**

$\mathcal{W}$henever a first marriage lasts, I imagine it's because of incredible good luck or incredible stubbornness.

—**MADONNA, DURING HER SECOND MARRIAGE**

$\mathcal{I}$ think second marriages prosper because all too often the parents of the bride or groom, or both, have a hand in the first one.

—**BILLY JOEL**

$\mathcal{I}$t's very simple. For those who remarry, the second time around is the charm because we're older and wiser. What do kids in heat know? —**GARY MORTON, LUCILLE BALL'S SECOND AND FINAL HUSBAND**

Warren has his imperfections. Thank goodness for them! Living with a saint would be worse than being one. . . . We try to be perfect parents . . . but I'm not sure very many people would really want a perfect mate. **—ANNETTE BENING, WIFE OF WARREN BEATTY**

I'm married four decades now, very happily. It's her. I'm not the perfect husband—no debate there—but she's the perfect wife.
**—MARTIN SHEEN** *(THE WEST WING)*

My aim is to follow in my dad's footsteps. To go from wild to mild—just take that w, turn it around, and you got an m.
**—SON CHARLIE SHEEN, FORMER BAD BOY AND HEIDI FLEISS CLIENT**

Happiness is having a large, loving, caring, close-knit family—in another city. . . . Contentment is knowing your wife's nearby and so's the next meal. **—GEORGE BURNS, HUSBAND OF GRACIE ALLEN**

There's a French saying that to learn a new language is to live a new life. It's proving true for me and Vanessa [Paradis], and now I'm studying the language harder than ever. This, I'm convinced, is for keeps . . . it's new and wonderful. **—EXPECTANT FATHER OF TWO JOHNNY DEPP IN 2002 (HIS LIFE PARTNER IS A FRENCHWOMAN), LIVING IN FRANCE**

It was wonderful, and the reason it outlasted many [legal] marriages was that neither of us felt trapped. We were together because we wanted to be. **—FARRAH FAWCETT, REFLECTING ON HER LENGTHY RELATIONSHIP WITH RYAN O'NEAL**

Sometimes the kids say they want us to get married. . . . Kurt and I have it so great, we feel why tamper with it? It couldn't get any better for us. **—GOLDIE HAWN, LONGTIME COMPANION OF KURT RUSSELL**

My marriage to Tony and my nonmarriage to Franco were both big human adventures . . . both felicitous. I did not feel as bound to Franco, I didn't feel the same weight of other people's expectations—and when his eye wandered, I resented it fractionally less.

**—VANESSA REDGRAVE, WHO HAD TWO DAUGHTERS BY DIRECTOR TONY RICHARDSON AND A SON BY *CAMELOT* COSTAR FRANCO NERO**

There are worse betrayals than the sexual kind. A man may be cheating on you in his mind, turning the love to hate or contempt. . . . Some men use extramarital conquests as a weapon. For most, it is a weakness, like eating too much candy is for some women.

**—FASHION DESIGNER GABRIELLE "COCO" CHANEL**

We had a meeting of minds, of wit, a convergence of lifestyles and old age. I would have stayed with her until I died, gladly. . . . Why she did what she did, I cannot and will not explain. The knowledge of it shattered me. Had I found out while she was alive, I don't know if I would have chosen [divorce]. **—VINCENT PRICE, WIDOWER OF ACTRESS CORAL BROWNE, WHO COMPLAINED OFTEN TO FRIENDS THAT SHE HAD TO DO WITHOUT DUE TO PRICE'S STINGINESS; AFTER SHE DIED, IT WAS FOUND SHE HAD A SECRET FORTUNE, REPORTEDLY LARGER THAN HIS**

*I* could understand my wife looking at other men. In her place, I would too. I think the real disloyalty wouldn't automatically be a fling or something, it would be talking against your spouse behind their back. That would hurt much more.

**—ROTUND COMIC ACTOR JOHN CANDY**

*My* current relationship has outlasted my marriages for a number of reasons, most of them personal. And I think what's between you and your significant other should remain personal, your own little world, and a retreat from the more public arena of your professional life. Privacy nurtures relationships, I have found.

**—TV AND FILM ACTRESS STOCKARD CHANNING**

*A* private life is, by its very definition, not something one discusses publicly. Yet very few people in Hollywood decline to dissect their private lives for the media and the paying public. Those few who do guard their private lives are usually happily married or gay.

**—FORMER JAMES BOND ROGER MOORE**

*I* became less ambitious once I fell in love. I gather that, from what people and history show, anyone who's ruthlessly ambitious, like where their career is first and last, that's who's gonna have an unhappy marriage, or a bunch of them.    **—KURT COBAIN**

*Few* lips would be moved to song if they would find a sufficiency of kissing.    **—RUDYARD KIPLING, THEORIZING THAT MANY ARTISTS ARE THWARTED IN LOVE**

Robert Browning, during the first three years of his celebrated marriage to Elizabeth Barrett, wrote one poem . . . which makes me wonder about the marriage of the prolific horror novelist Anne Rice.
                                                    **—HISTORIAN MARTIN GREIF**

You can get good advice about marriage, but is it right for your marriage? Maybe a beautiful poem about love is more relevant. And helpful. But maybe not. Depends whether one's willing to listen to advice, let alone act on it.                    **—DEBBIE REYNOLDS**

I always pass on good advice. It is the only thing I ever do with it. It is never of any use to oneself.                    **—OSCAR WILDE**

My advice is, think of divorce, if you must, but never use the word. Don't use threats, and don't make divorce into a possibility by verbalizing it.                    **—DIANA ROSS**

My wife couldn't divorce me. I'm her credit card, she's a shopaholic. She'll buy anything that's marked down. Yesterday she brought home two dresses and an escalator.                    **—HENNY YOUNGMAN**

I would never have the heart to divorce my wife. She's so optimistic. Yesterday she was at the beauty shop for two hours—and that was just for the estimate.                    **—HENNY YOUNGMAN**

Divorce? Never. But murder often!          **—DAME SYBIL THORNDIKE, WHEN ASKED IF SHE'D EVER CONSIDERED DIVORCE DURING HER LENGTHY MARRIAGE TO SIR LEWIS CASSON**

The very fact that we make such a to-do over golden weddings indicates our amazement at human endurance. The celebration is more in the nature of a reward for stamina.   **—ACTOR-AUTHOR ILKA CHASE**

Well, my present relationship with Jonathan [Thomas] is going on twenty-eight years. I tend to have long-term relationships.
**—PLAYWRIGHT EDWARD ALBEE *(WHO'S AFRAID OF VIRGINIA WOOLF?)***

My wife is my best friend and we spend a lot of time talking. If we have problems, we try and sort them out. . . . It's great when you have a long-term relationship. You have something that is very valuable to the both of you. It's our friendship that transcends a lot of stuff and gives both of us strength.
**—WRITER-PRODUCER STEPHEN J. CANNELL *(THE A-TEAM)***

May 8 [2002] will be our thirty-fifth anniversary—of our wedding. On paper. But we were together four years before that. That's certainly a part of our relationship.
**—ANN-MARGRET, MARRIED TO ROGER SMITH, FORMER ACTOR**

We'll be celebrating our fifty-fifth anniversary on May 15 [2002]. The secret? I found the right person.
**—FYVUSH FINKEL *(PICKET FENCES, BOSTON PUBLIC)***

𝒥 think gay marriages are often lengthy because there's less resentment. The two people—two men or two women—are peers, and nobody has an expected "role." As in women's work, who's the head of the house, who has to do this, who isn't allowed to do that. . . . It's two individuals, not two people forced into slots whether they like it or not. —SIR ELTON JOHN

𝒴ou notice in restaurants how often straight couples don't seem to communicate? Gay people do, even if they've been together for decades. Because we have the same interests. Men and women tend to have different, separate interests. —DAN BUTLER *(FRASIER)*

𝒯he law doesn't keep us together. Our love keeps us together, law or not. —FASHION CRITIC MR. BLACKWELL ON LIFE PARTNER ROBERT SPENCER, WHOM HE MET IN 1949

𝒲hen most people think marriage, they see a bride and a groom in their traditional costumes. They don't necessarily see two people in love who wish to share their lives. People have to get used to the idea of gay marriage. In several European countries, including France, it's already a legal reality. —ELLEN DEGENERES

𝒮ecretly, we wish anyone we love will think exactly the way we do. —WRITER KIM CHERNIN

𝒲ell, he was quite wealthy and I've always liked to shop. . . . It's very expensive to be me. —ANNA NICOLE SMITH, WIDOW OF AN OCTOGENARIAN, EXPLAINING HOW SHE SPENT $6.7 MILLION ON JEWELRY, CLOTHES, AND HOMES DURING THEIR FOURTEEN-MONTH MARRIAGE

There is probably nothing like living together for blinding people to each other.   **—IVY COMPTON-BURNETT**

The sign of a good marriage is that everything is debatable and challenged; nothing is turned into law or policy. The rules, if any, are known only to the two players, who seek no public trophies.
**—WRITER AND EDUCATOR CAROLYN HEILBRUN**

It takes a long time to be really married. One marries many times at many levels within a marriage. If you have more marriages than you have divorces within the marriage, you're lucky and you stick it out.   **—ACTRESS RUBY DEE**

Believe me, if there is some secret formula to making a marriage work, it's something most men do not know. It's the wives who know. And it's the husbands who, for better or worse, decide to end it, regardless.   **—DIRECTOR JOHN HUSTON, WHO HAD FIVE WIVES**

When you educate a man you educate an individual. When you educate a woman you educate a whole family.   **—PART OF A SPEECH BY CHARLES D. MCIVER, DELIVERED AT THE NORTH CAROLINA COLLEGE FOR WOMEN**

Successful marriage is an art that can only be learned with difficulty. But it gives pride and satisfaction, like any other expertness that is hard won.   **—DR. BENJAMIN SPOCK**

𝒜 man is either a better husband the second time around, or he's unquestionably worse. He either learns from his mistakes or he compounds them, rather like the abused child who becomes an abusive parent. Human nature being what it is, too often the victim of a bad first marriage is the second wife. **—PRODUCER JULIA PHILLIPS**

ℳarriage is like plastic surgery. Don't do it for relatives or for your career or for what others will think. Do it only if you really desire it. Otherwise you won't be happy with it. **—VICTORIA PRINCIPAL *(DALLAS)*, WHO MARRIED A PLASTIC SURGEON**

𝐼 could have been developing a long, loving relationship with another bloke, which is my natural inclination. Instead, I avoided that, and then I married a female, thinking I could change. None of which made anybody happy. Remember, if you don't let us marry each other, we instead marry your daughters. **—SIR ELTON JOHN**

𝒯he basis of a good affair is lusting, while the basis of a good marriage is liking. When the lust's spent, think of the long haul. . . . **—COMEDIAN KATHY GRIFFIN**

𝒞an he say "I'm sorry" when he ought to? If he can, there's hope for a long run. **—CYNTHIA NIXON *(SEX AND THE CITY)***

𝐼t helps if your mate has more than a bit of the boy in him. I don't mean irresponsible or immature, I mean the little boy in him hasn't died or been smothered. There's charm and sweetness in a man's inner boy. **—YOKO ONO, WIDOW OF JOHN LENNON**

Eddie Albert is my handsome, charming gringo. . . . I'm very proud to be Mexican, and Mexico has had one of the great cultures in world history, but I did not want a Mexican husband. A Mexican man, most of the time he just wants a servant or a mistress, and sometimes they are the same person—his wife! With an American man, there is the possibility of [being] equals. With a Mexicano, forget it! —MARGO *(LOST HORIZON)*, WHO WAS MARRIED TO THE *GREEN ACRES* STAR UNTIL HER DEATH

Some husbands don't say I love you very often. But as we all know, actions speak louder than words or declarations.

—BETTY WHITE *(THE GOLDEN GIRLS)*

Lots of men say I love you to their wives and actually mean it. After all, men love their cars too. They "love" sports. "Love" is such an easy word; it's too easy. The proof of love is good treatment. In a word: kindness. No kindness, no love. —ACTRESS EILEEN HECKART

To handle yourself, use your head. To handle your beloved, use your heart. —ANONYMOUS

It's whatever works for the two of you, whatever you agree on. My good friends Robert Sterling and Anne Jeffreys, beautiful couple, literally—if you've ever seen them on *Topper*. Anne decided to retain her looks; she still looks great. Bob let his hair go white and he eats what he wants. Anne loves to go out to parties—and I'm her escort—while Bob prefers to stay at home, watch TV, read, snooze, do whatever, or do nothing.

But you know something? When Anne returns home, she and Bob talk and they laugh. They're so happy to see each other again—and I'm very happy for them.   **—ACTOR AND SOCIALITE CESAR ROMERO**

A happy marriage takes two people. Happy, relatively independent people. The wife who keeps embracing you, who is too needy, becomes a clinging vine. She needs outside interests, she needs strength from within herself. Nobody can get everything they want or need from another human being.

**—UK WRITER ANTHONY BURGESS *(A CLOCKWORK ORANGE)***

Successful marriage requires successful individuals. They should be happy together, and they should be happy at those times when they are apart.   **—TIM ALLEN *(HOME IMPROVEMENT)***

Even if my marriage is falling apart and my children are unhappy and my spouse is unhappy, there is still a part of me that says, "God! This is fascinating!"   **—WRITER JANE SMILEY**

That old maxim: There's no place like home. This is so greeting-card. There are lots of places like home. But there's no place, whether you travel near or far, like your own bed. That is your private, comfy, inviolate nest for two.   **—TONI COLLETTE *(MURIEL'S WEDDING, THE SIXTH SENSE)***

$\mathcal{W}$e travel a lot . . . and sometimes we're glad to return home, sometimes not so glad. But "There's no place like home"? The real meaning of "home," in my opinion, is any place where the two of us are alone together. By now, we are each other's home. **—MICHAEL CAINE**

$\mathcal{S}$eems like we're always working and traveling, but everywhere we go, Terri and me, we got one huge interest in common—apart from our daughter Bindi—and that's animals, the world's wildlife, and preserving it. We're so dedicated to that, and so also to each other. It's all so organic—loving animals and loving each other.

**—STEVE IRWIN, A.K.A. "THE CROCODILE HUNTER"**

$\mathcal{W}$omen are more interesting when they have backbone and stand up for themselves. Doormats may be useful, but they grow dull fast. I've reached the conclusion that women should raise more hell and fewer roses. **—CARROLL O'CONNOR *(ALL IN THE FAMILY)***

$\mathcal{I}$f a man's thirty minutes late for lunch with his wife, he's just late. But if a woman puts her husband on hold for three minutes when he calls her at the office, she's ruthless or insensitive. You know what? So what. If you ignore these labels people automatically use, you'll be happier in your relationships and within yourself—and you'll live longer, which is the best revenge. **—KATHY NAJIMY**

𝔉red Astaire's longtime wife Phyllis was a little tiny woman. She'd been previously married, already had a son, and she was insanely jealous of Fred. She didn't let him dance with Ginger Rogers at parties—she was insanely jealous of Fred. He wasn't allowed to kiss Ginger Rogers—on the screen either! I don't think Phyllis needed to worry, because I don't think Fred wanted to kiss Ginger anyhow, or anybody else. **—FRIEND AND HOLLYWOOD HOSTESS JEAN HOWARD**

𝔏ouis B. Mayer ordered Nelson Eddy to marry. Eddy agreed, but he didn't want a virgin bride or some insatiable creature, and Mayer understood. Sometimes the least sexual marriages last the longest. . . . Mayer found him an older divorcée who'd been married to a movie director—she was wise to the ways of Tinseltown, she was not sexually demanding or needful, and she was pleased to live the comfortable life of a movie star's life. She was satisfied, Eddy was satisfied, the studio was satisfied, the public was satisfied. **—SIR NOEL COWARD**

𝔜ou can always tell the gay actors. They're the ones who have the plain or ugly wives. Or live with an ugly girl. Look at Tyrone Power or Rock Hudson, to mention two I can legally name. Or that famous TV star or that homely male singer. Besides, most of the gays in Hollywood are good-looking. . . . In real life, gay men get handsome men and straight men get beautiful women. Of course the irony is that these pretend marriages can outlast the genuine thing where the straight actor sheds his wife for a younger model or actress. **—ANNE BAXTER *(ALL ABOUT EVE)* IN THE 1970S**

You know Bette Midler? Big talent but a face like a lemon. Have you seen her husband? He makes her look almost beautiful. These star broads don't marry for love, they marry for contrast.
**—SAM KINISON (AS OF THIS WRITING, MIDLER REMAINS HAPPILY MARRIED)**

Without naming names, I will admit I find it incredible when a stunningly beautiful woman is married to an ugly man, regardless of his age. Such a woman can get any man she wants, and not all rich men are old or plain. I believe such females want to be the couple's sole, shining star. Isn't that called the Beauty and the Beast Syndrome?   **—JULIE WALTERS *(BILLY ELLIOTT)***

Grace Kelly . . . arrogant, anti-Semitic, snobbish, and alcoholic, and talk about social climbing! . . . We all know that Aristotle Onassis, who owned the Monte Carlo casino, ordered Prince Rainier to marry a Hollywood blonde for the publicity and tourism. It was rumored that Rainier almost chose Marilyn Monroe. If he had, no doubt she too would have been immortalized by the media as virginal, talented, and a nonaddict. . . . At least Marilyn wasn't a hypocrite. Unlike Grace she didn't pretend to be a sanctimonious virgin.
**—ANNE BAXTER, AN OSCAR WINNER FOR *THE RAZOR'S EDGE***

Poor Jack Benny. He was Lucille Ball's neighbor, and she knew that he was trapped in that marriage of his. Till death did him part. The older she got, the more dictatorial Mary Livingstone became. But she had a hold on him. It had been a marriage of convenience, and eventually those grow awfully inconvenient.
**—GAY ACTOR CESAR ROMERO (LUCY'S FRIEND AND DANCING PARTNER),**
**WHO RESISTED INDUSTRY PRESSURE TO WED**

*I*t's strange, and if you think about it, deliberate, but the media fed the public all the details about Truman Capote's friendships and feuds with famous [female] socialites. Yet they barely ever touched on the fact of his long-long-running personal partnership with Jack Dunphy. **—NOVELIST CHRISTOPHER ISHERWOOD (DUNPHY WAS A DANCER TURNED NOVELIST)**

*S*he is my other daughter. **—LANA TURNER ON "JOSH," THE LONGTIME FEMALE COMPANION OF HER DAUGHTER CHERYL CRANE**

*I* knew her better than a husband would. . . . **—BEATRICE LILLIE ON HER LENGTHY ROMANTIC FRIENDSHIP WITH STAGE STAR *(THE KING AND I)* GERTRUDE LAWRENCE (IT OUTLASTED ANY OF THEIR MARRIAGES)**

*P*eople thought, naively, "What good friends they must be!" Because Mary Martin and her husband lived right next door to Janet Gaynor and her husband—in Brazil. In a jungle in Brazil, on adjoining ranches. Of course. Privacy. She was her longtime love, he was lovers with him. You can't do that in Beverly Hills without other neighbors getting suspicious. **—HOLLYWOOD COLUMNIST JOYCE HABER (GAYNOR WAS THE FIRST ACTRESS TO WIN A BEST ACTRESS ACADEMY AWARD)**

You can never really tell. However, a lot of arranged marriages do last. And remember, most of the world is still pushed into arranged marriages. Some turn out pleasantly because the two make the most of it, others because they happen to fall in love—and knowing that divorce is all but taboo, they resolve to make the best of the bad times.

Such a marriage can also endure if the husband has, um, outside outlets and the wife is a willing martyr, which those patriarchal cultures encourage them to be.   **—STEVE PARKER, LONGTIME AND ONLY HUSBAND OF SHIRLEY MACLAINE (HE LIVED IN JAPAN)**

At the worst, a house unkept cannot be so distressing as a life unlived.
**—DAME ROSE MACAULAY, ENGLISH WRITER**

Love at a distance may be poignant; it is also idealized. Contact, more than separation, is the test of attachment.
**—ACTRESS-AUTHOR ILKA CHASE**

If it's gonna last, watch your tongue. Think twice before you speak. The names you call your spouse will linger longer throughout the marriage, like ugly little stepchildren that never leave home.
**—ESTHER ROLLE *(GOOD TIMES)***

One must be chary of words because they turn into cages.
**—THEATRICAL PRODUCER-DIRECTOR VIOLA SPOLIN IN *THE LOS ANGELES TIMES* (1974)**

Ohat's really weird about a lot of marriages—and sometimes you only have to look as far as your parents' or relatives' marriages—is how the two people seem to enjoy being in a rut. Or seem so resigned to it. You want to say, "Life is not a dress rehearsal—this is it," but they'd just shrug and go, "Nyeh."—**NATASHA LYONNE** *(AMERICAN PIE)*

The hardest thing to believe when you're young is that people will fight to stay in a rut, but not to get out of it.  —**NOVELIST ELLEN GLASGOW**

The way I felt about my marriage was, first, he's far older than me, one must make allowances—and wait. . . . Second, he can't be all wrong. After all, even a stopped clock is right twice a day.
—**NATALIE SCHAFER** *(GILLIGAN'S ISLAND)* **ON ACTOR LOUIS CALHERN,**
**ONE OF WHOSE OTHER WIVES WAS ILKA CHASE**

The long-term accommodation that protects marriage and other such relationships is . . . forgetfulness.
—**WRITER ALICE WALKER** *(THE COLOR PURPLE)*

Love seems the swiftest but it is the slowest of all growths. No man or woman really knows what perfect love is until they have been married for a quarter of a century.  —**MARK TWAIN**

$\mathcal{I}$ once fell to talking with a gentleman who told me that his parents had been married numerous years and that the father had been a poor husband as well as a poor father. However, in old age he lost much of his short-term memory and became more pliable, less full of malice. He semi-reverted to childhood, and so the wife, to her barely concealed joy, became a sort of mother again. After the man died, she canonized him, and posthumously, it had been a "wonderful" marriage.

Another proof that most of the fiction in this world is not in the movies.                              **—JAMES MASON *(A STAR IS BORN)***

$\mathcal{Y}$ou want a wonderful, a husband for keeps? Do like I did. Marry a doll. A terrific human being usually makes a terrific partner. Don't marry a bastard and expect to change him. Unless you define "change" as divorce, of course.                    **—DAME JUDI DENCH**

$\mathcal{T}$he thing about marriage is you should participate in it but also look at it. Be objective. If it's not working, analyze your role in it. What can be changed, and what can't? Even if it's working well, take mental notes—for the future, when perhaps it isn't working as well. . . . Don't take matrimony for granted. Like any enterprise or undertaking, it requires some effort, some planning, and in the case of marriage, it's no better than the two people involved in it.

**—SCREENWRITER ISOBEL LENNART *(FUNNY GIRL)***

$\mathcal{I}$ believe that we all should wise up and recognize that a marriage is a small business and that married couples are business partners.

**—CLINICAL PSYCHOLOGIST DAVID HOPKINSON**

(Tlot of marital unions, nowhere more so than in politics and show business, are basically facades. They may have been the genuine article once upon a time, but they become shells; however, a shell is an ornament, and the public likes ornaments. Others, of course, are fakes from the start—usually due to social pressure. . . . These purported unions last as long as they continue creating profit and/or prestige.
—CANADIAN PLAYWRIGHT JOHN HERBERT *(FORTUNE AND MEN'S EYES)*

Long or short, most marriages have two or three levels. There's the reality between husband and wife—or man and wife, if she's less lucky. The united front presented to the outside world. And if there are children, the level of marriage which *they* experience at close secondhand.
—FRANCES LEAR, MAGAZINE EDITOR AND EX-WIFE
OF TV PRODUCER NORMAN LEAR

There was that old song about "love and marriage." How they go together like a horse and carriage—which gives you an idea how old it is. In point of fact, love and marriage, like quantity and quality, may or may not go together. To be on the safe side, don't assume that they always do.
—DAME CELIA JOHNSON *(BRIEF ENCOUNTER)*

Marriage can be like joining a religious habit [sic]. It might bring you joy and then contentment, or it might be a form of penance you submit to permanently. It's best not to get too wrapped up in yourself or even in your partner; unlike a monastery, marriage is in and of this world. Don't lose your links to the outside . . . work and friends should always count.
—RICHARD KILEY, STAGE AND TV ACTOR *(ALLY MCBEAL)*

ℬefore you congratulate a couple on how long they've been together, is it a marriage or a cage? An obsession? A mindless habit? Not all neurotics are individuals; I've met a lot that are couples.

—FILM CRITIC GENE SISKEL

ℋe's my whole life, even more than my career, and anyhow his is more important than mine. . . . We met doing summer stock in 1957 and it's been a double act ever since.   —STAGE ACTRESS GWYDA DONHOWE
*(APPLAUSE)* IN 1987; THE FOLLOWING YEAR HUSBAND NORMAN KEAN,
A PRODUCER, MURDERED HER WHILE SHE SLEPT, THEN LEAPT TO HIS
DEATH FROM THE ROOF OF THEIR APARTMENT BUILDING

ℬy 1945 Noel Coward and Graham Payn were deeply in love and committed to each other, although like most couples they did stray from time to time. They were together until Sir Noel's death in 1972, but when Coward was finally knighted not long before he died, rather than taking his life partner to this, the apex of his social and professional life, he—yes, cowardly, what else?—took two platonic female friends. For show. You still view this sort of charade at the Oscar ceremonies. . . . If you're gay and single and closeted, that's one thing. But if you closet the longtime love of your life, your other half, what kind of success can you call that?

—SIR ROBERT STEPHENS *(THE PRIVATE LIFE OF SHERLOCK HOLMES)*

𝒪ur friends often think I'm Don and vice versa [on the telephone). When we're working on something together we sometimes use a tape recorder, and it's the most extraordinary thing. Even we can't tell the voices apart! That's what twenty-six years have done.
—CHRISTOPHER ISHERWOOD, TOGETHER WITH PARTNER AND ARTIST DON BACHARDY
FOR THIRTY-THREE YEARS, UNTIL THE WRITER'S DEATH IN 1986

*I*'m the longest-married woman in my family.
**—LESBIAN AUTHOR DOROTHY ALLISON**

*A*bsolutely [legalized gay marriage] has to happen. Absolutely. I've met couples who've been together for fifty-four years, thirty-five years, . . . and they have no legal rights. This nonsense that [the government] has to have a Defense of Marriage Act, this is ridiculous. Defense against what? The divorce rate is 50 percent or something. . . . Gay marriage in no way threatens anyone else's marriage; marital problems come from the inside, not the outside.
**—BETTY DEGENERES, AUTHOR AND ELLEN'S MOTHER**

*C*ertainly, under the present social set-up, a homosexual relationship is more difficult to maintain than a heterosexual one. . . . Because it demonstrates the power of human affection over fear and prejudice and taboo, it is actually beneficial to society as a whole—as all demonstrations of faith and courage must be: they raise our collective morale.
**—CHRISTOPHER ISHERWOOD**

*G*ore Vidal has been . . . with Howard Austen since about 1950. But of late he's [saying] they haven't had sex for years, that it's now loving but platonic. . . . In saying [so], he diminishes their marriage in most people's eyes. Because many, possibly most, longtime heterosexual couples haven't had sex either, not for decades or since having their kids. But they do not go around announcing "the fact" for public approval.
**—POET ALLEN GINSBERG**

*I*s it me, or is the truth that the longer you're married, the more conformist you become?
**—GILDA RADNER, MARRIED TO ACTOR GENE WILDER**

When you're on your own, you can do wild and crazy things. But boy, the minute you're half a couple, you have to think about all the ramifications, repercussions. . . .    **—STEVE MARTIN**

Being married for so long has given me a peaceful confidence I would not have thought possible, way back when. Of course whether that's enough confidence to deal with widowhood someday, I don't know.    **—JAMES STEWART'S WIFE GLORIA STEWART, WHO DIED FIRST**

Love is what you've been through with somebody.
**—CARTOONIST JAMES THURBER**

In a good and ongoing marriage, you fall in love several times. Always with the same person.    **—CANDICE BERGEN *(MURPHY BROWN)***

I'm not a real movie star—I've still got the same wife I started out with twenty-eight years ago.    **—WILL ROGERS, ACTOR AND HONORARY MAYOR OF BEVERLY HILLS (1879–1935)**

My husband doesn't want any part of the show biz world. Fine. When you're suddenly, temporarily hot, your life turns into a gold-fish bowl. If I insisted on dragging him to Hollywood parties or he insisted I play the little wife and always put myself second, it wouldn't go very far, and if it did it wouldn't be worth it.
**—ESTELLE *GOLDEN GIRLS* GETTY**

Especially during the 1930s, with the upheavals caused by the Great Depression, Hollywood movies sought to influence audiences' behavior. The most apparent way was nearly every film ending with a marriage. Before modern times, a large percentage of people lived in common-law marriages, which church and government dislike because it diminishes their influence. In 1934 Hollywood agreed to endorse a very rigid censorship code pushed by government and the churches.　　　　　　　　　　　**—HISTORIAN MARTIN GRIEF**

I guess one reason divorce was so seldom talked about openly was that you didn't even see it in the movies—and you saw nearly everything in the movies! There was a real stigma if your marriage didn't last a lifetime. Desi and I had a long marriage by today's standards [in the 1980s], but when it ended between us, we were afraid to take it to the public. We didn't know how they'd react.　　　**—LUCILLE BALL**

An actor and an actress who join up, sincerely or not, get more than double the publicity together they could ever get solo. . . . An example was [Alfred] Lunt and [Lynn] Fontanne. Neither was even close to movie-star material . . . but together, as a husband-wife team, they were a Broadway box-office attraction for a very long time. People wondered why they never had or even adopted a child, but they loved that Lunt never looked at another woman and Fontanne never looked at another man. People were naive—they didn't guess.

**—ACTOR BRODERICK CRAWFORD** *(BORN YESTERDAY)* **ON THE SECRETLY GAY PAIR**

If a [gay] guy marries a woman for two months, it'll be in his obituary. If he marries another guy and they're together two decades, don't count on it being in the obit. The rulers of the country and its media do not want you to know about gay love.

—GAY COLUMNIST BOYD MCDONALD

Tony Perkins didn't marry [a woman] until about age forty. But he told friends it would last, it would be for the rest of his life precisely because it was the perfect cover. He'd wanted kids, not a wife—and they had two [sons]—but having a wife enabled him to continue having affairs with other men but without the fear of being revealed as gay. His mindset was from the Victorian era.

—MARTIN BALSAM, PERKINS'S COSTAR FROM *PSYCHO* AND *MURDER ON THE ORIENT EXPRESS* (PERKINS—1932–1992—DIED OF AIDS)

A good marriage would be between a blind wife and a deaf husband.

—MONTAIGNE

Well-married, a man is winged; ill-matched, he is shackled.

—HENRY WARD BEECHER IN 1870 (PREACHER BEECHER WAS THE BROTHER OF *UNCLE TOM'S CABIN* AUTHOR HARRIET BEECHER STOWE)

I can appreciate a nicely formed bod as much as anyone, but men, until about the age of twenty-nine, lack conversation. . . . Marriage requires quite a bit of conversation.

—KATHLEEN TURNER *(BODY HEAT)*

Twenty years ago, I married for richer, for poorer, for better, for worse. Fang's so lazy he hasn't been any of those things.

—PHYLLIS DILLER

After they retired from the White House, Nancy wanted to get Ronald Reagan a going-away gift, something to remind him. . . . She finally found the perfect gift: a certificate from Naps-R-Us.

—**COMEDIAN TURNED CBS VICE PRESIDENT TIM FLACK**

For our anniversary my wife wanted to go someplace she's never been before. So I took her to the kitchen. —**HENNY YOUNGMAN**

The wife's been nagging me to get her a chinchilla coat for our anniversary. I said, "You'll get your chinchilla when a man walks on the moon." Just my luck. —**CORBETT MONICA *(THE JOEY BISHOP SHOW)* IN 1969**

I don't know what to get my wife for our anniversary anymore. First she wanted a mink. I got her a mink. Then she wanted a silver fox. I got her a silver fox. It was ridiculous. The house was full of animals. —**HENNY YOUNGMAN**

It's 1990 and for our anniversary, Edgar bought me something I've been wanting since 1972: a 1972 convertible car. —**JOAN RIVERS**

Leona Helmsley's beloved husband Harry has never forgotten their wedding anniversary. I mean, if you were married to her, would you forget the day that happened? —**COMEDIAN MARIO CANTONE**

William Wyler, the great director, wanted to marry me. I truly was foolish not to! I understand that Jewish husbands usually stay the course, and I might have had one long, happy marriage instead of four relatively short ones. My friend Joan Blondell calls my four husbands the "four skins." She married a Jewish man [producer Mike Todd] . . . but he left her for Elizabeth Taylor. . . . When it comes to husbands, there really are no guarantees, except headaches along the way. Brother!                                                        —BETTE DAVIS

Anne Bancroft married Mel Brooks. Shirley Jones married Marty Ingels. What can these people possibly have in common? Are those marriages or stunts? I can't figure it out.     —LUCILLE BALL, WHO ALSO HAD
A LONG MARRIAGE TO A COMEDIAN, GARY MORTON (BORN MORTON GOLDAPPER)

Life can be depressing enough without having a comedian for a husband. I'm not expressing myself right: What I'm saying is, being Gene Wilder's wife makes my life a little less realistic. Comedy is grounded in reality, but it can't be tied to it. What I'm really trying to say is, I wouldn't want to be married to Clint Eastwood.
                                            —FELLOW COMEDIAN GILDA RADNER

Charlie [Bronson] isn't the handsomest man in the world, but he is very three-dimensional, and our marriage is for keeps.
                                            —JILL IRELAND *(DEATH WISH II)*

If Clark had one inch less, he'd be the "queen of Hollywood" instead of "the king."     —CAROLE LOMBARD ON HER HUSBAND CLARK GABLE

What initially attracts us to a mate is seldom what binds us to them.
—JOHN FORSYTHE (DYNASTY)

Old meat makes good soup. —ITALIAN PROVERB

I married late; my husband [actor Stringer Davis] married late. We are the best of friends. He told me he had a crush on John Gielgud, and I respect that. We two are loving companions—no less and no more. —DAME MARGARET RUTHERFORD *(BLITHE SPIRIT)*

The great secret of successful marriage is to treat all disasters as incidents and none of the incidents as disasters. —GAY DIPLOMAT HAROLD NICOLSON, HUSBAND OF LESBIAN WRITER VITA SACKVILLE-WEST (THEIR SON NIGEL NICOLSON WROTE THE CLASSIC *PORTRAIT OF A MARRIAGE*)

After I had that terrible stroke and seemed, temporarily, to have become only part of a person, my husband was lifting me onto my bed. I whispered in his ear, "I apologize for ruining your life." And he said the most wonderful, truly husbandly thing. "Nonsense, Aggie, you've made me a better man." —CHOREOGRAPHER AGNES DE MILLE

In matrimony, the more you genuinely give, the more real of a marriage you make it. —HARRY HAMLIN *(L.A. LAW, MAKING LOVE)*

Who we are never changes. Who we think we are does, and marriage has a lot to do with that. —DICK VAN PATTEN *(EIGHT IS ENOUGH)*, PARAPHRASING "SOME PHILOSOPHER WE HAD TO READ IN HIGH SCHOOL"

This gentleman friend who was a divorced marriage counselor once said the most insightful thing, anyway: that the difference between a good marriage and a so-so marriage is leaving two or three things a day unsaid. **—RUE MCCLANAHAN *(THE GOLDEN GIRLS)***

The longer you're married, the more down to earth you feel. It's a good feeling for most people. Not everyone wants to soar or feel like a bird. Being earthbound's not a bad thing.

**—ANETA CORSAUT (HELEN CRUMP ON *THE ANDY GRIFFITH SHOW*)**

Most adults feel primarily like either a parent or a spouse or an individual. All of it's fine. The prize is staying happy with whichever role you feel. **—GERMAN ACTOR KLAUS KINSKI *(NOSFERATU)***

If you let something or somebody unpleasant become a regular part of your day, you can get used to anything. But do you want to? And if so, why do you feel you should have to? Quality of life is the best concept. **—ALISON ARNGRIM *(LITTLE HOUSE ON THE PRAIRIE)***

In time, a couple's joys, secrets, and sins become their marriage. Shared and confidential experience become their mutual skin.

**—AUTHOR RAY BRADBURY**

It's strange. Unlike with our relatives, the longer you live with your significant other, the more you become like them.

**—JUNE LOCKHART *(LOST IN SPACE)***

$\mathcal{A}$ great marriage doesn't always mean your sexual needs are fulfilled, especially if it's a longer marriage. Yet you cannot consider cheating with anyone who knows you, because they'd think less of your commitment and your partner. So it would have to be with a stranger or on vacation. And strictly safe sex. So, almost, in a way, why bother? **—EMMA THOMPSON**

$\mathcal{I}$n a good marriage, you think twice about anything you do publicly, because it reflects on you both. So in a way it's definitely a limitation . . . a tender trap. **—DIAHANN CARROLL**

$\mathcal{M}$any wives wish to lose themselves in marriage. Very few men do; most keep a deliberate distance from it, especially at work and among other men. **—STEPHEN BOYD** *(BEN-HUR)*

$\mathcal{W}$hat a pair: Dan and Marilyn Quayle. Made for each other. Who else would have them? **—KATHY NAJIMY**

$\mathcal{M}$arriage is about the biggest thing most people can do in life. And if you do it right, it even outlasts having a child. But like a career, marriage can't take up your whole life or substitute for the other things that are missing. You have to actively make your marriage rounded and yourself a rounded individual.

**—PATRICIA ROUTLEDGE** *(KEEPING UP APPEARANCES)*

$\mathcal{D}$on't confuse childless with child-free. Or assume everyone wants to add to the overpopulation. . . . I'll bet if they ever did, or dared do, a survey, they'd find child-free couples are usually happier with each other and stay in love longer. **—AVA GARDNER**

$\mathcal{T}$reat each other like romantic best friends. Because as marriage wears on, there's a strong tendency to treat each other like talking furniture. —**MICHAEL LEARNED** *(THE WALTONS)*

$\mathcal{J}$ackie married Jack Kennedy for love, I suppose, but didn't get it. She married the Greek [Onassis] for money and got it. You tell me which was the more successful marriage. . . . —**"COCO" CHANEL**

$\mathcal{O}$ne size in marriage does not fit all. Different marriages are undertaken by differing people, and at different times of life perhaps, for various reasons, for assorted goals. . . . One wife's life sentence is another woman's perfect marriage, and one man's mate is another man's poison. —**ACTOR TURNED SCULPTOR GEORGE MONTGOMERY** **(DINAH SHORE'S FORMER HUSBAND)**

$\mathcal{J}$ couldn't believe it! After Bill [Frawley] left our show *[I Love Lucy]* and got onto *My Three Sons,* this puff piece in one of the fan magazines had a headline about his "Secret Yet Long-Lasting Marriage." I had to show it to Lucy, because everyone knows Bill hated marriage and ran away from his wife without saying good-bye or making it official. In fact, he hated all wives—including those of us unlucky enough to play his wife. —**VIVIAN VANCE**

$\mathcal{W}$ell, I think of Richard Denning as a little more than a good friend. After all, he played my husband for quite a while [on her radio series *My Favorite Husband*] and we got along beautifully. . . . I think the role of husband is a wonderful one, even when it's make-believe. —**LUCILLE BALL [CBS ORIGINALLY WANTED DENNING TO PLAY LUCY'S HUSBAND ON *I LOVE LUCY,* BUT SHE INSISTED ON HER REAL HUSBAND OR NO SHOW)**

$\mathcal{I}$ couldn't imagine ever leaving my wife [actress Rita Wilson], but if I did, the only person I'd leave her for would be Antonio [Banderas].
—TOM HANKS ON THE SPANISH ACTOR WHO PLAYED HIS
LIFE PARTNER IN *PHILADELPHIA*

$\mathcal{N}$ostalgia is not what it used to be, and dating is the most overrated activity you can do outside the home—you figure that one out. . . . Most folks look back on their courtship days as the best of all. Not me! Courtship is tough. You're nervous, insecure, on tiptoes with best behavior. . . . You settle into marriage, it's like an armchair that gets more comfortable as it adjusts to your contours. Romance is great if you can sustain it, but comfort is best. Comfortable is the way to live, and the only way to stay married. —ROXIE ROKER (*THE JEFFERSONS*;
THE ACTRESS IS ALSO THE MOTHER OF MUSICIAN LENNY KRAVITZ)

$\mathcal{M}$arriage is forever—with time off for bad behavior.
—ROBERT DOWNEY JR.

$\mathcal{T}$hey ought to hang a sign in all courthouses and wedding chapels that says, "All decisions are final." —ROSE-MARIE (*THE DICK VAN DYKE SHOW*)

$\mathcal{A}$fter a lengthy, excellent union is ended by a death, the very excellence of it will bring memories of grateful joy as well as lingering, sometimes intense pain. However the predominant emotion, for both partners' sake, should be gratitude. Gratitude that one experienced and has shared such a sublime love. —HINDU PHILOSOPHER KRISHNAMURTI

𝒜 marriage which continues for life is simply one where both halves remember what they said about for better or worse, until death does them part. —JAMES STEWART

𝒮o far as I know, Jim never stepped out [cheated] on me. I think other women scared him somewhat. But I remember the time we were sitting at a sidewalk café in Rome and a beautiful girl was passing by who seemed to recognize Jim. She smiled at me, then came up to him and whispered a quick something in his ear. I was dying of curiosity to know what she'd said.

Jim said, "She just said to try the house wine, it's very good."

Years later, he told me what really happened: Jim had been waiting for me on the sidewalk in front of our hotel while I was getting ready for our afternoon stroll along the Via Veneto, where the best cafés are. This beautiful Italian prostitute approached him and offered her wares. Jim said, "No, thank you," and she said, "But for $50 you get the best in Rome." He declined again, saying, "I'm sorry, I only have five dollars," so she left.

Later, when she saw him sitting with me at the café, she couldn't resist going up and whispering to him, "See what you get for $5?"

—HENNY BACKUS, LONGTIME WIFE OF *GILLIGAN'S ISLAND*'S JIM BACKUS

𝕸arriage is for a lifetime. Actually, it's for two lifetimes—served concurrently. —SAM LEVENSON

It's been said that the bitterest tears cried over graves are for words never said and deeds never done. Sad to say, the same holds true for a marriage, before it's ended by death or by choice. Make the most of it, before it ends—and maybe it won't have to end. Don't hold back—assume this is the only marriage you'll ever have.

**—NATALIE SCHAFER *(GILLIGAN'S ISLAND)***